FRONTIERS
OF
LEARNING

In memory of my mother-in-law
Mrs Tjan Sioe Bie † 1986

Pjotr Hesseling

FRONTIERS OF LEARNING

The Ph.D. Octopus

1986
FORIS PUBLICATIONS
Dordrecht - Holland/Riverton - U.S.A.

Published by:
Foris Publications Holland
P.O. Box 509
3300 AM Dordrecht, The Netherlands

Sole distributor for the U.S.A. and Canada:
Foris Publications U.S.A.
P.O. Box C-50
Riverton N.J. 08077
U.S.A.

CIP-data

ISBN 90 6765 249 0

Printed in the Netherlands by ICG Printing, Dordrecht.

Contents

VI

Preface

The origin of this book dates back some twenty years. When I had finished my doctoral dissertation on 'Strategy of Evaluation Research' in the field of supervisory and management training in 1966, my director of the Technical Efficiency and Organisation department at Philips, Prof. D.A.C. Zoethout, asked me why I had not included the evaluation of university education. An honest answer would have been that I was ambivalent about my own exposure to academic rituals. The emphasis seemed to be more on formal issues, such as language, punctuation, quotations and references, than on the content. Also during the public defense of my thesis in the old Lutheran cburch in Amsterdam the questions raised by the academic forum seemed to reflect a debate between competing faculties and schools rather than a discussion of the content. Indeed, much later I discovered that there was disagreement whether my thesis subject belonged to sociology or psycbology and whether my promotor, Prof. S. Hofstra an anthropologist, was qualified to assess the quality. At that time, bowever, I was ignorant about the procedures. My assumptions were that agreement with my promotor was the necessary condition and that the dissertation required original, independent work.

In the Dutch academic tradition the usual graduate degree is 'doctorandus' meaning somebody who is able to or has to become 'doctor'. The Latin phrase in some Dutch universities is, when becoming drs., that you are admitted to strive for the highest honours in scholarship. It is a natural complement of graduation, be it after many years of work. However, my exposure to other academic traditions in Germany, the UK, France, Scandinavian countries, the USA and Japan at that time made me aware that university traditions are not universal. Even in my own country actualization of this privilege became in some disciplines exceptional, although the assumption was not challenged and there were regularly senior officials and professionals who presented their dissertation at a later stage, even after retirement. What was the value of such prolonged concentration of one particular theme or issue usually outside work hours without any direct career perspectives? Why are people motivated to search for approval by a rather fragmented academic community with a seemingly abnormal cost-benefit balance? Of course, in medical and natural sciences there were clear cases of pre-career dissertations, but the cultural tradition of coming to the fore at any stage was widely spread under graduates. On the other side a doctorate was not a necessary complement, even not for top academic positions. In my own network of colleagues and friends I discovered that a doctorate was sensitive requiring particular explanations, almost a conspiracy. There were also too many examples of rather useless academic rituals or doctorates awarded by obscure universities abroad.

How could I escape oral history and anecdotical evidence, generate valid and reliable knowledge about doctorate phenomena, and even discover universal trends? Is a cost-benefit analysis feasible and at what level of aggregation, an individual, a university or a country? How to assess the relationship between supply and demand at a national level? What value is exactly added by a doctorate rather than by other academic degrees or professional certificates? How universal is the doctorate for access to the mainstream of research and development, scholarship or professional excellency? What are the alternatives programmes, tutorials, editorial assistance, publication outlets or special institutes for advanced studies? Because of personal interest and the nature of comparative organization studies my main objective became establishing interlinkages between disciplines, countries and cultures in order to stimulate universality of advanced learning.

Since my appointment as professor of business economics, especially internal organization, to the Netherlands School of Economics in 1970, I became gradually more involved in the academic assessment of the quality of thesis proposals and drafts. Decisions for pass are easier to trace than decisions for rejection. Each of the (attempted) dissertations presents its own learning episode. Each episode consists of an irregular series of drafts, tutorials and discussions over some years, where one concentrates on designing, pruning, improving, adding and editing a particular thesis with a changing balance between teacher/tutor/supervisor/promotor/advisor and student/fellow/assistant/colleague. After some interpersonal consensus between promotor and promovendus on the state of the art and the proposed addition to received knowledge frequently other members of the academic forum or other resource persons are consulted. Of course, one cannot expect a complete consensus, but one can agree on certain standards for judgment. 'it is often impossible to disagree with some assertion of standards without appearing to disagree with the very idea of quality' (Raymond Williams, 1976) but parameters change at the frontiers of learning. Formal regulations for the appointment of a committee vary, but the process of intercollegial auditing seems similar: an independent assessment of quality in a particular field of study.

One cannot easily arrive at cumulative evidence on the nature of doctorates from participant observation, because each episode sets its own conditions. When I interview senior colleagues with an impressive record of doctorate 'generation', I am frequently struck by their careful reference to their particular field of study and their reluctance to generalize for other disciplines. The experience seems idiographic reflecting one's own priorities and preferences in promoting paradigms and developing intellectual maturity within a discipline. A change of promotor implies frequently another style of learning. Because the number of doctorates under supervision of one professor never reaches a sufficient quantity for generalization and reflects a particular style and discipline, only a micro network analysis seems possible.

My first approach to extend the empirical basis for understanding the doctorate process and product was to establish a regular Ph.D club. Every month candidates discussed a particular dissertation usually introduced by a recent doctor or a particular design by a candidate. The emphasis was on the feedback of the process, its critical stages and the role of a promotor. Since 1982 these monthly sessions of some fifteen members proved to be stimulating and rewarding especially for candidates, but it remained a floating membership with no clear programme and restricted to a personal network and style. Since 1985 this Ph.D club has become a Ph.D platform with invited speakers and a thematic programme. It is a continuous source of inspiration.

My second approach was initiated by an invitation from the Japan Foundation to revisit Japan in March 1984. The Japanese case of the new Ph.D as adopted only in 1953 by the MacArthur reforms has created a dilemma between the harmony of professorial patronage after initial selection and individual prominence at the basis of originality especially in social sciences and interdisciplinary studies. Discussion with colleagues and officials in the ministry of education and research institutes revealed many paradoxes and specific and different networks within universities. Some finish a doctoral programme without expecting to complete a dissertation. There is an old Chinese-Japanese tradition of doctorship *hakase* which connotates with wisdom as the three 'kings' in the Bible and which might be awarded much later even as professor. It might be also compared with a doctorat d'état in France. For foreigners, mainly Asian, other rules seem to apply. There is a strong conviction that Ph.D's are useless outside academia, but there are exceptions. The number of Japanese with a foreign Ph.D is unknown, only the number of Japanese who study abroad on official scholarships. Internationalisation is a key issue. This visit raised more questions than answers. A cross-cultural approach to Ph.D's and equivalents prevents easy generalizations and triggers off fundamental questions about equity, selectivity and quality.

My third approach was initiated by the opportunity of a visiting fellowship at the Netherlands Institute for Advanced Study in the Humanities and Social Sciences in Wassenaar from September 1984. I focused on the history of advanced higher education in various traditions and became especially fascinated by the major changes in higher education at the turn-of-the-century in the USA. In 1904 William James of Harvard wrote already his 'The Ph.D Octopus' warning against the tentacles of overspecialization and abuse of doctorates. On 14 May and 14 June I convened two symposia at NIAS under the title 'Frontiers of Learning: the Ph.D Octopus' with an impressive participation. The title was chosen to reflect the double edge sword of each Ph.D: an heroic effort to push the frontiers of learning a little bit further in the American tradition of a frontier society and of exploring new territories, but at the other side a continuous threat of narrow specialization and lack of communication between (sub)disciplines. The core of a Ph.D must remain a fundamental effort to provide an independent and original contribution to a chosen field of study rather than only reflecting a codified body of knowledge as in the bachelor's or a mastery of advanced methodology and theory as in the master's. In that sense a Ph.D will never be a necessary complement of higher education for all graduates but only for those who are ready and able to grasp the opportunity. If the Ph.D becomes ossified in formal regulations, it loses its function and one has to invent another shiboleth of originality. The participants of the symposia challenged me to specify questions, framework or even a theory of advanced learning. They refuted an accounting approach. At the time of writing there is an acceleration in policy proposals for restructuring Ph.D education along American lines and for abolishing the traditional apprenticeship without teaching.

Although I have still more questions than answers how to guarantee the international quality of a Ph.D, in this book I try to indicate the major pitfalls, confusions and opportunities of doctorates for individuals, universities, societies and the world of learning. I acknowledge the contributions from too many for explicit recognition but especially from doctoral candidates who reflected on their lonely journey in terra incognita. The final result may not pay off immediately, but a sense of mission and a disciplined effort of extending frontiers of learning will have its own reward.

Actually this book is based on a continuous discussion with colleagues and fellows. It centers around the humanistic value of a Ph.D, both in the sense of his personal qualities and interests and in the sense of his culture-of-origin and role. My main purpose is to stimulate a more fundamental discussion than on the level of completion rates and approved programmes. I gratefully acknowledge the patience and care of my secretary Alice Moerman and the support of the publisher.

Let me state very clearly that the responsibility for errors in the use of English in this book is solely mine.

Chapter I

Doctorates

The Kingdom of the Octopus

The first man to describe the habits, appearance and anatomy of octopuses was Aristotle (Historia Animalium). An octopus is a backboneless animal belonging to the cephalopods, head-footed. These animals have an ancient lineage. Fossils of a small cephalopod have been found in rocks believed to be at least 400 million years old. Although some 650 species of Octopoda and Decapoda have been described, it is impossible to give the exact number in the world today. Moreover, the systematists whose work is to classify animals are not agreed how to group the available material. Many of the 650 or so species are known from only one specimen and some from an incomplete specimen.

Octopuses are the best known. There are about 150 species and they live in nearly all the seas of the world, from the tropics to the Arctic and Antarctic. They vary in size from 2 inches towards 32 feet. The better-known species are found in shallow water, but there is little doubt that some actually live nearly three miles below the surface. Pressure at this depth is about three tons per square inch.

All octopuses have eight arms, which grow from the head - 'eight radiating, supple, tapering tongs' or 'supple as leather, though as steel, cold as night'. Patience in hunting is their most evident virtue. They are active mostly at night. Their diet shows a remarkable adaptability. Ink or sepia is their chief means of defence against enemies. The ink is so durable that the ink from cephalopods fossilized over a hundred million years ago can be diluted and used for writing today. Although there is no doubt that the ink confuses the enemy, exactly how or why is still debatable. The theory that the ink cloud is merely an aquatic smoke-screen is now known to be an oversimplification. The ink might have a paralysing effect.

Ages before man discovered jet propulsion cephalopods were jetting through primeval seas. The adult common octopus nearly always swims backwards when travelling by jet. An octopus can (also) crawl about the sea-bottom on its arms, and even make brief excursions on shore. There is a story of a wandering octopus in a library. Gilpatric, a teuthologist as an expert on cephalopods is called, brought a newly captured octopus in a bucket, which he put on the floor while he talked to the librarian. The octopus climbed out of the bucket, meandered across the room, and was then crawling up the bookshelves. The octopus reached the third shelf, stopped at one of the books, turned colour, and dropped dead. Gilpatric maintains that the book where the octopus stopped was one of his own.

The eyes of the octopus are remarkably similar to the human eye. The brain behind the cephalopodon eye is the most highly developed of any invertebrate. The brain is divided into 14 main lobes governing different sets of functions. Octopuses can crawl through unbelievably small openings several times smaller than the diameter of their body. This Houdini-like trait proves embarrassing to teuthologists. They continuously escape. Octopuses penned in an aquarium are never quite satisfied. They escape not because they want to go foraging, but because they want to get to a more comfortable place. (Frank W. Lane's book of 1957 was a rich source and dr. J.H. Reuter of our medical faculty a guide for consultation).

Reading for amusement about the octopus stimulates my curiosity. Nature is intriguing and one is tempted to dig into the extensive documentation systems and search for new knowledge on memory, learning, colour changes surpassing the famed chameleon, bioluminiscence, reproduction, ecological niches and the giant kraken. Frank Lane used four years to cover some 900 odd entries in the bibliography and he exchanged 5000 letters with experts in more than 40 countries. Recently the amount of scientific literature is doubling approximately every ten years. This is only a compilation by a layman and out of date.

Until the beginning of this century our knowledge of how these animals behave was due almost entirely to the anecdotal method - to what people said they had seen animals doing. All too often the anecdotal method confuses observation with interpretation. A better method is the experimental method. This means that every experiment can be checked and re-checked, either with the same or with a different animal. Variations in procedure can generally be introduced to eliminate possible alternative explanations of an animal's behaviour. Besides new observations in habitat each hard-won fact which experiments yield, however trifling, helps us to understand nature a little better. Such experiments, although seldom undertaken for economic reasons, have sometimes proved of great practical value to mankind.

The Ph.D Octopus

In 1903 a famous Harvard professor, William James, published an article with the title 'The Ph.D Octopus' in the Harvard Monthly. This small anecdotal paper has survived anonymity. Burton R. Clark (1983) refers to it as teaching Americans how to curse 'the Ph.D octopus' with its tentacles of specialization. Statesmen attempting to revive general education some seventy years later bemoaned its condition in the U.S. system as 'disaster area'. In this article he describes an incident where a brilliant student had to produce a Ph.D thesis only for a teaching appointment. For William James this incident is characteristic of American academic conditions at the turn of the century.

'Human nature is once for all so childish that every reality becomes a sham somewhere, and ....the Ph.D degree is in point of fact already looked upon as a mere advertising resource, a matter of throwing dust in the Public's eyes. (There are) two antagonistic passions, one for multiplying as much as possible the annual output of doctors, the other for raising the standard of difficulty in passing, so that the Ph.D of the special institution shall carry a higher blaze of distinction than it does elsewhere. Thus we at Harvard are proud of the number of candidates whom we reject. America is thus as a nation rapidly drifting towards a state of things in which no man of science or letters will be accounted respectable unless some kind of badge or diploma is stamped upon him....a decidedly grotesque tendency. Other nations suffer terribly from the Mandarin disease. Our higher degrees were instituted for the laudable purpose of stimulating scholarship, especially in the form of 'original research'. It is well for a country to have research in abundance, and our graduate schools do but apply a normal psychological spur. But the institutionizing on a large scale of any natural combination of need and motive always tends to run into technicality and to develop a tyrannical Machine with unforeseen powers of exclusion and corruption....The truth is that the Doctor-Monopoly in teaching, which is becoming so rooted an American custom, can show no serious grounds whatsoever for itself in reason....In reality it is but a sham, a bauble, a dodge, whereby to decorate the catalogues of schools and colleges....All the European countries are seeking to diminish the check upon individual spontaneity which state examinations with their tyrannous growth have brought in their train. Whatever evolution our state-examinations are destined to undergo, our universities at least should never cease to regard themselves as the jealous custodians of personal and spiritual spontaneity.... Universities ought to keep truth and disinterested labor always in the foreground, treat degrees as secondary incidents....It is indeed odd to see the love of titles –and such titles- growing up in a country of which the recognition of individuality and bare manhood have so long been supposed to be the very soul. The independence of the State, in which most of our colleges stand, relieves us of those most odious forms of academic politics which continental European countries present. Anything like the elaborate university machine of France, with its throttling influences upon individuals is unknown here. The spectacle of the 'Rath' distinction in its innumerable spheres and grades, with which all Germany is crawling today, is displeasing to American eyes; and displeasing also in some respects is the institution of knighthood, which aping as it does an aristocratic title, enables one's wife as well one's self so easily to dazzle the servants at the house of one's friends'. (pp. 329-347 passim).

In another address (1907) William James refers to college education as higher, because it is supposed to be so general and so disinterested. 'Geology, economics, mechanics, are humanities when taught with reference to the successive achievements of the geniuses to which these sciences owe their being. Not taught thus literature remains grammar, art a catalogue, history a list of dates, and natural science a sheet of formulas and weights and measures. The sifting of human creations! – nothing less than this is what we ought to mean by the humanities'

The Ph.D: a problem of classification

The Ph.D is a particular testcase of the classification of knowledge and a taxonomy of learning. In contrast to the biosphere of the living where one can observe species and, after Linnaeus, classify them, the noosphere of knowledge is invisible until it is recorded, transmitted and utilized. The concept of academic degrees is validated through the responsibilities of universities to certify people who have obtained a specified level of competence in some academic, technical or professional field. The Ph.D or Philosophiae Doctor is a traditional credential attribute of an individual awarded by an institute of higher education after the successful defense of a dissertation, recording the candidate's independent and original contribution to knowledge. It is the highest degree in most educational systems. Any discussion of the nomenclature leads straight to some of the most perplexing issues facing graduate education (Mayhew, 1974, p. 154). Excessive numbers of doctorates lead to limitations or complementary degrees.

William James belonged to the first generation of graduate education in the United States, which has gradually reached a level of achievement that has made it 'the envy of the world' (Jencks and Riesman, 1968, p. 513). Professor Tom F. Pettigrew, a fellow at NIAS and formerly of Harvard, told me that in his undergraduate days William James' Memories and Studies (London, 1912) were an obligatory introduction. Reading his studies, I am struck by the clear vision of advanced education at the turn-of-the-century. There was then a healthy scepticism toward academic ritualism and narrow specialization but a high regard for new knowledge. This period is sufficiently distant for historical reconstruction but it still can be traced in a family-like fashion of intellectual grandfathers.

The last turn-of-the-century represents the first great period of academic reform in American higher education (Clark Kerr, postscript, 1982). After the Civil War there was the land-grant movement and the modernizing efforts of strong presidents of universities, such as of Eliot at Harvard, White at Cornell, Gilman at Hopkins and others. The national efforts were to industrialize rapidly and to settle the whole continental United States, especially the introduction of new agricultural crops in new areas. Higher education became a source of science and technology, of engineers and farm agents, going far beyond the earlier classical education for the historical professions of teaching, medicine, the law and the ministry. The reforms attracted the upwardly mobile and docile children of farmers and immigrants with a strong puritan ethos. The central theme was enhancement of expertise, of science and scholarship. Graduate work, self-governing departments and student electives were a complement of the traditional, 'colonial' colleges. University presidents with charismatic power were the great agents of change, stimulating new curricula, research and public service.

The earlier American colonial colleges which acted *in loco parentis*, were originally Harvard (1636), the college of William and Mary (1693), Yale (1701), the college of New Jersey, later Princeton (1746), the college of Philadelphia (1764), King's College, later Columbia (1754), Brown University (1746), Rutgers (1766), and Dartmouth (1769). They stressed the traditional English education with Latin as a core. During the nineteenth century the impact of German scholarship and university life upon American university ideas replaced the English prototype. Ten thousands of American students attended German universities as modeled by von Humboldt. However, one tried to establish an American tradition, no copy from Germany. 'In following, as we are prone to do in educational matters, the example of Germany, we must beware lest we accept what is there cast off, less we introduce faults as well as virtues, defects with excellence' (Gilman, Cordasco) American higher education thus was founded on two different national patterns: a German university superimposed on the English college that had been the model for U.S. undergraduate instruction. The resulting strain has characterized American higher education since (Katz and Hartnett, 1976, p. 4).

The origin of advanced higher education in the U.S.A. is part of a long historical process. The first American Ph.D was awarded by Yale in 1861, but the first resident graduates were there already in 1814. Graduate studies in Yale were initiated by Porter in 1841. Some historians date the 'official' beginning of graduate studies in the year 1876 when John Hopkins was founded and at first offered only graduate instruction (R.T. Hartnett and J. Katz, 1976, p. 5). Graduate instruction at first was rather informal. Graduate students registered by merely giving their name and address to the President's secretary. They were not required to select formally a major or a minor subject. 'There were professors who proposed to lecture and there were students who proposed to study; what more was necessary?' No marks or grades of any kind were given (Versey, 1965, p. 169). One focused on a thesis subject and used the opportunities of going to lectures or seminars. This informality is still a very desirable part of the creative pursuit of knowledge. It is still the core of some European doctorate practices as in the Netherlands without special post-graduate education.

In the U.S.A. the growth of graduate education resulted gradually in prescribed curricula and structured requirements for certification via the doctoral degree. This formalization found its critics from the beginning. It diverts the attention of aspiring candidates from direct dealings with truth and problem solving to the passing of examinations (see William James). Some criticized the graduate school also as rigidifying intellectual pursuits and forcing candidates into conformity with narrow criteria of scholarship, and stifling creativity. It is possible to describe the quantitative growth of doctorates since the start and especially the period between 1920-1974 has shown a remarkable increase of the population of living U.S.A.-generated Ph.D's from one thousand in 1920 towards almost half a million in 1974 (see Figure I-1). The American Commission on Human Resources has made visible also the fluctuations over time in relative growth (Figure I-2). However, the major problem is not so much this quantitative growth but the quality and its impact on the educational system, business and society. Quantitative growth and selective quality might even correlate in a negative direction.

Evaluation of Ph.D degrees

Classification of knowledge leads to evaluation. Evaluation is assessment of value. Value is an abstract concept, which defines for an individual or for a social unit what ends or means to an end are desirable or desired. Primary values are related to primary needs such as safety, protection, salvation, health, justice and welfare. Also knowledge is a primary value for individuals and society. In human evolution the transfer of received knowledge has gradually developed into an educational cascade of various levels. At the end of this cascade there is a research imperative.

'This imperative entails a specific conception about the nature of knowledge; in every field there is an accepted body of truth' but this body of truth is only a stage in our knowledge about the world. Science is an investigative process through which our knowledge is tested, deepened and perfected, which means that the process, scientific research, is itself integral to the transfer of knowledge through the teaching function'. (Locke, 1985, p. 167).

These ideas about the nature of knowledge are deeply rooted in human civilization (see chapter II).

In its modern form the Ph.D is a German invention in the sense that they had managed by the nineteenth century to institutionalize these ideas in their forms of higher education. In the Germanic world of Middle Europe the Ph.D was a research degree as was the *Habilitation*. Few who aspired to a professorship in German universities attained their goal unless they had proven their research capacities by the completion of a doctoral thesis and a *Habilitationsschrift*. The term science, *Wissenschaft*, applied there to all fields of knowledge because knowledge in every field was subject to systematic, disciplined research and development. Since this was the university tradition, no self-respecting discipline or institution of higher education could hope to find acceptance in Germany unless it conformed to the research model. Consequently, when the engineers, merchants, businessmen and educators founded technical institutes and business schools in Germany, they sought to make much more of them than glorified trade and commercial schools. It is therefore no surprise that a survey of top managers in a major German industrial region shows that 61 percent of the members of corporation boards, and other surveys show that half of the degree holders in their manager sample hold doctorates (Locke, 1985, p. 168, p. 201). Indeed, as Locke aptly remarked 'The End of The Practical Man'.

Originally, also the English term science applied to knowledge as such, as in Shakespeare: 'hath not in natures mysterie more science then I have in this Ring'. By 1867 we can find the significantly confident, yet also significantly conscious, statement' we shall use the word 'science' in the sense which Englishmen so commonly give to it....as expressing physical and experimental science, to the exclusion of theological and metaphysical'. That particular exclusion had profound consequences in other areas of human learning, where a particular and highly successful model of neutral methodological observer and external object of study became generalized, not only as science, but as fact and truth and reason or rationality (Raymond Williams, 1976). Consequently, engineering and business studies experienced a very different fate from the German. It is no surprise that almost no British managers hold doctorates.

One could collect data on the percentage of doctorates in various disciplines, professions and occupations in each country and indeed scattered evidence shows large variation. However, degrees are not really comparable. One has to compare educational traditions and the place of learning in a society. The Ph.D as it has moved from Germany to the U.S.A. (1861), U.K. (1917), Japan (1953) and gradually has penetrated each higher educational system is in any case the most comparable distinction in itself, not in its distribution over disciplines, professions and occupations. Of course, the Ph.D is no monopoly for original and independent work neither is each doctoral dissertation a proven example of such work. I have selected *an attempt to provide evidence of original and independent work for an acade-*

mic forum as the shortest and most common description of a doctoral thesis, but it is restricted to the best available knowledge at a particular time and place according to a particular university and its selected representatives. Is there a common standard for evaluation?

The meaning of *standard* ranges from a source of authority as in Royal standard towards levels of achievement as in educational standards. Standardization came into use in the last period of the nineteenth century, from science (standardizing the conditions of an experiment) and then from industry (standardizing parts). If we apply standard to universities, we might find at any given time certain precise standards, but universities change standards and disagree about them and vary between different societies, disciplines and periods. If one does not specify judgments of fact, value or interest, university standards can be used to override necessary arguments or to appropriate the very process of valuation and definition to its own particular conclusions (Raymond Williams, 1976). Applied to originality standards are particularly elusive. At the symposium of 14th May a participant suggested that we have to get rid of originality. In the many medical dissertations under his supervision only one out of ten was original. Doctorate programmes are training devices in the definition of a problem, in writing, in application of methodology and theory, 'but I never wanted them to be original'. It sometimes happens, but is no standard to be aimed at. Young wrote in 1759:

> 'an Original....rises spontaneously from the vital root of genius; it grows, it is not made; Imitations are often a sort of manufacture, wrought up by those mechanics, art and labour, out of pre-existent materials not their own'. (Raymond Williams, 1976).

These explorations lead to the conclusion that university standards and attributes such as original, and the same applies to independent or other terms in use, can only be made meaningful if one agrees on evaluation procedures. This brings me safely back to my original thesis on 'Strategy of Evaluation Research' twenty years ago. I use 'original' here of course in the retrospective sense of my first academic work. There is a remarkable parallel between the post-war expansion of industrial training from standardized import packages as in Training Within Industry towards analytical training and experimental, self-exploring group sessions and the present industrial approach to mass higher education with standardisation, credit points and time budgets. In the mid sixties one started to realize that teaching and learning in higher education were frequently based on intuition and prescientific experience. The increasing number of students with vocational goals and growing specialisation made the evaluation problem urgent. Within Dutch universities centres of research of education were established and a new interuniversity centre was proposed which would collect, exchange and disseminate facts about teaching and learning in higher education (Report of the Committee of the Academic Council, in Universiteit en Hogeschool, June 1965, pp. 363-407, and Onderzoek van Onderwijs, Eindhoven, 1964 and 1965). Actually it took almost twenty years before such a new centre became operational.

Historically, evaluation of universities from a managerial perspective is of recent origin. The transformation of guilds towards plants or from individualized labour (craft) towards mass production triggered off the need for professional management and its logic of action and reflection. In the 'Handbook of Organizations' (J.G. March, 1965) only public elementary and secondary school systems were considered. This choice was forced by the almost complete absence of empirical research dealing with universities (Ch.E. Bidwell, o.c. p. 972). In 1967 the leading journal 'Administrative Science Quarterly' devoted an entire issue to universities as organization. The explosive growth of higher education, coupled with the puzzling complexity of university organization and their neglect as empirical research sites led to this decision. The resulting collection was meagre. In a bibliographical survey it is concluded that the attention given to college and university administration has been minuscule. Existing theories of evaluation and organization may not be applicable to universities: the goals are not specific; the product is not tangible; the customer (student) exerts little influence; the employees (faculty) are dedicated to their discipline, not to the employing institution; the decision-making process is diffused. The turbulent years of the sixties did result increasingly in literature on the changing role of universities but expressed more ideology and normative statements than empirical evidence. It is outside my terms of reference to describe this period in more detail. Presently it is not difficult filling a library with books and articles on higher education and its administration. The recent survey and bibliography of Philip G. Altbach and David H. Kelly (1985) give in their 7000 selected books and articles an impressive overview. Moreover, there are some 269 'national' journals devoted to higher education.

However, the problem of the nature of Ph.D's or other doctorates is hardly touched, as far as I could discover. There are some studies on reform in graduate education, on the quantitative growth of doctorates and some on the Ph.D as learning process, but there are few attempts for a comparative approach of the value of Ph.D's. Renate Simpson wrote in her *How the Ph.D came to Britain* (1983) that the circumstances surrounding the introduction of the Ph.D have been more than elusive and the general university historian has tended to evade the subject. As a motto of her book she uses Ernest Rutherford's statement of 1918 'The Ph.D.....will be a real and very great departure in English education – the greatest revolution, in my opinion, of modern times'. Another author on Ph.D's, Estelle M. Phillips wrote that very little is known about research at the postgraduate level or what it is that is being assessed when candidates are examined for the Ph.D (1980).

Despite this lack of systematic knowledge there are many negative views of the Ph.D as a training device to do original research or to become a skilled writer. The period of preparing a Ph.D is too long, it inhibits creativity, it is too specialized or tries to cover a too broad field. In any discussion on Ph.D's one observes a large variety of objections to a phenomenon that has never be systematically studied. There are many fundamental issues at stake. I would speculate that mass higher education offers more opportunities for the many who are enabled to come to the fore, but that there is 'a pool of ability' or 'reserves of talent' that can be drained. If universities stick to the standards of originality, even a major increase in doctoral fellowships will not increase the number of doctorates, if we are scraping the bottom of the barrel (Wilkins, 1964 p. 101). Of course, these same arguments have been appllied also in the past to an increase of primary and further education. Is the doctorate only for the few or does it need to increase in numbers as the whole higher education system?

Typology of dissertations

How to define a doctoral dissertation as a phenomenon? The common core is a scientific work presented by a qualified candidate to a university and judged as an independent and original contribution to a field of knowledge according to the university standards at a particular time. For an operational definition each of the terms requires specification. It is not difficult to collect from the scattered literature a long list of characteristics which sometimes have been selected, such as the number of pages, the writing style, language, the number of copies, birthplace of the candidate, the promotor or name of rector magnificus/president, the particular faculty or discipline and a curriculum vitae. The best available Doctorate Records File is maintained by the Office of Scientific and Engineering Personnel of the National Research Council and concerns a survey of earned doctorates awarded in the U.S.A. The cumulative file goes back to 1920. Each year a sample of doctorate recipients is selected for inclusion in a longitudinal research file. Field of specialization, educational preparation of degree recipients, their sources of financial support, the length of time required to attain the degree, postdoctoral employment plans, personal characteristics of recipients as sex, age, citizenship, 'race', marital status, physical handicaps and educational background of parents are included in the survey. The resulting reports as A Century of Doctorates – Data Analyses of Growth and Change (1978) are impressive but do not include an assessment of quality or impact. Moreover there are no comparable data files in other countries.

A doctorate records file belongs to statistics and indicators which strive to describe phenomena by means of classification and counting of certain things, in the forms of sequences of numbers, tables and diagrams. It is of special importance that statistical indicators are selected or constructed from empirical data, in a way to

- form a coherent system based explicitly or implicitly on some theoretical model of the phenomenon under study;
- permit aggregation and segregation as required;
- render possible the uncovering of trends in form of time series;
- offer a basis for policy options by comparison, analysis and extrapolation of data.

Given the high costs of information and transaction for a coherent system over time, one measures only what one values. Statistical indicators have been used first a century ago to compare the economy of nations and have become general e.g. GNP. The systematic use of social indicators has become accepted only during the last decades. Data concerning science occupy a relatively minor place among social indicators. The 'science indicators' movement in the United States resulted from a reaction against the 'anti-intellectual' climate of the end of the sixties where the expansion of science and technology were seen as a source of social and economic troubles. It was imperative to provide both the government and the public opinion with data –instead of anecdotal information– reflecting the state of scientific enterprise. The first volume Science Indicators 1972 was published in 1973 and has been followed since by similar volumes every two years. Within the science indicators movement the Science Citation Index (SCI) has become one of the world's most significant interdisciplinary bibliographic databases concentrated in recognized international journals and in highly structured sciences (Braun, 1985). It is therefore no surprise that doctoral dissertations with their wide range of assessment procedures and their low degree of publication are not integrated in scientometric approaches. As a social indicator doctoral dissertations are seen as higher education, not as an indicator of scientific progress.

Presently, the nature of postgraduate education and research is becoming one of the main policy issues in many countries. It is at the crossing line between higher education and science policy with different concerns and priorities and rarely adequately co-ordinated. Research is not any more the natural complement of the first four-year cycle of higher education as in the 19th century German idea of university study (OECD, 1986). The question becomes then whether the new generation of postgraduate research needs a special focus and needs to be integrated in science policy. Is it useful and feasible to design a monitoring system for doctoral dissertations as a steering device for science policy? Higher education's priorities are seen in an industrializing effort towards the first cycle with planning, management and budgetting for the many. Above certain participation ratio's it becomes more important to deliver within a given period and budget the highest output as in any other industrial effort than to stick to the research imperative of the past. Science policy priorities are in selected fields of high potential for technology and industrial development and in excellent research centres whether they are inside or outside universities. The traditional integration of scientific education and research within universities seems at stake. Perceived exigencies of the labour market are more important than lofty ideas of advancement of knowledge and scholarship in a society. Of course, the outcome of present reorganizations is the result of collective bargaining at various levels. As an individual one can only provide arguments for the role of advanced higher education and research.

I have selected three dimensions for characterizing doctoral dissertations:

(a) The first dimension contains the continuum from a narrow disciplinary focus towards neighbouring fields, the intellectual community, consumers of knowledge and society. It is the definition of the audience (forum) for whom one writes a doctoral dissertation. At the one extreme within an established paradigm and a highly structured discipline one could conceive the doctoral dissertation as a specialist contribution. Shigeru Nakayama gives as an example that someone who succeeds in working out the expansion of copper wire correctly to one more decimal place may be awarded a Ph.D for his work. This achievement may not be particularly relevant for the author's own scholarship, but since sooner or later someone in the field will almost certainly make use of it, his peers consider it worthy of recognition (Nakayama, 1984, p. 145). In similar sense there might be professional scientists who work with problems that become increasingly subdivided and specialized. This leads to even more sharply defined problems, but insofar as these problems are divorced from the concerns of society, the scientist finds himself engaged in a very exclusive enterprise. I remember a dissertation defended by J.B.G. Frenk at our university on 'Renewal theory, Banach algebras and functions of bounded increase' in 1983. Except the Dutch summary and the last proposition only specialists could read the thesis. This touches a very old problem in doctoral dissertations. There has been a continuous movement from subjects of general interest for a broader discussion towards narrow specialization only for a restricted audience. In the Dutch academic tradition there are still the separate propositions which are supposed to cover partly other fields of knowledge. Moreover, in the public defense the candidate is expected to explain his contribution for a broader audience.

There seems to be a danger where Ph.D's as a pre-career device become focused on the demonstration of a particular methodology and theory within a narrow field and isolated from general academic interest or further objectives. It is efficient and might reduce the period of completing a dissertation but at the costs of integration and academic traditions. If a subspecialization remains closed for a longer period and contacts become largely confined to those in the same specialty, an evolutionary perspective suggests that overly specialized organisms lack the capacity to survive in the face of sudden changes in the environment (Nakayama, 1984, p. 147). In an organizational perspective there is a need for dynamics between closing up for specialization and opening towards other disciplines and professions. New ideas and paradigms usually grow at the frontiers of disciplines. The history of sciences is full of a succession of differentiation and integration.

There is an equally serious danger when Ph.D's directly reflect issues of immediate social concern without substantial disciplinary knowledge. An organizational action perspective is especially prone to such an abuse, when the candidate tries to prove a particular preference of action. The distinction between judgments of fact, value and interest and the relation between phenomena is the core of a scientific enterprise.

(b) The second dimension is based on the role definition of the candidate. As a researcher in a particular field of specialization he might focus on a career as professional researcher either in an academic setting or in an industrial setting. As a teacher in a faculty or school he might be interested to show the particular place of his thesis subject and the research process in a curriculum for a certain range of students or, what frequently happened in the Dutch setting, to prepare himself as teacher in secondary education for teacher in higher education. The doctorate is then seen as broadening his scope as teacher. As a professional outside the university he might focus on establishing a solid scientific core for his profession e.g. as medical doctor, lawyer, accountant or engineer. A doctorate is then a measuring rod for professionalisation (e.g. Touw-Otten, 1981). As a policy-maker, official or manager the perception of a doctorate might include broader objectives as influencing society or business in a more responsible or otherwise qualified direction. Sometimes a candidate has no other definition of his role than as somebody who is interested in developing a thesis for an intellectual or personal challenge out of curiosity or some sense of mission. He looks for an empathic supervisor or promotor. He is not interested in advanced methodology or theory for its own sake neither in attending lectures or seminars unless it fits his particular interest

I don't think that there is a continuum of roles. There might be a succession of roles in a life cycle but roles reflect also the particular environment or social context of a candidate. I don't much care for an overall, superimposed, pattern of doctorates, as one of my respondents, Prof. H.C. Allen expressed it. Let a reasonable number of flowers bloom. We can not be dogmatic about knowledge cycles. We need only to keep a reasonable balance between the different types of doctorate roles and, I would strongly argue, prevent that a doctorate becomes a monopoly of research as a professional career within specific specializations. Role is an interpersonal concept and therefore a candidate needs access to a broad range of qualified supervisors or promotors who are willing and capable to screen proposals or to refer candidates to more suitable colleagues. It is a time consuming and hardly productive activity and especially interdisciplinary topics meet considerable obstacles in finding empathic attention. The major distinction in the role set between supervisor and doctoral candidate seems to be a student role definition as somebody who has to be trained and educated in a certain discipline as applied to fresh bachelors or first-stage graduates, and a fellow role definition as somebody with interesting experience and ideas who has to be guided in academic discipline, language and procedures in order to classify, analyse and present his personal research according to university standards.

(c) The last dimension consists of the continuum between local and cosmopolitan. Nakayama makes the point, that wherever modern science has been accepted not simply as positive knowledge but as a mode of scholarly practice, research has begun with 'local science': studies that focus on problems with a particular relationship to or meaning for a specific country or region as opposed to the more general and universalistic problems that typically occur in fields like physics and chemistry. In such activities as the classification of native plant and animal life and the study of endemic diseases, 'local science' was being practised by local inhabitants. Gradually, by the collection of materials for introduction to the Western academic community, by survey projects related to local development, and by (higher) education of the local population local science becomes internationally recognized. However, the first stage of this universal mainstream in the East is usually second-grade normal science. J.D. Bernal e.g. spoke of Japanese science as pedantic and lacking in imagination because the Japanese scholars followed ready-made institutional patterns. There are exceptions as in Terada Tokahiko's local geophysical studies of earthquakes that became known as 'Terada physics' (Nakayama, p. 226). In Japanese science dynamics there is an interesting trend from Chinese studies through Dutch Western learning towards Western studies and internationalization.

'Local science' is a particularly sensitive term. If Stephen C. Ferruolo studies the 'Origins of the University' in Paris from 1100-1215 (1985), it is of course local history, but given the Paris university model as paradigm for Western civilization it will be classified as universal. If Ho Ping-ti studies 'The Ladder of Success in Imperial China' (1962), it is of course national history: but without evidence of the impact of the Chinese examination system e.g. on the French Grandes Ecoles and the British civil service system it might be excluded from the academic mainstream. 'International science' is therefore an equally misleading term, if it reflects only the dominance of a particular scientific community at a certain time.

Forum, role and locus

These three dimensions might lead towards a meaningful typology of Ph.D's for higher education and science policy. Such a typology with nx3 cells in a cube might charactarize doctoral dissertations at different levels of aggregation, in fields of study, in institutes and in the form of time series, if we find a satisfactory way of measuring each unit of analysis. The major problem seems to me the distinction between an intended meaning of a dissertation and its realized impact. Let me give a historical example. On 10 March 1742 Jacobus Elisa Joannes Capitein, born in what is presently called Ghana, defended in Leyden University a political-theological dissertation on slavery as not in contradiction with Christian freedom (Dissertatio politico-theologica De servituti, libertate Christianae non contraria). It was printed in the international language of that period, Latin, and has been translated in Dutch with frequent reprints (S. van der Woude, 1963). On our dimensions it would be characterized as at least multidisciplinary. His role perception seems that of an official, a preacher. In the perspective of the time it was international. I assume that this is a rare case of an influential doctoral dissertation and it might be the first written by an African.

Another more recent example might be Robert K. Merton's Ph.D 'Science, Technology and Society in Seventeenth-Century England' (1935). The original thesis has become the base of a rich intellectual offspring. According to our dimensions it would be characterized as crossdisciplinary, because he was developing a new field of study. His role perception seems that of an academic researcher but his scope might have been characterized as national or regional. However, because he was studying the England of Newton with his international impact the dissertation has an international perspective. A direct comparison of the content between the two dissertations is of course meaningless without the context of time and discipline. However, forum, role and locus provide a framework for comparison.

For operational purposes it seems only feasible to record the intentions of the authors at the time of completion. The score on a continuum from mono towards interdisciplinary can be made reasonably objective. It is no value judgment for an individual dissertation. Each score is respectable, but some might object to multidisciplinarity without attempt to integration. Over time multidisciplinary approaches might become interdisciplines or new disciplines as in biochemics. The definition of one's role might meet some obstacles, if one accepts the position of a neutral observer as the only valid entrance point for a scientific work. However, in the motivation of the selection of a thesis subject one might find an implicit or explicit reference to a career. Part-time doctoral candidates have usually a more professional or societal role perception than full-time candidates. Of course, the core of each scientific enterprise is the role definition of a scholar. The scope of a dissertation from local towards international is more a matter of explicit elaboration than the actual focus on a locus. Language and publication are critical variables.

The actual content of dissertations cannot be directly compared. It belongs to the history of science and disciplines. The three dimensions try to characterize dissertations as particular forms of inter-cultural communication (Gudykunst, 1983). How narrowly does one define the forum which has to assess the value of a dissertation? In highly structured fields of study and research institutions one might restrict the communication only to experts within the same field, but in new fields of study or without strong scientific institutions one might need to address a broader forum. Role definitions or the concept of self are cultural phenomena. The familiar observation of more collective modes of expression as in the East and more individualistic modes of expression as in the West is simplistic, but one can observe a refusal of highly individualistic, competitive definitions of a researcher in its own field in many non-Western universities. The same applies to the impact of maturation and experience on the concept of self. Mature persons seem to be less inclined to restrict their role within a narrow set of paradigms than fresh graduates. Locus is more ambivalent. One might observe the world in a grain of sand, as the anthropologist Clifford Geertz once remarked. However, an international scope characterizes the vanguard of scholarship

My main hypothesis is that doctorates at the end of the educational ladder need to reflect a concerted effort to broaden the forum, to socialize scholarship and to expand its scope to international dimensions. If, at the reverse, doctorates become restricted to a narrow forum of specialists, are reduced to a professional researcher's role, or remain confined to local dimensions, they become only academic rituals without meaning for the advancement of science. Basic education is a need for all and might be extended until the age of fifteen or later, but the type of the highest degree reflects the place of knowledge in society as a cultural mission. It is a natural selection process for those who manage to complete. But as with biological natural selection some waste and frustration result from the process: a good deal of time is devoted to pursuing fruitless topics, there are periods of demoralisation, and quite a few candidates fail.

Successive approaches

Taking forum, role and locus as anchor points, the following successive approaches seem useful:

1. An evolutionary approach describing the transformation from prototypes to the ideal types in modern universities;
2. A cultural approach describing the cultures of various scientific communities;
3. A functional approach focusing on the role of doctorates in a life cycle and academic traditions;
4. A structural approach emphasizing institutional means for the production of doctorates;
5. A development approach in the particular case of the Third World;
6. A system's approach where one tries to integrate the key variables as a manageable enterprise for policy.

In the next chapters I will elaborate each approach.

Review and summary

A description is given of the octopus, which has been used as a metaphor for the Ph.D. In contrast to our knowledge of cephalopods studied by teuthologists there is no similar systematic body of knowledge about Ph.D's. Of course, in each individual case representatives of universities have certified that a doctoral dissertation made an independent and original contribution to a field of study, but a descriptive account of physical characteristics of dissertations as title, the number of pages, copies, form of reproduction, language or of doctoral candidates as age, sex, nationality and educational background is not very meaningful without a theory or policy. Quality is the most important characteristic, but qualitative data are notoriously hard to come by. I have wondered why there are no comprehensive files of doctorates except in the U.S.A. The American higher education system is heterogeneous and market-oriented. There is a strong empirical tradition and the Ph.D has an established pre-career function with taught courses. European higher education is fragmented with different traditions. There is no clear function for the Ph.D except for the 'Habilitationschrift' in Germany. The experience of individual candidates and supervisors is ideographic and cross-disciplinary or cross-national comparisons are rarely made in any systematic way. We do not have a prosopography of Ph.D's as we could label the specialization of describing common characteristics of a specific intellectual élite in order to obtain insight in their mobility and position in society (Stone, 1971; Mayeur, 1981).

Doctorates have an uneasy place. Considered as student' products they might be worthy, in part, of publication as is usually stated, but they are not kept in libraries as real books and might be found in microfiches, archives or special bookshops (S. van der Woude, 1963). In relation to mass higher education their numbers tend to be too small for special consideration. From a science policy perspective doctorates are only interesting if proven to cover new grounds and then international journals are better gatekeepers than university records. Doctorates might give entrance to an intellectual elite but there is too much ambivalence in their contribution to treat them as a special distinction.

I have selected three core variables of doctorates which might lead towards a meaningful typology: forum, role and locus. In the following chapters a number of successive approaches are tested to discover whether a general typology of doctorates is feasible and relevant, and what contribution a data base according to what dimensions could make to science dynamics.

Chapter II

The Roots of Higher Learning and Education

Introduction

Evolution consists of ongoing interaction of populations of species which affect each other, under conditions of constantly changing parameters. One might distinguish biological species like octopuses, physical species like molecules, and human artifacts like educational credentials. Individual phenotypes come into being as a result of processes of production. Biological species carry their own genetic instructions within the phenotype. In social species the genetic material consists of knowledge in the heads of persons or in libraries or computers. A particular species as a doctoral dissertation results from learned images and behaviour, such as observing, thinking, talking, writing and reflecting. These 'academic' skills are acquired in the course of previous education and life experience. Decoding available learning material and designing a new synthesis result from interaction and communication with other persons and by the learning processes in the body. There is not yet an evolution theory of the noosphere as in the biosphere although there are some drafts (Kenneth E. Boulding). Knowledge is invisible and multiparental. It can only be observed by its expression, distribution and utilization.

Looking at higher education from an evolutionary point of view one cannot but observe a rather painfully slow and intermittent progress, interspersed with catastrophes and reversals. For understanding the meaning of higher degrees and its expression in written evidence I have selected five periods or better episodes: (1) prototypes, (2) the origin of universities (3) the German research university in the beginning of the 19th century and its impact (4) the rise of American graduate schools and its adoption, (5) the turbulent years of the student' revolt in the sixties.

I do not claim a comprehensive history of advanced higher education. It is a bird's view with some case studies.

Prototypes

In *Western* civilization one might start with the Aristotelian writings, which

were completed in 322 B.C. He found existing educational practice perplexing.

> 'For men are by no means agreed about the things to be taught, whether
> we aim at virtue or the best life. Neither is it clear whether education
> should be more concerned with intellectual or with moral virtue. Existing
> practice is perplexing: no one knows on what principle we should proceed.
> Should the useful in life, or should virtue, or should higher knowledge, be
> the aim of our training? All three opinions have been entertained. Again,
> about method there is no agreement; for different persons, starting with
> different ideas about the nature of virtue, naturally disagree about the
> practice of it'. (Politics, book 8, chapter 2, transl. B. Jowett).

The natural ambiguity of purpose of higher education has set insiders always
for a cruel dilemma. Surely, outsiders say, you can tell me what your
enterprise is about, why in sum, you are doing what you are doing. But as
knowledge materials expand and fragment, insiders seek reassurance in
formulations that promise to pull things together again and provide some
overarching meaning. Thus, we witness a steady stream of purportedly new
statements, that, in their small alteration of phrases, become like old 'whines'
in new bottles: manpower training and/or cultural transmission and/or
individual development, and always back to scholarship and research and
public service (Clark 1983, p. 20). In that sense, the evolution of higher
education has shown a shifting balance between pragmatic, scholarly and
moral qualifications. Presently the horizon has shrinked to pragmatic considerations. Especially the meaning of virtue seems to be left out in present-day
discussions on the role and function of universities. The meaning of $\alpha\rho\epsilon\tau\eta$ is
excellency with moral qualifications of something what is highly valuable
and desirable for individuals and society. (WNTI, Bauernfeind, pp. 457-460).
Of course, Aristotle is also an eponymic concept identifying the classic
origins of Western civilization. Traditional education centred on learning
Latin and Greek in order to get insight in the classic world of thinking.
Unfortunately this requirement is also in decline but the original ideas are still
valid, I assume.

In *Eastern* civilization one might start with the Chinese classics. The
Chinese style of learning upon which Japanese and Korean traditions are
based is documentary, centered around the keeping and ordening of written
records. The famous imperial examinations in China began in the Sui (622
A.D.) and linked scholarship directly to national job opportunities. The
system replaced an earlier method of appointment which relied heavily on
personal recommendation. It seems to have been inspired by a desire to
strengthen the central government on the base of intellect and knowledge
rather than on cliques and wealthy families. W.J. Boot made an interesting

comparison between the Japanese and Korean adoption and adaptation of these examinations (Boot, 1985). The examination system demonstrated the capacity to provide authoritative public standards for judging among prospective candidates. In China it was an open competition and it was rare that the same family produced during two or three successive generations the mandarins (Ho, 1962). In Korea the entrance to the examinations was restricted to the aristocracy, yangban. In Japan there was also a feudal restriction based on birth but examinations were only introduced in 1790 (Boot, 1985).

According to Nakayama, the examinations consisted of both oral and written sections, the former being chiefly a test of the examinee's ability to memorize. One of the favorite Chinese methods of doing this was to select a line of a classical text, cover the surrounding passage plus three characters in the text itself. In the written portions of the exams, scholarly essays and discussions of policy left some room for originality (Nakayama, 1984, p. 63). My resource persons in Leyden university explained the use of case studies and the impact of this examination system on the British civil service and the French 'grandes écoles', but I am unable to check the original sources or to test different opinions.

Comparing the two styles of learning, Nakayama distinguishes a documentary style of learning and rhetorical learning. Especially Chinese astrological records are seen as exemplary of scholarly activity in the documentary style. There were speculative dogmas (such as the theory of Yin-Yang and the Five Elements), but the ancient astrologer regarded past records as an independent and virtually absolute source of power. Only unprecedented anomalies generated enough tension to require new interpretation. As a result, revolutionary theories were almost unheard of as the records continued to increase year after year. Although it does not necessarily call for a creative mind, it demands the same painstaking care, the same devotion to clerical routine, as bookkeeping. Rhetorical scholarship was largely the creation of the Greek natural philosophers and Sophists and the pre-Ch'in (3rd century B.C.) philosophers of China. Forged and honed in the direct democracy of the Greek city-state where citizens hammered out public policy through discussion and debate, this was a spirit that regarded words as souvereign and saw in persuasive techniques a means to personal advancement. The locus of true education is dialogue, for it is there that new ideas and pattern of thought emerge (Socrates, Plato). Hence they preferred to entrust thought to the living minds of men rather than to the skins of dead sheep.

Of course, the two styles of learning are not a simple dichotomy. It is also useless to glorify one of the styles. Each scholarly style has functioned in the history of science and learning whereever we find it. However, the distinction between root-learning and memorizing received wisdom as in the East and rhetoric learning through discussion and debate as in the West seems still to explain present-day preferences in higher education.

Another over-arching typology has been made by Ron Dore. He counter-poses two alternative ideal-typical patterns of achieving balance between equality and diversity in higher education. The first one is based on assumptions of Original Sin. This pattern places great emphasis on the effort of passing selection hurdles, 'if a rough equality of opportunity has allowed one man to go further than another, he earned the unequal reward –income, status, authority– which goes with that success' (p. 182). The main driving force is self-interest and hard work. The second pattern he calls the romantic Confucian system based on Original Virtue. This pattern stresses the luck element in the distribution of talents: a social atmosphere which channels intelligence into productive self-fulfilment and the performance of social duty rather than into self-regarding achievement. Those who reach the top are not encouraged to claim privileges on the ground that they deserve them, that they have earned them by their efforts; they should rather, feel humbly grateful that fate has 'called' them to interesting and worthwhile jobs. The main driving force is productive self-fulfilment.

Of course, this distinction between Original Sin and Original Virtue is highly moralistic. 'There is no such thing as Original Man capable of being virtuous or sinful. Actual men, in actual societies, are shaped by the culture of their society' (p. 19)). The place of learning in a society cannot be entirely derived from pragmatic considerations. Indeed there is a technological impe-rative which became dominant at the turn of the century, but there are also educational traditions on the intrinsic and moralistic value of knowledge. The design of educational institutions is based on a particular philosophy and ideology. Educational degrees as those established in Ph.D's or doctoral dissertations cannot be seen in isolation from this particular philosophy and ideology translated into a policy and supported by career patterns in govern-ment and industry.

This selective description of the prototypes of higher education indicates constant changes in parameters what a final degree means at a particular time and place. When one reads about the postwar development of mass higher education in its explosion of reforms, committees and special journals, it is difficult to discover what has been left of an Aristotelian or Confucian sense of mission for the university. It seems as if mass higher education has become a closed world with its own rules, bureaucracy and internal market without constant interaction with society and without reflection on its mission. However, individual differentiation within the higher education system at the level of a doctoral dissertation continues to challenge the meaning of higher education in its original dimension. One cannot escape the original questions. I assume that a new reflection on learning styles and ideal-types is needed in order to obtain a balanced growth of advanced higher education. Neutral uniformity in higher degrees does not exist, but broadening forum, function and locus from a cross-cultural perspective in each national policy seems a realistic target.

In other civilizations there might be other venerable learning traditions such as the samnyasin and the university of Texila in the third century before Christ (Staal, 1980). A recent discussion with professor P.N. Agarwala (Oxford and Harvard educated) made clear that there is no connection between the Calcutta University Commission (1917-1919) and these old universities. In the Arab world the old university of Al-Azhar still exists but does not easily fit into modern advanced higher education. A discussion with the Indonesian chairman of Nahdatul Ulama, Abdurrahman Wahid (Al-Azhar and Bagdad educated) revealed a fundamental problem of connecting modern advanced learning systems with the traditional wisdom and scholarship of the Islam. There is a remarkable parallel between the design of madarsah djamiah (Islamic university) and that of Oxbridge colleges. One wonders how relevant are the prototypes of advanced learning for present practice, but especially in non-Western higher education one observes an increasing reflection on the origin of their noosphere and some opposition against a dominance of Western pragmatism.

The Origins of the University

The medieval universities from c. 1200 transformed Greek and Graeco-Roman education to Christian Europe. This transition was characterized by an increasing emphasis on educational utility. Greek education was not designed to equip for a professional career or to cultivate a particular art, but rather to develop personality and his ethical being. The medieval university was essentially an indigenous product of western Europe: privileged corporate associations of masters and students with their statutes, seals and administrative machinery, their fixed curricula and degree procedures. Former centres of higher education (Athens, Beirut, Constantinople) might have anticipated in terms of embryonic organization, but there does not appear to be any organic continuity between the universities c. 1200 and these schools. There is an intellectual impulse from tbe past Greek, Graeco-Roman, Byzantine or Arabic traditions, but their institutional crystallization was a new departure born of the need to enlarge the scope of professional education in an increasingly urbanized society (A.B. Cobban, 1975).

The earliest efforts to construct universities in medieval Europe pose us for the question why Bologna and its imitators in northern Italy survived but an earlier and equally promising effort in Salerno did not. According to Cobban, the history of medieval universities reinforces that institutional response must follow quickly upon academic achievement if the intellectual movement is not to be dissipated. The absence of a protective and cohesive organization to sustain its intellectual advance may initially provide a fillup for free-ranging inquiry, but perpetuation and controlled development can only be gained through an institutional framework. Salerno failed to develop this organizational network.

Hastings Rashdall concluded in his 'Universities of Europe in the Middle Ages' (1895) that the original universities had shown a great deal of versatility and flexibility during the first centuries. Despite this 'perpetual modification' or perhaps because of it, the university had managed to preserve and expand upon its essential form. To Rashdall, the university was more than a well-established institution made venerable by time and tradition. It represented three important educational values: a commitment to providing not only useful professional training but also the highest intellectual cultivation possible; a desire not only to conserve and transmit knowledge but also to advance it by research and writing; and, most essential of all, the idea of joining together teachers of diverse subjects into a single harmonious institution, the ideal of making the teaching body representative of the whole cycle of human knowledge. Professionalism and specialization need to remain subordinate to a higher ideal of learning.

Stephen Ferruolo has recently analysed the schools of Paris and their critics from 1100-1215. By 1215 the university of Paris got recognized its rights and privileges by both the King and the Pope. This 'university of masters' was but one of the first prototypes of the university. By 1193 a 'university of students' had formed at Bologna, whose scholars had earlier (in 1155 or 1158) been granted the first of the academic privileges. And before the 'university' was securely established in Paris, there were educational foundations modeled on those in Paris and Bologna at Oxford, Cambridge, Naples and Toulouse, which were regarded by contemporaries as essentially the same type of institution and referred to by the common term 'studium generale'. By the later Middle Ages the term 'universitas' which originally meant any legally defined guild or corporation, was specifically and exclusively applied to this new institution. With a significant degree of local autonomy and the right of self-governance the university was an association of men of diverse social status drawn from a wide geographical area beyond the local region, studying a variety of subjects at different levels of expertise, and united only in that they were all involved in the pursuit of knowledge in the same place at the same time. Teaching took precedence over all else.

There were three basic characteristics which distinguishes the university of other schools. First, it was an enduring and autonomous corporate body. Second, the professional identity of the university consisted in teaching or being taught: the sharing and transmission of knowledge. Third, the university was intended to subsume the specialization of academic disciplines and division of faculties within a broader institutional structure defined by common educational goals and purposes. The first 'university of masters and scholars' in Paris resulted not so much of the pragmatic need of scholars to secure their interests against an external adversary as from the prevailing interests of certain exalted educational values. Of course, there were increased demands for utilitarian learning and professional training, but the university originated out of resistance to these pressures. The university was a victory, if never a complete one, for a higher educational ideal (Ferruolo, 1985). The core was a studium generale and there were 'supranational' pretension as the ius ubique docendi by papal or imperial decree. The rich and kaleidoscopic pattern of university organization which spread over medieval society, ranging from extreme student republicanism to magisterial governmental forms, has ensured that the collective European experience has known virtually every organizational permutation that can be devised. In that sense present day universities are still the lineal descendants of medieval archetypes, and they continue to perpetuate a competitive degree system and habits of ceremonial procedure, which, however disguised, are fundamentally derivatives from the medieval universities (Cobban, 1975).

The Dutch case

As a nation of traders and a delta country Dutch tradition in higher education has been continuously exposed to the major European educational philosophies. In a certain sense the Dutch system can be considered as a cultural pilot experiment in cross-fertilization or a hybrid. There were no clear geographical frontiers. 'Natio' was used for student houses in the university of Paris. In medieval times the Dutch participated in the academic perigrination as students and professors in Köln, Heidelberg, Paris, Bologna and Oxford (R. Calcoen, M.A. Nauwelaerts, A.G. Weiler). As a member of the recently coined Erasmus University I cannot escape mentioning Desiderius Erasmus (1469-1536) as a European scholar.

After Louvain (1425) the first 'Dutch' university of Leyden in 1575 was stimulated by the French prince of erudition Joseph Justus Scaliger 'le monstre sacré de l'érudition batave'. Also in Rotterdam the French Pierre Bayle acted in 1681 as an intellectual foster-father for the predecessor of the Rotterdam university. According to Willem Frijhoff's pioneering Ph.D study (1981) the former five universities (Leyden, 1575; Franeker, 1585; Groningen, 1614; Utrecht, 1636; Harderwijk, 1647) promoted 22.933 graduates during almost two and a half century (1575-1814). As early as 1644 the university of Utrecht started to use the title 'Philosophiae Doctor et Liberalium Artium Magister', which became in use from then. The first degree was extremely rare and mainly required by foreigners. In this period 5356 foreigners were promoted in Dutch universities (23.4%). The majority Germans and some 25 Americans. The difference between the second (licentiate) and the third (doctorate) was mainly a financial question. Since 1600 the thesis was usually printed and either privately (in senatu) or in public (more majorum) defended. Dutch students preferred the Doctor's title, also at a later stage. It was a practical and moral education for the ruling elite of the Republic. 1877 Dutch students got their final degree at foreign universities, mainly in Orléans (1292). I cannot resist the temptation of mentioning one other doctoral dissertation by G. Henk van de Graaf, who published in 1979 in Hungarian a thesis about the role of Dutch universities for Central European protestantism between 1690-1795. S. van der Woude (1963) collected originally some 20.000 titles of printed products of academical instruction in Dutch universities until 1800. In libraries theses are neglected and a great number of these old Dutch theses, all in Latin, were actually traced in London, Dublin, Edinburgh, Oxford, Uppsala, Leningrad, Gluj, Marburg, Herborn and Paris. Since 1963 the catalogue has been doubled and includes the total range of academical products. There were for higher degrees two types of printed products.

(1) The 'disputatio sub praeside' where the student had to defend a set of printed propositions, later a short essay, sometimes based on the work of his professor, under chairmanship of the professor. In Utrecht university since October 1643 one needed 200 copies and the printer was supposed to keep one copy of each 'dispute'. The printing costs were paid by the university and the president got a fee. Usually the participants were drinking wine. It was a festive occasion sometimes.

(2) The 'dissertatio pro gradu doctoratus' where the candidate within one hour had to defend his thesis against oppositions from 'studiosi' and 'doctores and magistri'. Also here the promotor got a fee, called 'chirotheca', formerly given in natura as a glove. The defense of the doctoral dissertation and the solemn promotion were two distinct activities usually at different days. The private promotion (in senatu) was less expensive than the public promotion (more majorum). During the public promotion, as described in article 33 of the laws and statutes of the University of Leyden in 1631 and elsewhere, the rituals were extensive: a long procession of professors in black gowns, the promovendus also in gown with two secondants (paranymphs) like a best man in weddings, a prescribed promotion formula and a 'laudatio' on the qualities of the new doctor by the promotor following detailed regulations, and after an equally solemn return, the day was completed with a promotion dinner.

Every observer of a present-day Dutch academic promotion (or for that matter an Indonesian one) will recognize the continuity of old traditions. Even the number of printed copies(500 in Utrecht by 1685), complaints about the quality in some universities as Harderwijk, and scandals about accepted, printed and at the last moment retracted dissertations can be found in present-day Dutch universities. In that sense, academic rituals reflect a social structure of 'rites de passage' for a society rather than an expression of rationality in science dynamics.

A more detailed case study of a Dutch university provides the three hundred year commemoration of the University of *Franeker*, established at 29 July 1585 and abolished in 1811 by the French reorganization of higher education. The 500 pages of the commemoration book published in 1985 give a lively picture of a once famous university which after a careful start flourished especially in the seventeenth century and gradually shrinked towards a provincial and local university. I have selected a few indicators of the life cycle of this university. In figure II-1 one can observe the entrance (immatriculation) of new students in Leyden and Franeker. Except for a short period from 1665-1684 there is a similar curve, be it that Leyden has around four times as many students as Franeker. In figure II-2 and II-3 the number of foreign students and doctores are separately shown in graphs. There is also a separate chapter on the 177 professors with their geographical origin. There was clearly a supranational, at that time time a European, concept of scholarship and university. Around one third of the students were foreigners and the same applies to the faculty: 33 from Germany, 6 from France, 6 from Switzerland, two from Poland, and one from England and Sweden. After 1750 one did not try anymore to attract foreign scholars. The reformation and contra-reformation has been one of the major motives for establishing new universities since the religious peace contract of Augsburg in 1555, where many regional sovereigns started their own university as an 'instrumentum dominationis'. However, science was seen as supranational, be it in a protestant and catholic mode. Especially the academic peregrination where students visited more than one university made univeristies international centres. Also the use of Latin as a lingua franca has been helpful, but gradually national languages in academic instruction reduced the internationalisation.

Although it is difficult to generalize from a particular case study, I cannot escape the hypothesis that universities need an international dimension in forum, role and function for survival. This internationalisation does not prevent a particular local or national style. In the Dutch case e.g. Franeker had a special Frisian style but generally following the pattern of the other four Dutch universities of the time. Frijhoff describes this pattern as follows:

Qualitatively, (1) Dutch educational philosophy attempted to strike a balance between speculative theory and praxis. It was not a 'Gelehterschule' as in seventeenth century Germany but a practical and moral education for the ruling elite of the Republic. "Froid bon sens, goût du concret, contact étroit avec l'expérience, réalism, curiosité multiple, tendance aux applications pratiques" as a French historian wrote (Frijhoff, pp. 25-26). However, engineering, trade and vocational skills developed independently from universities.

(2) The academic perigrination was a Dutch habit for rich families; "their

youths, after the course of their studies at home, travel for some years .....
chiefly into England and France, not much into Italy, seldomer in Spain, not
often into the more northern countries" (Sir William Temple, quoted by
Frijhoff).
(3) The Dutch electicism was receptive to foreign ideas and culture rather
than showing their own cultural heritage. "They somewhat resemble their
brokers, who trade for immense sums without having any capital" (Golds-
mith, quoted by Frijhoff, p. 286). The Dutch-Japanese relationship from
1609-1856 is a perfect example of brokerage. The few Dutch graduates in
colonial service did not use their knowledge for academic explorations
(Frijhoff, pp. 206-207).

For a historical survey the standing conference of rectors, presidents and
vice-chancellors of the European universities (CRE) has published in 1984 a
preliminary document, where the chronology of some six hundred 'university' institutions has been indicated. Of course, this compendium does not yet
allow a comparison, but I assume that in future studies the role and function
of doctorates can be made explicit in an international perspective.

The German Research University

In scientific activity, structure and curricula the early German universities
followed the patterns of Paris and Bologna, which are specifically mentioned
in their statutes. The main features of university organization (called universitas, academia or Hohe Schule without uniform terminology) were and are
faculties, a constitutional rectorate, senate and deans. In the wake of the
humanist movement and in connection with the Reformation there were
important changes. After the middle of the 16th century universities became
confessionally divided: Lutheran and, on the Catholic side, belonging to the
Jesuit order, but everywhere they pursued the ideal of humanist reform,
namely that of 'sapiens et eloquens pietas'. The intensification of the religious
debates resulted in a manifest decline in the universities in the second half of
the 17th century. The universities were rescued by a rationalist, secular view
of science in conjunction with the needs of and the corresponding pressure
exerted by the princes. The foundation of Halle (1693) and Göttingen (1733)
resulted from this rationalist movement. This scientific optimism was maintained in the second half of the 18th century, despite its too shallowly
rationalist orientation, but the effects of the French revolution led to the
dissolution of many universities (Hammerstein, in Compendium, 1984, p.
25).
In the victory over the influence of Napoleon's educational measures in
university practice and theory, the real landmark was the foundation of the

University of Berlin in 1810, in accordance with the plans produced by the State Minister and humanist scholar, Wilhelm von Humboldt. It confirmed a victory of the 'universitas litterarum', i.e. the institutional unity of all sciences over the specialized college principle, ensuring the continuity of the historical structure, in the shape of a state-protected corporation with academic autonomy. The 'Abitur' of a humanistic gymnasium (introduced in Prussia in 1788) became the official prerequisite for admission, and the 'Habilitation' the necessary qualification for the post of 'Privatdozent' as the first rang on the academic teacher's ladder. The newly founded or revived universities: Berlin (1810), Breslau (1811), Bonn (1818) and Munich (1826) expressed the new conception of science in the sense of research as well as teaching (see p. 6, the research imperative). it were again high educational ideals, where, as in the past with virtue, Humboldt's idea of 'Bildung' became jeopardized by the rapid growth of specialization in the individual sciences. The universities were not transformed into national institutions, as radical forces at that time desired. They remained under the education authority of each 'Land', even after the foundation of the 'Reich' in 1870, but were seen as equivalent. This is still the case (L. Boehm, in Compendium, p. 27).

The impact of the research imperative: the French case

The German research university became the most important worldwide academic institutional model of the nineteenth and early twentieth century. Centered on the research imperative, this modern prototype integrated research and teaching in the full professor, reinforcing his dominance as director of his research institute and as part-time policy maker at other levels of university administration (Clark, 1983, p. 47). In contrast to the teaching priorities from the guild model with elaborate examinations, exercises in the techniques of teaching and ceremonial investiture, the production of new knowledge as in a laboratory or industrial pilot plant became dominant. The French system has long incorporated the belief that the university tests and teaches. According to Joseph Ben-David, France was the Western European country least influenced by the German model. (Ben-David, 1977, pp. 106-107). Research needs the support of a separate structure of academies, institutes and centers. Its most prestigious sector, the leading 'Grandes Ecoles' consists principally of places devoted to strict professional training that leave the research function out almost entirely. It seems an anomaly (Clark, 1983, p. 98).

Is the French case indeed an anomaly? C. Maury remarked in a presentation on the duality of the French educational system: 'It is a true "tour de force" to present exactly and throughly the French higher educational system. Its complex organization has obviously roots in history. But a full understanding goes through a reference to the social mission of higher education, that is to prepare the insertion of graduates into professional life and social positions' (Maury, 1985). For an outsider the French system offers even more of a challenge.

Jacques Verger (Compendium, 1984, pp. 32-35) describes the breakdown of the great medieval universities in Paris, Montpellier, Toulouse, Orleans, Angers and Avignon as the result of many new colleges, frequently controlled by the Jesuits, and on the other side by protestant academies. Moreover, the traditional universities became mere diploma mills without any serious intellectual control and without analysis of social needs and new ideas. The French revolution could easily suppress the universities, because they had lost their original function, 'elles ne furent guère que de formes vides n'ayant pour fonction, outre la collation des grades, que l'organisation de quelques cours public devant un public clairsemé' (p. 33). The major part of the nineteenth century can be characterized by the stagnation of the university as an institute and the rise of the 'Grandes Ecoles' and similar institutes outside the university. However, in the reorganization of the French faculties and universities at the end of the nineteenth century the German model has played a major role, although the 'Grandes Ecoles' maintained their leading position.

George Weisz offers in his 'The Emergence of Modern Universities in France, 1863-1914' (1983) a remarkable analysis of this reorganization. This book is based on an American Ph.D and a 'doctorat de 3è cycle' in Paris and focuses on the internal changes in French society and its educational system. The growing prestige of German science and universities awakened fears that France's intellectual status within the international community was on the wane: these fears intensified after the German victory of 1870. The research sector of the education system was fairly peripheral and the reformers wanted intellectual production to become a prime function of professional life, closely linked with demands for more academic freedom and institutional autonomy, increased resources and salaries, and the creation of universities to replace the dispensed professional faculties (p. 7). After 1895 there was an intensifying military and commercial rivalry between France and Germany, which heightened interest in technical and commercial education (p. 12).

The thrust of French reforms seems to be transforming faculties into institutions of science and research rather than merely disseminating received scientific truth. The German example is always in the backyard, but of course within the French dual higher educational system, making a clear distinction between the prestigious and highly selective 'Grandes Ecoles', and non-selective universities for the majority. From the beginning of its history, France has shown a firm attachment to a strong central state and puts therefore a strong emphasis on the early selection of a satisfactory set of graduates for higher technological and business positions. This educational mission is strictly defined and gives much importance to school results between the age of 16 and 20. It is highly competitive. Priority was given to know-how linked with defense problems of strategic interest: the building of roads and bridges to facilitate transportation of troups, the extraction of minerals to produce powder and so on. Ecole de l'Artillerie et du Génie (1802), Ecole des Ponts et Chaussées (1747), Ecole des Mines (1783) were all specialized educational institutions in response to specific needs. The most prestigious is the Ecole Polytechnique (1794) in response to the need for state engineers. It provided a grounding in mathematics and science. The existence of a well defined selection and ranking process is the key which separates the Universities and the Schools. In a competitive entrance examination ratio's of one to ten are common and the selection starts already at the 'classes préparatoires' and the last cycle of secondary studies between the age of 15 and 18. This selection process seems to be inspired by the Chinese imperial examinations as they have become known by French Jesuits (Zi, 1894; Teng, 1942).

Research was delegated to universities and academies. The ideal of the teacher-researcher was adopted enthusiastically in the French universities. The dean of the medical faculty in Toulouse wrote e.g. in 1901 after describing teaching activities, that the more elevated mission of faculties is to be a center of scientific production, as organs of the state and as depositories of national renown. 'Our "mâtres" will have small numbers of students, an elite on which they will lavish the best of their thought, this is the noble task which goes together with the more modest and more pressing task of being a professor to students who aspire to become practitioners' (Quoted in Weisz, 1983, p. 199).

Quantitative indicators of this growing importance of research in the modern French universities are also based on doctorates. Victor Karady, for example, examined the size of doctoral theses in the faculties of science and letters. During the first half of the nineteenth century it is suggested, that doctorates in both institutions were elaborate initiation rites of little scholarly value. During the second half, however, they became increasingly substantial, at least in terms of length. Before 1840, for instance, 83 percent of all theses for the doctorate of letters were less than 100 pages long; after 1881, 72 percent were longer than 300 pages. In the case of the doctorate of science, 63 percent of all theses before 1850 were less than 40 pages in length, after 1876 only 7 percent. Of course, such statistics tell us nothing about the quality of work accomplished. In the case of medicine and law the situation was different. The doctorate of medicine was a degree certifying competence to practice medicine. The thesis - which linked it to research doctorates in other faculties - was a short, largely symbolic affair. The doctorate of law was a somewhat more serious research degree; but after 1889 it served mainly as a way of getting students an exemption from military service and as a framework for the many newly created courses in the social sciences that could not fit into the 'Licence' programme (Weisz, 1983, p. 201, p. 213).

In the years before the First World War, complaints about the decline of French science became increasingly common. Politicians were disturbed by the apparent superiority of German research. Firstly, one complained about the lack of research facilities, a familiar criticism. Secondly, individual research often took place at the margins of an organizational system whose deepest logic was based on the need to train and certify middle-class professionals. There existed no real 'islands' of research equivalent to the German institutes and seminars. Also a rather familiar sound. Thirdly, scientists complained, that the pressure of teaching and examinations took too much time away from research. 'We do useful work, but work that is inferior and foreign to the very essence of our function' as one professor wrote (RIE 35 (1898) p. 233). This is also hardly new.

The basic problem of research in France went deeper than lack of facilities and time or the excessive demands of teaching future practitioners. The dilemma specific to French higher education seems the structural inability to separate training for the research role from training for the liberal and teaching professions. Except at the 'Ecole Pratique des Hautes Etudes' (1868), French higher education was incapable of making room for a formal system of graduate studies. The three examinations (excluding the 'baccalauréat') were 'licence', 'agrégation' and doctorate. Only the doctorate was a dubious test of research ability. 'Agrégation' was in fact required for most university positions and required a rather long effort made more difficult by the fact that many candidates continued to prepare for the competition while teaching in 'lycées'. Emphasis was placed on the development of rhetorical skills and the mastery of knowledge that would have to be communicated. There were specific courses for 'agrégation', but there existed no formal training for research beyond the advice that a patron or older colleague could offer (Weisz, 1983, pp. 212-213). The 'agrégation' is a peculiar examination, where a candidate has to prepare a lecture on a special subject within twenty four hours and deliver it for a forum of some seven academics. The selection of this forum seems to determine the outcome. In 1886 a new degree was inaugurated at the Sorbonne: Diplôme d'Etudes Supérieures (DES). The new diploma was supposed to enable students to demonstrate research competence before they undertook to prepare for the 'agrégation' competition. By 1904, the DES had proven its value and was extended to all disciplines in the faculties of letters and science.

Reviewing the French case of adopting the research imperative as initiated by Germany, it becomes clear that (advanced higher) education is teleological in nature and cannot be reduced to pragmatic and economic considerations. In Germany it was not a question of teaching a body of acquired knowledge to students. 'Wissenschaft' was what one did with the body of knowledge acquired, and what one did was research i.e. crèate knowledge. The German research seminar, the doctoral dissertation and the 'Habilitation' thesis are

expressions of this scientific attitude. It began as much in the humanities
–solid German philology– as in the natural sciences (Locke, 1984, p. 310).
The French case (and for that matter any other national case) is not an
anomaly. It reflects French society with a strong central government and a
need for selecting a dominant administrative elite based on highly intellectual
qualities, the mandarins (Suleiman, 1974; Dogan, 1975). From a French
perspective the dominant forum was the centre of power, Paris. Virtually all
of the 'Grandes Ecoles' and institutions of research and erudition were
situated in the capital. In the mid-1870s three quarters of all doctors of
medicine, science and letters were trained in Paris (Weisz, 1984, p. 23). Of
course, this forum includes exporting language, culture and higher education
world-wide. The dominant role in French higher education seems to be the
administrative elite rather than one of an independent scholar or researcher.
There seems little doubt that the capital was seen as the locus of power and
intellectual leadership.

In a historical perspective Humboldt's concept of a research university has
added a new dimension to higher education. The doctorate became more
explicitly a research degree, whereas in medieval universities the distinction
between various degrees was unclear and sometimes mainly of financial
nature. This new concept cannot be seen as a recipe or model to be adopted by
other higher education systems, but needed to be adapted according to one's
own educational traditions. Of course, broadening the frontiers of learning
has been always included in the mission of universities but the role conflict
between teaching future practitioners and research at the leading edge of
one's specialization became explicit. For research one needs more freedom to
enter the academic arena with new propositions, whereas in teaching one has
to agree what needs to be taught and how it should be organized. Research
requires an international dimension, whereas teaching concerns those who
are actually addressed as students with their particular background, ambi-
tions and perspectives. For teaching the forum consists of students and their
future employers, whereas for research the forum consists of colleagues and
editorial boards of international journals.

American graduate schools

In the first chapter I have described the origin of the American graduate
school as the result of two different national patterns: the concept of a
German university superimposed on the English college system. It is a
remarkable historical coincidence that also German has been considered as a
national language for the United States. The graduate school is, however, not
a copy of continental traditions. The American graduate school is at the
moment clearly the dominant mode and in the first stage of my study I tried to

restrict myself to the origin of American graduate education, because in its variety and richness it seemed to encompass all elements of previous experience. Moreover, most studies on higher education are of American origin. However, I became gradually more curious about what exactly is the contribution of the American concept and whether it has integrated all previous traditions.

It is difficult to generalize about 'the American model'. The differentiation of American higher education is so extensive that one needs some twenty categories of types of institutions. Less than a fifth of American students and faculty are in the research universities that couple research and teaching to a major degree since the last quarter of the nineteenth century. The traditionally heterogeneous university category has become even more so as various state colleges have developed advanced programmes and some research. Adding such places to the many private universities that have long had the character of service rather than research universities means that the images of the Ivy League and such leading state universities as California, Michigan, and Wisconsin are poor guides to reality (Clark, 1983, p. 61).

The rise and spread of the graduate school in the United States as a solution to the problem of underpinning research and advanced training was never a centrally planned solution, nor was it apparently even a tacit agreement among a small group of leaders. It was more a social choice, a resultant rooted in the competitive interaction and voluntary imitation of autonomous institutions. This choice came out of a disorderly competition as emerging universities faced the common problem of how to accommodate research and advanced training in a setting already occupied by the college, then already a two-hundred-year old form. Institutions were free to experiment in how to make these accommodations. For instance, Charles W. Eliot as Harvard president (1865-1909), was initially no great supporter of the new research imperative, but he changed his mind and his tactics in the face of losing renowned professors to John Hopkins where Gilman stressed graduate programmes.

The history of educational degrees in the U.S.A. followed originally a European pattern: the first bachelor's degrees at Harvard in 1642 and at Yale in 1702. Later by 1644 Harvard began to grant master's degrees and in 1692 the Harvard corporation awarded Increase Mather, in a ceremony of medieval precedent, a doctorate in theology. However, as expressed by Gilman the new modern Ph.D's since 1861 abolished the old ceremonial habits. The distinctive nature of American Ph.D's results from the freedom to experiment. The 1819 decision of the United States Supreme Court in the so-called Dartmouth College case established the inviolability of publicly as well as privately chartered university corporations (Herbst in Compendium, 1984, p. 72). It is therefore no surprise that the largest variety of doctorates has developed in the U.S.A.. The pragmatic and commercial connections of American higher education have been the almost perennial topic of attack by critics. But the critics have often overlooked the ability of the American professoriate to use at least part of the money that came to them for the advancementof pure scholarship and science. This use has been facilitated by the uncertain distinction between pure and applied science and even more by the utility of the two to each other. As a result, American graduate schools –in a country so often characterized as materialistic– have been able to support pure inquiry on a scale in equipment and numbers of people unprecedented in human history (Katz, 1976).

The American graduate school is indeed an amazing phenomenon. From a production of 239 Ph.D's by the year 1900, this number increased to just over 2,000 by 1930, and on up to nearly 3,600 by 1941. Gaining momentum after a few years hiatus following the Second World War, productivity climbed to over 6,000 by 1950 and 10,000 by 1960, the beginning of the most dramatic growth in graduate education's one-hundred-year history. During the 1960s, the production of Ph.D's nearly tripled, and by 1971 American universities produced over 32,000 doctorates. Over the years, doctorate production became spread over a greater number of institutions with the general trend being more toward state universities and less concentration in what was regarded as the dozen or so elite institutions of the 1920s and 1930s. By 1971 the top 20 institutions produced only 37 percent of the doctorates. Far and away the largest single provider of dollars for the support of graduate education was the federal government. Historically, the graduate school had lived budgetarily of the undergraduate college by a sort of 'overhead'.

With respect to the nature of Ph.D production, it clearly became increasingly impersonal. Many academic departments which began as small, intimate groups of scholars with mutual concerns and interests, blossomed into large collections of diverse individuals, and in orientation and value, often so heterogeneous that it became difficult to discern any central purpose or vision. Grant-swinging became the name of the game, as the volume of research applications and research grants became astronomical. There were few conceivable questions that someone did not try to put to some empirical test in some grant application. At the same time –and most likely as a consequence-concern for Ph.D candidates was neither respected nor rewarded. There was, first, a virtual explosion in the number of outlets for scholarly reports, and, second, an increasingly constricted notion of professional societies and allegiances. As more and more scholars prepared increasing numbers of manuscripts (usually dealing with increasingly narrow and esoteric topics), the number of insignificant publications increased as well. Though we have no clear evidence for this assertion, the percentage of publications that are so seriously deficient on one or more important criteria that they should not be published in the first place may be higher now than was the case twenty years ago (Katz, 1976, p. 12). Pierre van den Berghe wrote a stimulating book on 'Academic Gamesmanship How to make a Ph.D pay' (1970).

Presently, the American Ph.D seems to be everywhere the model to be followed. In most meetings and discussions with colleagues one blames the 'European' pattern as too long, a life-work or too uncertain and admires the structured and taught approach of the American graduate school and indeed, especially in fields that have a method which can be articulated and taught, graduate schools make a contribution. If one likes to increase the knowledge of particular methodologies and theories, the American graduate school offers opportunities for effectiveness. However, in new fields or interdisciplines it is not sure whether the graduate school can be seen as an institutional invention to promote organized creativity. (Berelson, 1965). Methods are in constant flux and there is dispute about the appropriateness and effectiveness of different methods for different purposes. In the American graduate system there are complaints about an undue allegiance to a specific 'school of thought' and a loss of theoretical breadth, community of inquiry and civility (Katz, 1976, p. 262).

Of course, one cannot easily generalize about "the" American system. There are sufficient voices of Americans who strive for the unity of science, the cultural mission of Ph.D's and for increasing the standards of evaluation (Lederman, 1984). Especially the notion of granting candidates the right to originality only after they have passed a graduate programme seems not to be supported by evidence. The traditional apprenticeship was based on the notion of long time involvement in tbe actual application of knowledge. In our framework of forum, role and locus, it seems that the American Ph.D constraints thinking in the direction of conforming with professorial ways of thinking. The forum is frequently too narrow and specialized. The role of a Ph.D in the American system tends to be too much in terms of career prospects rather than the advancement of knowledge. With the exception of the great centers of learning quite a few Ph.D's have only a local dimension.

The main contribution of the American graduate school is that it expanded considerably beyond its German model with strong departments allowing for large numbers of professors in contrast to the German domination of one field by one man. The emphasis on research permeated the professional schools. Each new field of study, whatever its academic status, could become subjects taught and investigated on the same level as the old established fields (Ben-David, 1972, p. 93). Every specialization seems possible for graduate development. However, without similar conditions of voluntary monitoring on the base of output and evaluation, without a similar function of Ph.D's as pre-career devices and without the openness for market forces the American graduate school is only a partial solution for training methodology at an advanced level.

The Roaring Sixties

What has been the impact of the student activism in the sixties, exemplified by Berkeley 1964 and Paris 1968, on the roots of higher learning and especially the Ph.D phenomenon? It seems still too early for a reasonable judgment. A future historian might conclude that the turbulent events of the sixties are only symptoms of the demographic growth towards a mass university and a changing function of the university (Hesseling, 1981). However, as Altbach remarks (1971, p. 271), without the dramatic growth of student activism in the sixties, many universities would have remained silent and would clearly not have begun to think seriously of academic reform. For the most part political goals or a wide-ranging dissatisfaction with the establishment have been at the root of the movement, but the student unrest brought the university in the public attention and stimulated the over-all academic crisis. Universities are marked by their inability or unwillingness to deal with key problems until they are of crisis proportions.

In a general sense, one could observe a change in the value of knowledge from validity and reliability towards social responsibility, but in the countless studies on student protest the emphasis is mainly on student attitudes, reforming the (undergraduate) curriculum and participation in policy making. Ph.D candidates or graduate students were not particularly active in the more militant groups and have not received special attention in the studies on the student movement. Only as teaching assistants or employees they played a major role e.g. in The (American) Teaching Assistants Association, in laying the foundations for the New Left of the 1960s and in radical journalism as in New University Thought (Chicago), Studies on the Left (Wisconsin) and Root and Branch (Berkeley). However, it seems that the student revolt does not touch the Ph.D system as such. In a memorial book on the university of Amsterdam e.g. (de Jong, 1981) the doctorate is hardly mentioned in the flood of stencils of the day, except once in suggesting less ceremony in formal dress.

The origin of a reflection on science as a social responsible activity is much older than the student movement. The English physicist J.D. Bernal wrote his book 'The Social Function of Science' in 1939:

'Science has ceased to be the occupation of curious gentlemen or of ingeneous minds supported by wealthy patrons, and has become an industry supported by large industrial monopolies and by the State. Imperceptibly this has altered the character of science from an individual to a collective basis and has enhanced the importance of apparatus and administration'

The fascism in Nazi Germany and scepticism about Sovjet science led to the foundation of the Society for Freedom of Science in 1941 with scientists as J.R. Baker, Sir Solly Zuckerman, and Michael Polanyi. This was partly a liberal answer to the more radical Association of Scientific Workers. Self-coordination of the scientific community was needed, but scientific considerations in the production of knowledge, such as originality and personal responsibility were predominant. In analogy with Adam Smith, Polanyi suggested also 'an invisible hand' in the coordination of scientific production (de Boer, 1981). Whatever one's personal appraisal of the function of new knowledge as in Ph.D's, it is quite clear that knowledge production is part of the public domain and that the external influences of the environment has increased enormously in the personal choice of what to study. The student movement has accelerated this process of reflection.

The origin of the structural changes in universities dates back from the postwar period. Especially the Marshall plan brought the attention of many to the more effective American university and its graduate schools. In the Netherlands e.g. the first proposals for structural changes which starts now to be implemented were made since the commission Reinink (1 May 1946). Also in other countries reform proposals were made before the student movement (see e.g. Wheatcroft, 1970). However, especially the violent climax in Paris and Amsterdam in 1968 of radical protest stimulated the transformation. Universities lost their introverted attitude and had to cope with their image and respectability. It might be that the time spent on internal re-organization and public relations has decreased the readiness of supervisors for accepting candidates but I have no evidence on time budgets. Moreover, time pressure has been frequently used as an excuse for those who never or rarely supervised doctorate applicants.

The main impact of the roaring sixties seems to have been the differentiation between a four-years cycle for the many with planning, programming and budgeting and, after some time interval, further separate stages for the few. Gradually also in the second and third stages considerations of efficiency and effectiveness became dominant, e.g. in discussions about completion rates (Meeks, 1985; Hodges, 1985). Fragmentation of the academic forum made the applicability of 'universitas' even more dubious than in the past. In the Dutch case, the only one to the best of my knowledge, the senate as symbol of the scientific community has been even abolished in 1971. Only in the case of doctorates a relict in the form of a committee of deans is the official authority to award a doctorate and is usually represented by the rector and a promotion committee. I frequently wonder whether the abolishment of the senate in the Dutch case cannot be characterized as a historical failure.

Review and Conclusions

History never finishes. In the next chapters I will continuously return to the origin of cultures, functions and structures. It is rather arbitrary to include these five episodes and even this selection has not been fully described. Universities have shown a great deal of versality and flexibility during the centuries. Of course, most historians warn us that some knowledge of the past is a condition of practical wisdom in the present, but the lessons of history seldom admit of formal deduction or didactic exposition (Rashdall, 1936, 3:464). If history is a teacher, it is a difficult one or we are slow in understanding its lessons.

In economic history one has identified many cycles: 'Kitchin' for investment in stocks, 'Juglar' for investment in technology, 'Kuznets' for investment in production capacity and the long cycles of some fifty years. There is a rich literature. Knowledge cycles are comparatively underdeveloped. It seems a reasonable hypothesis that new knowledge precedes economic development. It is a necessary condition as can be illustrated by the American, German and Japanese case. However, new knowledge and even know-how is not sufficient as can be seen in the Chinese case of inventing the loom (Needham). It seems also a reasonable hypothesis that economic stagnation results in decline of knowledge production, but is there an essential role for doctorates which can be specified?

An understanding of the prototypes of higher learning seems still essential for classifying present modes and designing new alternative doctorate programmes. Modern world-wide communication exposes candidates for higher degrees to different perceptions of what a Ph.D is supposed to be. The distinction between careful recording of received wisdom before one is allowed to offer one's own opinion and triggering off new ideas by debate and discussion seems still underlying eastern and western learning styles. However, it is not a dichotomy. It is the result of nurture, not of nature.

The original concept of a university in the thirteenth century reflects the idea of joining together teachers of diverse subjects into a single harmonious institution and of representing the whole cycle of human knowledge. This concept is too precious to be neglected, although we realize now that it will always be challenged. The idea of a unity of science has been a major force in developing the unity of humanity, which is much on the minds of those who struggle for mutual international understanding in these perilous times, as Leon M. Lederman wrote in Scientific American (November, 1984). Society must care about this ideal as a cultural mission. The Dutch case shows that Reformation and Contra-reformation has narrowed down the academic forum, role and locus, as in other European countries. The university became an 'instrumentum dominationis' for local souvereigns and the academic perigrination decreased, also because Latin became less the general language for lecturing.

The German research university as designed by von Humboldt in the beginning of the eighteenth century can be seen as a victory over the influence of Napoleon's educational measures with its emphasis on schools. The German concept confirmed the institutional unity of all sciences and added the research imperative. It became the most important world wide academic model, an industrial model, if one likes in contrast to the traditional guild model with teaching priorities. However, the German model cannot be blueprinted but needs to be adapted in each national educational philosophy. The French case shows a duality but has transformed also faculties into research institutes. The emphasis on research forced universities towards an international orientation. The forum became broader and the research role more explicit. Frequently special research institutes encompassed the work of many individual universities.

The American graduate school elaborated the German concept superimposed on the English college system. It is highly differentiated and has been the most productive in Ph.D generation. The distinctive nature results from the freedom to experiment, whether as state or as private university. It has added a strong competitive element to Ph.D degrees. As a result of scale it clearly became increasingly impersonal with large, heterogeneous graduate departments. Its main function is in fields that have a method which can be articulated and taught. The American graduate school has become the envy of the world, but without similar conditions of monitoring on the base of output and of openness for market forces it seems only a partial solution for training methodology in certain fields. It is clearly an extension of the German model. There are, however, many parochial fora, the role is usually a pre-career role of teacher or researcher and mainly the great centers of learning stress the international dimension.

The student activism in the sixties has accelerated the change from elite towards mass university. The differentiation between the four-year cycle for the many with budgeting, planning and programming and the further stages for advanced study has become acute. I have found no evidence that the student movement has touched the Ph.D system as such. Reflections on the role of science and the planning of structural changes in universities are older than the student movements. The university lost its introverted orientation and had to cope with its image and internal reorganization. The academic forum became more fragmented and the role of a Ph.D changed towards considerations of labour market. The more one stresses completion rates of Ph.D more than content or quality, the more local production becomes important. The major challenge seems to be whether the meaning of a Ph.D as an original and independent contribution to knowledge can survive the present forces of effective industrialization for useful knowledge.

The most important lesson which I learned from reading historical episodes is that higher education and its frontiers are teleological: noble objectives of learning, self-development and character building needed for key positions in society but never reduced to pragmatic considerations. To quote Daniel C. Gilman, the founder of the first American graduate school:

'The object of the university is to develop character - to make men. It misses its aims if it produces pedants, or simple artisans, or cunning sophists, or pretentious practitioners.....The graduate school should prepare for the service of society a class of students who will be wise, thoughtful, progressive guides in whatever department of work or thought they may be engaged. Universities easily fall into ruts. Almost every epoch requires a fresh start' (in Cordasco, pp. 142-143).

It is very difficult to prove the influence of prototypes, the medieval university, the German concept and American educational ideals on present reforms. Each period needs its own aspiration and a new clarification of aim and purpose. Although it is only a case, I would stress that the establishment of Franeker University in 1585 was not based on financial or pragmatic reasons. Only in the eighteenth century, when humanistic educational ideals were extinguished, one started to use economic arguments (Waterbolk, in Jensma, 1985, p. 53). Also our time needs its sense of mission.

Chapter III

Cultures, Niches and Dynamics

Another way of looking at the frontiers of learning or, may be more appropriately, at the limits of science is the cultural perspective. Raymond Williams rightly observes that culture is one of the two or three most complicated words. It is the result of human cultivation and civilization. A Ministry of Culture refers to artistic activities, sometimes with the addition of philosophy, scholarship, history. In association with class distinction it produced the mime-word 'culchah'. In its German form Kultur it raises the suspicion of propaganda and its American variation 'culture-vulture' suggests dangerous dimensions (R. Williams, !976, pp. 76-82). Culture and science in its restricted meaning are almost antipodes.

Meaning of Culture

One can distinguish three basic meanings (Bauman, 1973).

The *first* usage is deeply ingrained in the common pre-scientific layer of the Western mentality and refers to an ideal nature of the human being. It is understood hierarchically as the conscious, strenuous and prolonged effort to attain this ideal, to bring the actual life-process into line with the highest potential of the human vocation. This usage is related to some colonial and neocolonial claims where culture is exported to the underdeveloped.

The *second* usage refers to the apparent differences between communities of people over time, between regions or nations, and between social groups, such as business organizations and classes. In its anthropological sense it has been coined by Edward B. Tylor who received in 1884 the first university chair in Oxford and started the definition of culture for scientific use with its normative dimensions. A recent anthropologist Clifford Geertz (1973) warns us that cultural analysis must not lose touch with the hard surfaces of life, such as the technological, economic and political realities, in search of all-too-deep-lying turtles. He warns against turning culture into folklore and collecting it, turning it into traits and counting it, turning it into institutions and classifying it, turning it into structures and toying with it. The real challenge of the interpretation of culture is the enlargement and amplification of human behaviour where any observed culture has only been able to utilize a very selective portion of all the possible human behaviours. The suggestion of Geert Hofstede's impressive 'Culture's Consequences' (1980) is that one can capsulate universal dimensions of culture. It seems better to relate culture as the specific way people give meaning to the relationship with other men, with nature and with time. Explicitness of culture will make the complex relationships in coping with our environment better understandable, it is a projection (Trompenaars, 1985).

The *third* meaning of culture is a generic one as the quality of a universal feature of all men and of men only. The essence of the human culture is then being structured and being capable of structuring. Man is the tool-making, talking and symbolizing animal who seems to be able to change his environment. In this generic sense one attempts to define the common root of culture and society in perception, language and other symbolic behaviour.

The Scientific Community

If we would extrapolate the scientific community from the prototypes of higher learning, the medieval 'universitas' of persons and the whole range of knowledge, the German research imperative and the American graduate schools, we would expect the Ph.D or similar higher degrees as an initiation into this community. J. de Boer described this scientific community in 1981 with his own ethos and norms of universalism, communism, desinterestness, systematic scepsis and rewards for originality. As a reflection of half a century scholarship in the field of theoretical physics he indicates the trial and error of scientific development. It is not a continuous and accumulative process of growth. New paradigms meet opposition and new original ideas as expressed in dissertations and articles sometimes need a long period of dissemination and debate before they become accepted.

The Ph.D seems the most common belief in higher education. It is awarded by a university with the 'ius promovendi', formerly a right by pope and emperor and frequently still based on a declaration by a souvereign. In the Dutch setting it is awarded by the committee of deans, a relict of the abolished senate, expressing the unity of science. The implicit or explicit statement that a doctoral dissertation is an original and independent contribution to knowledge, can only be characterized as a judgment call. Actually, this judgment can only be tested by exposure to a wider audience and by longitudinal studies. The fact that the famous French historian, Fernand Braudel (1902-1985), needed more than twenty years to complete his Ph.D on 'La Mediterranée et le monde méditerranéen à l'épogue du Philippe II' (1949) is less important than the quality and influence of this work.

Most definitions of culture imply that culture is a kind of shared cognitive and evaluational structure. Culture is practically everything in human life which is learned and transmitted by symbols. Culture defines the criteria for choice and the area of rationality prevailing in a certain social context or society. The relationship between culture and behaviour is not contingent and empirical, but conceptual. Actions which are said to depend on culture are expressions of ideas and action precepts being part of the culture. Which actions have been followed cannot be told before the action itself has been observed. Culture defines the limits of what is possible to do in a society or community. The prototype for a cultural explanation is the practical syllogism (Macintyre, 1964). For example, Max Weber's classic study on the relationship between the Protestant Ethic and the rise of capitalism is such a practical syllogism. Weber compares the technical development in India and China with similar phenomena in Europe and concludes that Protestant premises lead to capitalist action and not technical development as such. This is not a logical conclusion but an interpretation of a highly relevant practical syllogism.

Ph.D systems are value-loaded because they provide a plurality of nested groupings that manufacture culture as part of their work and self-interest. One can distinguish cultures of discipline, institution, profession-at-large, and national system in the scientific community (Clark, 1983, 72-106). This distinction itself causes uneasiness, because a scientific discipline is basically meta-cultural and has universal precepts

Discipline. In advanced higher education new members are gradually inducted into their particular fields as physicists, economists or historians of art. As recruits to different academic specialities, they enter different cultural houses, there to share beliefs about theory, methodology, techniques and problems. A scientific community becomes then reduced to members who share a paradigm. In Whitehead's words 'Science repudiates philosophy. In other words, it has never cared to justify its truth or explain its meaning' (in Boer, 1981, p. 25). Disciplinary cultures are hard to pin down, since they are only vaguely sensed by their own members, difficult to perceive by outsiders, and easily dismissed. The clearest cases appear in the fields most structured by a body of systematic knowledge and arcane categories of thought. The culture of mathematics, for example, stresses the internal logic and consistency of a set of numerically specific ideas with elegance and precision. Only mathematicians are able to judge an original and independent contribution in their field of study. For a physicist, as an other example, whatever the differences in building up the subject in France, the Sovjet Union or Britain, the corpus of knowledge is seen as universal: 'what counts as a valid finding is not dependent on geographical or cultural considerations, and the process of establishing or refuting a claim knows no frontiers' (Becker, in Clark 1983, p. 78). Disciplines have their own common vocabulary, what outsiders usually call jargon. Professional areas of knowledge, such as medicine, law and management, also develop subcultures of their own that reflect the different technologies and work patterns of their respective occupations. The more professionalized the occupation, the greater the cultural separation. Hence medical and law schools seem to have the most distinctive subculture with a long history. Management and education show less firmness in the integration of their own ways of knowledge production. Moreover, outsiders or amateurs participate here more frequently in the evaluation of dissertations than in the highly professionalized or scientific disciplines (Lammers, 1972).

Institution. The second source of academic culture is that which is generated by individual universities. In most countries sheer age is the main source of hallowed symbols and of the sense of continuity of ideals and activities that comes from the stone and mortar of bygone centuries – a sense of institutional roots that is hard to come by on the new campus, whether it is constructed of plate glass, cement blocks, or old stone. Elders in the institutional tribe quite simply have more culture than the young because they have extracted symbols from experience over a longer period, including ideologies that legitimate position and power. In that sense the historical compendium of European universities (1984) seems an excellent start for tracing Ph.D's in the most veneral universities. I guess that the older universities have become even more restrictive in their selection of Ph.D's whereas the newer institutions use a more liberal policy in order to build up their reputation. However, I have only scattered evidence in the USA and some in the UK and Japan. It would require a special study. Of course, the institutional culture is not restricted to graduate schools. Small liberal arts colleges in the USA e.g. have constructed definitions of themselves that elicit deep personal and collective commitment captured historically in the deeply emotional appeal made by Daniel Webster on behalf of Dartmouth College before the Supreme Court in a famous case of 1818: 'It is, sir, as I have said, a small college and yet there are those who love it'. Burton Clark (p. 86) is of the opinion that European and Latin American universities are more loosely integrated symbolically than their American counterparts, but I doubt it.

There are typologies of subcultures in academic institutions, such as two kinds of locals – the 'disinterested' teacher-scholar and the practical professional – and two types of cosmopolitans – the researcher and the consultant (Gouldner, 1957). However, for the Ph.D phenomenon we have to probe much deeper in a particular supervisory style as an interaction of disciplinary and institutional cultures. In a thesis submitted for the degree of Doctor of Philosophy at the university of Oxford, the candidate Tasman A. Smith introduced his personal selection as follows:

'In the design of the study I tried to accommodate two objectives i.e. to be methodologically rigorous and to produce findings with a direct utility for practising managers......I realised that management research had undergone somewhat of a bifurcation, with the luminaries of either side being separated by the Atlantic Ocean. The American school, in its purest form, displays a preference for highly delimited and very elegant statistical studies.....and has sometimes resulted in rather wooden and even inappropriate application of methodologies. In Britain and Europe, students of management seem to have eschewed high empiricism, preferring to work at a greater level of generalisation, although with more practical application. I have, therefore, attempted to position myself intellectually somewhere near the Azores' (Smith, 1978).

In this case it was a mid-career thesis of an Australian candidate on cross-cultural factors of expatriate managers in Thailand, which resulted some six years later in a success story of adapting a multinational to the Thai culture (Masurel, 1985). Of course, I cannot prove causality. In the Netherlands School of Economics I was informed that the distinction between two types of professors, extra-ordinary with their main occupation outside the university, and ordinary with their main occupation inside the university, led to two types of dissertations i.e. 'actual issues' supervised by extra-ordinary and 'principal issues' supervised by ordinary professors. In any case, the selection of supervisors and their culture is much more complicated than can be found in formal regulations or programmes.

Profession-at-large. Sweeping across disciplines and institutions there is the identity of 'academic man'. The most eloquent peroration of this academic identity I found in J.F. Staal's 'The Academic as nowhere man' (1970) with the introduction of the Beatles:

Eminent Physicist
Polyglot Classicist
Prize-winning Botanist
Hard-biting Satirist
Talented Pianist
Good dentist, too

and the song

He's a real Nowhere Man,
sitting in his Nowhere Land,
making all his Nowhere plans for nobody.
Doesn't have a point of view,
knows not where he's going to,
isn't he a bit like you and me?

Of course, he finishes his plea for internationalisation of universities to characterize his vision as a utopia after a long excursion around ancient academies and old traditions. The culture of the academic profession everywhere and since the origins emphasizes personal autonomy and collegial self-government. It portrays altruistic commitment, suggesting that it is a high service to society to create knowledge, transmit the cultural heritage, and train the young to fulfill their highest potential.

How strong, how intense, how unified is the culture of the academic profession, and in particular of Ph.D's, across national systems? There is indeed in France an 'Association Nationale des Docteurs és Sciences' (Arlman). Traditionally, Dutch gymnasia were considered as places where teachers obtained a doctorate, whereas in the modern type of secondary schools the doctorate was an exception. In each national system one observes special features for stimulating doctorates but a comparative analysis of the doctoral dissertation writing process of what the Americans call an ABD (all but dissertation) shows much more similar characteristics as the stereotypes of national promotion cultures would suggest. The detailed analysis of case histories by Rooyakkers (1986, of Dutch, English and American dissertations show a rich personal experience of an always lonely journey to new insights. Also my personal sample of Ph.D candidates from various countries and in different national systems suggests an intensive exploration of some three or four years where each candidate has to exploit all personal resources for arriving at an acceptable thesis. Of course, there are differences in the intensity and frequency of supervision, but there is no evidence whether close or loose supervision is better. There are differences in facilities, but in most cases it is a highly personal exposure to chase, chance and luck where the individual motivation to generate new knowledge determines the outcome for those who succeed. Whether the product actually turns out to be an original contribution is open to judgment, but the over-arching belief in an academic system with its criteria of originality, creativity, desinterestness, universality and communality seems a 'conditio sine qua non'. A myth? Yes, as a system of operational rules. No, as a factor x explaining why individuals survive periods of anxiety and frustration in their search for order in chaos. A religion, may be.

How testable are these propositions on beliefs in academia and academic man? Policy makers and grant-giving councils will not be pleased by research proposals suggesting longitudinal and comparative studies across disciplines and institutions based on ego documents to prove an unmanageable variable x. Present evidence is scattered and inconclusive. I remember discussions with the rector of the United Nations University, Soedjatmoko, where he explained his project to compare learning patterns within the great world religions. It seems highly relevant but it touches the core of the scientific system of validity and reliability and does not fit in any of the appropriate disciplinary houses. There is indeed presently a revival of studies on organizational culture (Ouchi, 1985), managerial culture (Joynt, 1985) and the consequences of national cultures (Hofstede, 198; Trompenaars, 1985), but one needs to break it down in manageable units with specific hypotheses and methods to get support of policy makers and administrators in the present highly pragmatic mood.

The two cultures debate

One speculative and much published effort to distinguish cultures in the scientific community has been made by the late C.P. Snow. In May 1959 C.P. Snow gave the 'Rede Lecture' at Cambridge. By training he was a scientist, by vocation a writer (The Affair, The Masters, Homecoming). To his surprise his lecture of some 50 small pages triggered off, after considerable time, a flood of reactions from the whole world.

The essence of his lecture was rather simple and not very original, in his own words. In advanced western society we have lost even the pretense of a common culture. Persons educated with the greatest intensity we know cannot longer communicate with each other on the plane of their major intellectual concern. This is serious for our creative, intellectual and, above all, normal life. It is leading us to interpret the past wrongly, to misjudge the present, and to deny our hopes for the future. The most pointed example of this lack of communication is in the shape of two groups of people, representing the 'two cultures'. One of these contained the scientists. The other the literary intellectuals. Of course, there is no complete solution. Renaissance man is not possible. But he argued that the chief means open to us is education – mainly in primary and secondary schools, but also in colleges and universities. There is no excuse for letting another generation be as vastly ignorant, or as devoid of understanding and sympathy, as we are ourselves.

His main intention was to warn against a compartmentalization of higher education. Of course, as he admitted, a dichotomy is too simple: there might be something like a third culture: social history, sociology, demography, political science, economics, government, psychology, medicine and social arts, such as architecture. A mixed bag, but all of them concerned with how human beings are living or have lived – and concerned, not in terms of legend, but of fact. One might even distinguish two thousand and two, or any number you like to name. In a sense this is true: but is also meaningless. He used culture in two meanings as development of the mind (nurture) and in the anthropological meaning to denote a group of persons living in the same environment, linked by common habits, common assumptions, a common way of life.

He compares the English educational strategy with the German, American and Russian. The Germans started long before serious industrialisation had started there with good university education in applied science as a pre-career device. The Americans take almost everyone up to eighteen in high schools and educate them very loosely and generally. Real severity enters with the Ph.D. They find enough talent to turn around nearly as many Ph.D's in science and engineering each year as we contrive to get through our first degrees. The Russians, according to him, have a deeper insight into the scientific revolution than the English and American have. Because there is a sizable component of science and mathematics in high school education, the gap between the two cultures doesn't seem to be anything like so wide as with us. In England the cultural divide seems at its sharpest. The highly educated members of the non-scientific culture couldn't cope with the simplest concept of pure science: it is unexpected, but they would be even less happy with applied science. He would bet that out of men getting first in arts subjects in Cambridge, not one in ten could give the loosest analysis of the human organisation it needs.

His main message was that neither the scientific system of mental development, nor the traditional humanistic system of intellectual development is adequate for our potentialities. They have to be complementary. His plea for communication between those who have been educated in tbe logic of pure and applied science and those who have been educated in the logic of language and human organization is still valid. Presently there is a new dichotomy gaining momentum, that is between analytical and holistic approaches. Dialectic is a human process. In the original Greek meaning the dialectic referred to a discourse where ideas or opinions were examined, often by the method of question and answer, so as to determine their validity. Since Hegel and Marx emphasis has been put on opposition between polarities, such as between rich and poor, elite and mass, advanced and primitive, 'new' and 'old'. In higher education one might also divide subjects in 'hard' and 'soft', those with an experimental and quantitative logic such as in science and those with qualitative reflection and interpretative description such as in human behaviour and organization.

Niches

A more limited and therefore more operational term to distinguish disciplines and institutions within the universitas as symbol for the unity of science is niche. It cannot replace the term culture as Peter Mitchell concluded in the symposium, because it only indicates the receptacle. Niche refers to the particular situation which is fitted for a species. To use Boulding's phrase: the production of human artifacts is strongly affected by the value structure of the noosphere, which creates niches in the social ecosystems for things that people want and have the power to acquire (1983, p. 14). The human genotype has not been changed since the start of civilization. The differentiation of human phenotypes results mainly from the particular interaction between limiting factors of race, creed, time and environment on the one side and particular opportunities and challenges in technological and human development on the other side.

Learning is the major force for change and development. Formal education has greatly increased the transmission of knowledge from one generation to another, but might also hamper individual creativity. Because of its limitations each individual follows a specific track in accumulating knowledge and experience and therefore becomes particularly fitted to occupy a 'niche' or fill in an empty 'niche'. Each technology and discipline lead to expansion until a new equilibrium is found, but one needs always an image of the whole universe as it spreads out in space and time. Narrow specialization prevents the required variety for coping with the changing parameters in the evolution.

In organization theory niche is becoming an important concept in the population ecology of organizations. This approach (it is not yet a theory) must seek to understand the distributions of organizations across environmental conditions and the limitations on organizational structures in different environments. In this case, why are there so many kinds of universities, doctoral research programmes and dissertations? Some universities, for instance, specialize more by focusing on a narrower range of subject matter (engineering and science only etc.) or on a certain level (e.g. graduate only) or on the education of people of a single sex, creed or minority (e.g. students of developing countries). By contrast, others try to offer a comprehensive range of academic programmes to almost everybody.

Any distinct combination of learning programmes, faculty and students that is sufficient to support an organization form might be called an environmental niche. In general, specialist organization forms need to maximize their exploitation of the environment over a relatively narrow range of subjects and programmes and have little slack or excess capacity. Generalist organization forms can survive over a wider range of environmental conditions but are not optimally suited to any single condition. Traditional universities prefer a more generalist organization form in order to allow narrow specializations for faculty and students and, thus, have much slack or excess capacity. The present differentiation between professional and academic programmes, between levels and between types of clientele in higher education requires trade-off between risk and efficiency or the exploitation of the particular environment in greater depth (Pfeffer, Hannan, Freeman, Kimberly). The number of permutations is limited, but large enough to find empty niches (J. Bevers, 1981).

In times of contraction or, more nicely, consolidation doctorate programmes show an interesting 'nichemanship' or positioning according to supply-demand expectations. The top universities are choosing to restrict programme enrolments and are making entrance requirements considerably more selective to further upgrade the quality of graduate students and fellows. They remain essentially as they are. The second-level tier move towards extensively specialized graduate programmes. Reflecting their own specialization and market forces they develop hybrid programmes in their particular field with many variations: area studies, new technology, financial risk or marketing of arts. There is a high level market segmentation, where new activities or new labels must attract candidates and support. The third-level tier of universities become local and heterogeneous in a more vocational direction and gradually loose an attraction for graduate studies. I have only evidence on the role of about 500 graduate programmes in business administration in the USA as collected by Hugstad (1983), but I sense a general pattern. Only the best universities will stick to their original mission of a broad and comprehensive knowledge base, whereas others try to tailor their programmes for a specific audience or niche within required planning and budget horizons. This implies also a preference for a more quantitative approach, because qualitative approaches are known to be less manageable. Moreover, there is a tendency to restrict interdisciplinary areas, because one is more likely to be rewarded for doing research that is central to a specific discipline. Despite the need for a new orientation the internal dynamics of scientific communities tend to close frontiers. Diana Crane's analysis of the social organization of research areas shows examples of relatively closed systems that avoid competing paradigms and resist 'overlapping neighbourhoods'. In the Dutch case of the Erasmus university e.g. one can observe the reduction of the faculty of philosophy, the increase of new specializations, a strengthening of quantitative approaches and a decrease of interdisciplinary areas as peripheral (Steenkamp, 1985).

Balance and Dynamics

How can one describe, analyse and evaluate the dynamics of the various cultures in disciplines, institutions and academic professions?. Each doctoral dissertation is actually a product of the intrinsic worth of the thesis' subject and its elaboration, a particular supervisory style and the reputation of a university as selected by the candidate (Lawrence, 1985). In the selection process a candidate assesses a great number of factors with imperfect knowledge, such as scope, methodology, feasibility, opportunities for support and career perspectives within the constraints of his background and resources. The actual writing process is a highly individual experience at the stage of an all but dissertation (ABD). Presently there is concern about Ph.D's and their uncertainties e.g. 'Bleak view from the Ivory Tower' (Time, January 24, 1983, p.p. 37-38) or 'They labor in the Foothills of Academe' (New York Times, June 2, 1985) and a collection of manuals on how to write a doctoral dissertation is hardly helpful.

At a high level of aggregation one can observe e.g. that the around half a million American generated Ph.D's show an equal split between natural sciences (life sciences, mathematics physics, chemistry, earth sciences, engineering) and social sciences and humanities (education, languages, professions, psychology, sociology, history), but this applies to the male. Female Ph.D's show one fourth natural sciences and three fourth social sciences and humanities (see Century fig. 15). In the Dutch collection of around 22000 Ph.D's there are around three quarters of Ph.D's in natural and life sciences and one quarter in social sciences and humanities (Wyler, 1984), but what is the meaning of this balance? The interaction between different cultures and niches in the production, diffusion and application of doctoral dissertations would require a much more detailed analysis of differential growth in fields of study and methodology. In any case there is an unequal distribution of Ph.D's across higher education systems, but I have not discovered any theory or consistent policy to stimulate an overall balance.

Empirical Studies

Let me review some empirical studies on the Ph.D process and product in the Dutch situation.

The first empirical study on the Dutch doctorate has been initiated by the Prince Bernhard Foundation, established in 1940 to promote 'spiritual self-reliance' and its 'cultural technology' on the base of exact-scientific knowledge. Financial aspects of the academic promotion were considered critical in the post-war years and one was worried about the decline of doctorates since 1939. The Municipal Council of Amsterdam proposed interest-free loans to promovendi. The researcher, H.M. in 't Veld, had in 1953 recently finished her doctoral study. The problem of financing resulted especially from the increase in university population of lower-class students. At that time there were no more than ten or eleven thousands promoti in the Netherlands with a yearly increase of 200-250. At average in 1947 27% of the graduates obtained a doctorate with a range between 8% (dentists) and 63% (chemists). Eight years between graduation and promotion were an average period with a range of 2-14 for 80%. Between 1930-1938 one can observe reasonable stability within disciplines. The highest percentage of doctorates in relation to graduates was in natural sciences (87% in 1931) and the lowest in technical sciences (8% in 1931). From 1939 there has been a decline (33% in natural sciences), but a stability in engineering. She assumes that lack of motivation, loss of social status and unsufficient support of professors are the reasons for this decline. However, the depression of the thirties has kept the promotion drift for the humanities and social sciences at the same level, whereas natural sciences needed team research.

Her questionnaire data are based on 450 promoti in 1947-1949 (70% of the total). The majority of doctores worked outside the university. She observed a distinction between natural sciences with an actual team guided preparation and the other sciences with an individual initiative. Only for a minority mainly in natural sciences the doctorate is a pre-career degree. For some 59% the doctorate is obtained more than 7 years after graduation and is definitely a mid-career degree.

The costs of an academic promotion (publication, social customs as reception and dinner, stress) were seen in no relation to the benefits (salary increase, sales, new opportunities). Interviews give a vivid description of the strong motivation for such an abstruse academic custom, where fully employed individuals spent every evening during some three years in study, writing and typing for an expensive hobby. From the 700 approached professors for this study only a minority answered. It seems that only for this minority the academic promotion of candidates is seen as a core task. With the exception of natural sciences it is a rare 'mandarin' tradition, where initiative and effort of candidates to come to the fore with some evidence of originality is more important than a rational cost-benefit analysis. It is a Dutch cultural tradition without post-graduate courses as in other traditions. The *second* more restricted empirical study concerns the scientific value of the academic promotion in sociology. C.J. Lammers and H. Philipsen use the tenth anniversary of a major Dutch journal in 1964 to study the 'Ars Promovendi'. It is presented as a partial study, but there is no follow up. A specific feature of Dutch doctoral dissertations is that their publication determines for a very large part the total scientific production. In the USA and Germany, for example, professional journals are more important. Since 1950 Dutch higher education has generated a relatively large proportion of sociologists (IJzerman, 1985, p. 80). From an original list of 303 titles they select 71 and 66 of these authors answer the questionnaire. They assume that the frequency of promotion has been increased since 1950. Also in this study the average period between graduation and promotion was long, some seven years, and for one third more than eight years. The costs of promotion have been increased, but there is more financial support in comparison to 1954: government departments (38%), Foundation for Pure Research, ZWO (14%), Universities (12%) and employers (12%). The authors make an interesting distinction between older promovendi (graduated before 1951) and the younger generation. The younger generation write frequently a purely theoretical dissertation, whereas the older generation prefers a more empirical and descriptive approach. They conclude that the new theoretical orientation of the new generation tends to become a closed school without too much communication with the empirical and descriptive sociologists. Theorists tend to be concerned with their own conceptual constructs without bothering about empirical verification. Of course, they carefully stipulate that they can only design hypotheses, because their data are restricted. However, the further development of sociology seems to have proven this hunch to be realistic.

A *third* empirical study by P. Buis of the Academic Council was based on questionnaires answered by 215 doctores, who obtained their doctorate between 1966-1980. He selected four faculties: medical (5), humanities (60) social sciences (57) and natural sciences (47). His interest was the learning process between promotor and promovendus. His own Ph.D (1978) concerned the feedback process in higher education and he had analysed his own Ph.D process in a publication (1979). Originally he selected 700 names of doctores, but it was impossible to get more than 480 addresses. 52% answered the questionnaire. In comparison to 1947-1949 the Ph.D had become a more academic career degree: between 1947-1949 75% of 450 doctores worked outside the university, whereas in the sample between 1966-1980 only 28% worked outside the university. The growth of higher education has created an internal market for Ph.D's. The period between graduation and promotion has not been reduced: at average 9.4 years with 6.2 years for natural sciences and 10 years for the other faculties. The average age of 36.2 years has a range from 31.5 years in natural sciences and more than 37 years in other sciences. The costs in terms of outside-work hours and social losses were seen as the highest in humanites and the lowest in natural sciences.

A *fourth* empirical study by G. Rooyakkers compares the quality of American, English and Dutch dissertations in the social sciences. This study has recently been published. The manuscript gives a detailed analysis of the perceptions of candidates, supervisors and the outcome of a re-appraisal by a panel of experts. The process of writing a doctoral dissertation seems rather similar in the three countries and the sample. Although the quality of dissertations seems slightly in favour of the Dutch doctorate, statistical significance is inconclusive. The age of obtaining a doctorate is higher in the Netherlands (39.7 year) than in the USA and UK (35.8 year), whereas the actual time spent on the dissertation is also higher in the Netherlands (5500 hours) than in the USA and UK (4200 hours). One needs, however, a more detailed analysis of research design and methodology before one can draw conclusions.

Codes of Practice

At the time of writing there is an increase in new initiatives for doctoral training and research. An OECD report on post-graduate education in the 1980s is in the process of circulation and discussion. Completion rates seem to be the major issue, but there is increasing awareness that one has to deal with the problems of promotion cultures in disciplines, institutions and national systems. The committee of vice-chancellors and principals (CVCP) published in January 1985 a code of practice regarding doctoral training and research for consideration by universities in the UK. The code does not propose a uniform system but commends good practices which are widely followed in many institutions. A European collection of good practices would be a major contribution.

Let me quote and comment on this document with some comparative suggestions.

- There is a clear trend where the ideal to develop and bring to fruition the quality of originality and independency through doctorates is complemented by a thorough grounding in research techniques as done in the American system. However, the CVCP stresses that the essential nature and purpose of Ph.D study remains affording the opportunity of making an original contribution to research and scholarship although there might be variation between disciplines and subjects. I strongly support this view and do not hope that we start to develop well-planned applications of advanced research technology as a Ph.D without originality as ideal.

- The CVCP stresses that candidates should be made aware that advantage may be derived from undertaking postgraduate work in a university other than the one in which they have studied for their first degree. In the Dutch practice there has been traditionally a large proportion of promovendi with first degrees from other universities. In Wageningen e.g. almost 25% of the thousand doctores since 1918 did not study in Wageningen (Crombach, 1984). In the new system of the two stages, which starts in 1986, there are intentions to consider doctorate programmes as a direct follow-up of the first cycle for a selection within the same university. I think that this is a wrong direction if it becomes the normal pattern. Moreover, the present budget policy where research assistantships and completed doctorates are used for special allocations might make Ph.D candidates more captive than before. Available evidence supports this hypothesis (van Hout, 1985). I have even seen cases where candidates for a Ph.D were prohibited to go to another university for a promotion. This seems bad practice.

  A European network of joint doctorate programmes as already exist in some institutions should be strengthened (see p. 185).

- It is recommendable that research candidates are admitted with no reference to a specific degree. This would allow that candidates who are not able or willing to complete a proper Ph.D can obtain another e.g. Master's degree, if they have satisfactorily completed research training. In most countries one observes the development of three-level systems, where only the last doctor's degree indicates the ideal of an original and independent contribution to knowledge. The three degrees are actually very old. Also in China one recognized three degrees: hsiu ts'ai indicating cultivated talents, equivalent to bachelor; chü jen indicating an elevation and recommendation, equivalent to master and licentiate; and chin shih, indicating entrance in scholarship (Zi, 1894). I do not see any need to invent new degrees but would strongly plead for keeping the Ph.D at the right level even if it needs a longer completion period.

- The CVCP seems to accept in appropriate circumstances a general trend to make the choice of a research topic dependent on industrial needs or research in progress or by an external funding body especially in natural science, social science and engineering. However, Harold Orlans formerly from the Brookings Institution warned already a decade ago that we 'should reject the simpler certitudes of social scientism, of obligatory relationships that bind ideas to social groups, actions to interests, words to convictions, respondents to words, complex facts to simple theories, and fallible observations to eternal laws like fitted carpets to the floor' (in Crawford, 1976, p. 40). Especially for mid-career candidates there must be sufficient room for selecting one's own research topic and offering guidance for appropriate supervision and support. Present Dutch policy starts from accepted research programmes in disciplinary clusters where candidates have to accept a role of research assistants within a restricted period. It seems a dangerous development, if it would not support independent, interdisciplinary and basic research outside accepted programmes.

- The CVCP elaborates supervision in ten points. Supervision is the responsibility of the university which appoints a qualified supervisor or joint supervisor. The supervisory relationship should be fully discussed to establish clear and explicit mutual expectations and to minimize risks and problems of personality clashes. One needs also regulations for a candidate about complaints or the possibility of changing his supervisor. Universities will have their individual mechanism for monitoring and ensuring that the various faculty and departmental arrangements and practices in regard to both supervisors and students are in accordance with university policy, but there are variations in arrangements between subjects and departments.

The Dutch term 'promotor' reflects another cultural dimension in the interaction than 'supervisor'. Promoting a candidate means helping forward and encouraging him to elaborate a research topic according to academic standards, whereas supervising means directing or watching with authority the work and progress of a research student. In actual practice each doctorate process seems to require a changing interpersonal balance on a continuum from instruction towards clarification. It tends to be highly personal within disciplinary and university customs. The major recommendation seems to me broadening the forum and making mutual expectations more explicit within an 'universitas' with a right of appeal for a candidate. I strongly support this recommendation, although there are limits to administrative regulations and one needs inter-university mobility for candidates who prefer another supervisor.

- The final examination which might result in a doctorate is the most critical. The CVCP recommends that the candidate's supervisor should be the internal examiner only in exceptional circumstances and that the supervisor should normally not attend any viva or meeting of examiners. There should always be at least two examiners, one external. When the supervisor is exceptionally appointed internal examiner, a third examiner should be appointed. The outcome of a doctorate examination ranges from immediate award, after amendments or revisions and re-submission towards rejection with no right of re-admission.

In this final examination culture is indeed the most pervasive and tenacious factor. By definition it is also the most obscure or hidden. I remember in a few cases to be asked by the external examiner before the viva whether we would have lunch with the candidate and I suddenly realized that this was an indirect way of exchanging a judgment about the quality. In the English system indeed the ideal of an independent external examiner outside the cosy culture of a department is very strong, but there are various subtle arrangements for consensus and approval. In practice one can appoint for almost every thesis a highly critical examination committee that will at least partly reject a thesis, but the reverse of a benevolent committee or external examiner is equally true.

The Dutch system requires an a-priori judgment, formally by authority of the rector magnificus, that the doctorate will be awarded after the public defense. This requires another set of negotiations in proposing the usually six members of the promotion committee. Formally the public defense is done in a public meeting of the deans of the university, and chaired by the rector magnificus. It is a 'senatus contractus', but the senate has been abolished in 1971, which I repeat seems to me a historical error. With the permission of the rector the committee might include outsiders, preferably doctors with special knowledge of the subject, such as a former minister or a business leader. Of course, faculty members of other also foreign universities can be part of the committee and this seems a highly recommendable practice. There are a few cases where the printed thesis had to be withdrawn, but this leads to wide

58

publicity and in case of lack of prudence the university has to pay the costs. Also in the past there were exceptional cases where the printed dissertation had to be destroyed (v.d. Woude, 1963).

A special complication arises, when there are special honour degrees as 'cum laude'. One has sometimes suggested to abolish these special distinctions. I think indeed that the judgment of an independent and original contribution to knowledge is already high enough an ideal and does not need to be complicated without specifying more than original. Of course, quality varies. Moreover, when I made a time series of 'cum laude' distinctions of Ph.D's, I discovered clusters over time. My interpretation is that when one starts with adding extra distinctions colleagues in that period or institution wonder why the dissertation of their candidate would not be equally distinctive. In some Indonesian universities there are even five distinctions 'satisfactory', 'highly satisfactory', 'cum laude', 'magna cum laude', and 'summa cum laude'. This leads to endless complications and I do not think it recommendable.

In a European doctorate network one would like to combine various good practices without aiming at uniformity. The core is the presentation of original and independent work, preferably for publication and not necessarily within the domain of one's first degree. The English custom of recommending how it might be published after the viva is attractive especially if it would provide more opportunities for the actual publication. The Dutch custom of public defense and wide circulation (some 400-600 copies) is also attractive but might be more restrictive for some subjects or disciplines.

The *forum* needs to be sufficiently comprehensive to cover the field of study. The invitation of qualified outsiders in the panel might prevent an ivory tower but does not need to be general practice. There is no need for any other consensus than that the thesis is defendable, although one might disagree with some propositions or would prefer another elaboration of some parts. In some universities all professors can formally participate in the discussion but in practice there is a selection. However, it seems recommendable that members of the senate in whose name the doctorate is awarded have access to the promotion. In Oxford e.g. I was informed that fellows with a gown could enter a viva, although it does not seem to happen. Although most European universities seem to allow faculty members of other also foreign universities to be examiner or committee member, there are usually practical obstacles in financing such participation.

For doctorates by independent research the *role* of a doctor does not need to be reduced to a selection for an academic or research career, but might include personal motives as curiosity, intellectual challenge, broadening one's interest, or reflecting on personal experience. I side with Spurr in his set of principles: The number of different degrees titles should be kept as low as possible, allowing for substantial variation within each as regards subject matter, emphasis, quantity and even quality of effort (in Mayhew, 1974, p. 163).

In France one has abolished the two types of doctorate. In the USA one has tried to introduce a Doctor of Arts degree which would require four years of study beyond the bachelor's (in theory the same as the Ph.D), but in place of a dissertation students would be asked to do within a chosen field an independent piece of work that was not necessarily an original contribution to knowledge. Also a Doctor of Social Science degree at Syracuse university especially catering for teachers was launched but when given the opportunity to exchange their degrees for the Ph.D, some 90 percent jumped at the opportunity. The same applies to the Doctor of Education degree, originally intended to be a practitioner's certificate and theoretically conceived of as equal in rigour but different in substance from the Ph.D degree. Either it becomes second-class or the demands become so modified that there is no perceptible difference with the Ph.D (Mayhew, 1974). As another analogy one can mention the introduction of a new more practical degree in the Dutch system (a bachelor's in economics). It did not work. Each national system has a preference for certain degrees. The Doctor's degree is the most common. If one sticks to the original ideals, there is no need for reform of titles, but one has to accept monitoring of quality differences between institutions, disciplines and departments as in the USA system.

If we search for the *locus* which satisfies all conditions of disciplines and scholarship as in the universitas, we can consider most institutions of higher education only as partial collections. In a more pragmatic sense I consider the three neighbouring universities of Leyden, Delft and Rotterdam as a satisfying solution. In this perspective the original five Dutch universities reduced to three in 1811 and expanded to thirteen represent still only some three or four university clusters. In the university of Indonesia as established in the interim period between 1945-1950 the concept of a universitas was expressed in a central circular university with a strong president and particular decentralized location for faculties (see p. 174). At a European level compared to the USA we might also be able to locate some ten or twenty university clusters covering the scope and depth of knowledge. These clusters would be the appropriate locus for Ph.D's.

One of the innovations in higher education at the present time is the open university. Communication technology allows networks of faculty members from various universities with internal co-ordinators which seems to offer rich opportunities for doctorate studies. The English psychologist Estelle Phillips conducted 100 open ended interviews with internal and external supervisors, current and former postgraduates and Heads of Disciplines between May 1982-1984. These yielded qualitative data from a comprehensive sample of people who had different perceptions of the system in operation including full time, part time internal and part time external, 'drop-outs' and successes. I refer to the full report that hopefully will be published, but select a few recommendations:

- Internal and external supervisors are confused about their role and have difficulty in defining the boundaries between them. It is suggested that induction seminars be arranged, a handbook provided and informal contracts be negotiated. It seems that an extended Ph.D platform as has been established recently offers a useful contribution for arranging informal contracts between supervisors, promotors and Ph.D candidates at a European level. There exist already various European groups in disciplines and fields of study, which could be used for a network of small groups of around 15 participants.
- Temporary resident facilities for ABD's in the final writing stage might improve the completion rate. The Nethertands Institute of Advanced Studies in Wassenaar could be such a residence, if there are flexible arrangements focused on Ph.D candidates rather than on senior professors.
- Ph.D seminars for discussing the intellectual, emotional and pragmatic problems of a research journey are of particular importance. It might act also as a clearing house for suggesting available taught courses which are relevant for some stages e.g. about the use of personal computers, publication outlets and alternatives within a broader network.
- Supervision needs to be included in the staff planning of academics' time and work load. In the present Dutch practice Ph.D supervision is considered as an average allowance of 150 hours a year for every professor. The uneven distribution of Ph.D candidates over faculty members makes this allowance unrealistic and prevents 'productive' supervisors to accept new candidates or to offer sufficient guidance. Time allocation and facilities become particularly critical especially if a doctorate project is not part of an accepted disciplinary cluster. Time budgets of faculty have been made, but there is no uniform standard.
- The Open University with its short history but roots within traditional universities might offer the flexibility needed for the monitoring of doctorate projects by individual research outside major programmes. There are sufficient data available, but one needs a clear policy or theory for interpretation. A regular interactive data base connecting trends at the macro level with the micro process of individual candidates is feasible with present communication technology.

The major recommendation arising from available evidence and personal experience seems to maintain the Ph.D by research as a demonstrated ability to organize and complete the full cycle of knowledge focused on a subject, including verification of old knowledge (the state of the art) and the search for new knowledge. It is not a magnum opus. Of course, in the life cycle of certain disciplines or institutions there might be need for highly specialized contributions but each doctorate project needs to be embedded in the full scope and depth of the field. A quantitative growth of doctorates is not in itself a sign of healthy development, if there are no multiplier effects in the scientific community. Historically, European universities were connected by the academic peregrination. Over time the scientific community has been split in many (sub)disciplines and over many institutions, but there is still the ideal of the international pool of knowledge to which a Ph.D candidate offers an intended original contribution.

Review and Conclusions

The cultural explanation of the Ph.D octopus is very strong. In contrast to the biosphere where one can explain variations by niches or a particular habitat the world of knowledge requires also an understanding of the meaning which candidates and supervisors give to the Ph.D process and product. It would require a symbolic interactionist approach in various disciplines, institutions and national systems. For each candidate it is a single journey exploring a new subject or approach where he becomes encapsulated in the particular supervisory style of a discipline and institution. He usually does not have many choices. It has been described as a monogamous relationship in the European tradition where one has to keep one's loyality during a period of some three years with a particular subject and supervisory style. In some American situations there is a larger committee with more choices but also there the Ph.D candidate is a captive audience. Supervisors tend to concentrate on their own preferences in developing sound and valid knowledge and are not particularly inclined to indulge in cultural reflections.

It is therefore no surprise that promotion cultures have not been studied. The few empirical studies describe either statistical trends without explaining the particular interaction between candidate, supervisor and thesis subject within a particular disciplinary and institutional network or are restricted to case studies or anecdotical evidence. There is a collection of manuals on how to write a doctoral dissertation but there is no evidence on their utilization or relevance.

The scientific community with its own ethos of universalism, communalism, desinsterestness, systematic scepsis and reward for originality is a powerful ideal for explaining the initiation rites of candidates. It is the core of most learning traditions. Of course, as a result of the explosion of knowledge and the massification of higher education a host of subcultures has been developed. C.P. Snow stressed a particular dichotomy between natural science and humanities. However, all these subcultures are variations within the scientific community. One cannot underestimate the intrinsic rewards of trying to make an independent contribution to the whole range of knowledge. In our time of managerialism one tries to structure projects around disciplinary clusters, but one needs to recognize the old concept of the universitas represented by the senate. Gilman remembered us that universities easily fall into ruts and almost every epoch requirs a fresh start.

In our time the European doctorate seems a particular useful contribution, where one revitalizes the traditional academic peregrination. Each national academic culture emphasizes particular dimensions. In the English system there is a preference for originality and a particular mixture of character, style and expression, but the publication rate of dissertations is poor. Moreover it is a rather closed system despite the external examiner and might be more open to abuse. The German system has a broad scientific tradition with an extra 'Habilitationschrift' for those who aspire an academic career. There are special publishers for dissertations but the organization in Länder with their own educational policy prevents a central policy. The French system with its duality has traditionally a high esteem for an elaborated thesis as in the now abolished doctorat d'état. It is highly centralized and elite. The Dutch system with the Scandinavian variants is the most public and ritual. In some Dutch universities the candidate is even asked to explain for laymen why he has started his study, how he has done it and what were his main conclusions. In these systems English can be used as a 'lingua franca' as Latin in the past. It is less open to abuse but is too dependent on the particular promotor. In each system foreigners are accepted as candidates and there is a large scope for European networks for dissertations.

The information about the Ph.D is scattered and mainly anecdotical, but even if we would have a European doctorate data base as in the USA, we need a European theory or policy to utilize the data. Moreover, there is a law of unresolvable ignorance as Pfeffer (1981) coined it. In the highly reactive process of learning over time we tend to select mainly successes in survival and to forget about the failures or mistakes. The population of Ph.D's which have escaped anonymity is not particularly a random sample. Failure rates are extremely touchy in the Ph.D process.

From a cultural perspective the Ph.D exemplifies the three basic meanings as explained in the first paragraph. It refers to an symbol of entering the scientific community or the world of scholarship as already denoted by tbe Chinese degree of chin shih or third cycle degree. Secondly, there are variations of the meaning of a Ph.D between disciplines, institutions and national systems. In that sense one can speak of disciplinary or other academic tribes with their own rituals. Lastly, there is a general concept of academic man as described by J.F. Staal.

The scientific community itself seems to be an ideal type with its own ethos and norms of universalism, communality, desinterestness, systematic scepsis and rewards for originality. It cannot be replaced by the independent application of advanced methodology or theory. The particular interaction of discipline, institutions and national system in the case of Ph.D's would require detailed studies. However, there is still a sizable minority of individuals who obtain a doctorate either outside the boundaries of their first degree discipline or outside their alma mater or national system. The recent international OECD seminar on higher education and the flow of foreign students (Zoetermeer, November 1985) presented background documents, but it is difficult to arrive at major trends from the past. I have the impression that the inter-European flow of doctorates is decreasing and being replaced by candidates from the so called Third World in some countries, but the evidence is not conclusive. The case of Cambridge for higher degrees in economics between 1981-1984 with 25% graduates from Britain, 29% from Europe, 18% from Asia, 13% from USA and 15% from other continents is a lofty example of an old ideal (Meeks, 1985).

Snow's introduction to the two cultures in the scientific community has accelerated the discussion. Presently we prefer a more detailed analysis of visible and invisible colleges. I do not assume that we can break the scientific community in dichotomies. There are life cycles in disciplines and institutions and a great variety of organizational structures (Whitley, 1985) but the underlying antagonism between natural science, social science and arts or between fundamental and applied does not die.

The cultural mission of a Ph.D to surpass boundaries of disciplines, institutions and nations, to offer an independent and original contribution to knowledge, and to strive for lofty qualities as universalism, communalism and desinterestness in the scientific community is rarely completed. However, this conviction need to be nurtured for human civilization. Scholars are only trustees not of civilization, but of the possibility of civilization, as Keynes once stated. Of course, there are always constraints of time, place and resources. The design of European doctorates with a code of practice, regular monitoring of quality and flexible arrangements between universities as in a European Open University would be an important contribution from our heritage.

Chapter IV

Life Chances and Information Markets

This chapter centers around two questions: what is the function of a Ph.D as a life chance and what contribution offers a doctoral dissertation to information markets? The differentiation between primary, secondary and tertiary education bas been established over time. The scope of the human heritage in knowledge increased and so did the division of labour in educational institutions and other training and apprenticeship systems. In organizational terms one can identify an educational cascade: primary schools needed to prepare their pupils for selection tests of secondary schools and secondary schools again for entering universities. The quality of each subsystem depended on the chance of entering the next level. Moreover, the scope of possible fields of knowledge required parallel streams for occupational, professional, teaching and research careers and their interlinkages. The cascade system of consecutive levels and the breadth of the human heritage gave rise to hierarchy, bureaucracy and standardization of learning modules. Each module along occupational or disciplinary lines requires its own entrance criteria. General education gets less attention than the obligatory subjects. There are no universal criteria on what constitutes a discipline, occupation or profession neither on when one has reached a level or obtained a degree, diploma or title. National or institutional conventions become blurred, when we look at comparative evidence. The actual acceptance depends on consensus between qualified individuals and parties, on performance and on legal conventions about equivalence.

There are many alternative routes to arrive at internationally acceptable final terms. Work experience, autonomous study and sandwich courses might contribute as much as formal higher education. Final degrees are assumed to encompass the outcomes of previous stages. What is the likelihood of a particular learning route for actually arriving at the full development of one's talents? There are system approaches to the world of education and training (e.g. E. Jantsch, 1972), but individual selection of available learning modules within one's environment and horizon does not allow an a priori structure. Moreover, there are many interlinkages possible to switch between professional, academic and general learning routes in one's life time. There is no comprehensive theory, model or blueprint from which we can arrive at the design of optimal learning routes towards excellency or completion. However, there are many partial and partisan views in disciplines, professions and occupations.

The higher education system

My image of the higher education system is presented in figure IV-1, as it has become partly transparent through the historical and cultural analysis of the previous chapters. I distinguish three types of careers: professional, such as medical, engineering and teaching; academic and research; and general careers in business, government or trade union.

The first cycle aims at the cultivation of talents as the first Chinese imperial degree, hsiu ts'ai, according to my resource person, indicates. Also medieval universities show the existence of a first degree as bachelor. Of course, at that time students could enter universities at the age of thirteen. Presently the first cycle consists of two to four years between, say, age 18 and 22. If we take a broad definition of higher education and include occupational training as in the USA and Japan, as much as 40-50% of the cohorts between 18 and 22 enter higher education. In Europe universities are traditionally more elitist and encompass only some 15% of the cohorts. The open university offers opportunities for a second chance higher education. The first cycle reflects the national educational system at primary and secondary levels and is usually given in the national language. There is a small sector of an international bachelor. In contrast to medieval universities with their high inter- European mobility of students and staff present European universities in the first cycle are mainly for nationals. For occupational careers, such as the medical and law profession, one cannot but follow the full professional requirements for qualified performance. There tends to be a numerus clausus given restrictions of the labour market. For general careers in business and government there is a growing trend to prefer young first-cycle graduates for apprenticeship and induction in companies and public agencies rather than to hire overqualified graduates. Japan is the dominant example of in-house training of young graduates. A relatively small percentage stays within universities for further degrees. The balance between general and specialist or occupational and scientific orientation in the first cycle varies between national systems.

The second cycle is the most complicated. It aims at advancement and specialization in particular skills, such as the MBA, but is used also as a weeding out or selection device. The second Chinese imperial degree indicates also advancement and recommendation. For professional careers there is usually a sequence of two cycles before one is accepted as medical doctor, lawyer or registered accountant. For general careers it is possible to enter the second cycle after work experience in a later stage. There is a whole range of chartered and non-chartered post-graduate courses. For academic and research careers there is much confusion whether one aims at the training of professional research skills or immediately at an independent and original contribution to knowledge in one's field of study. Professor Pettigrew distinguished in his Harvard experience a consolation degree for those who are not able or willing to continue for a Ph.D and an en passant degree for those who immediately aim at the Ph.D. Figure IV-2 represents his image of these degrees. Professor Lawrence distinguished five types of master degrees in the English system. The M.Phil seems an appropriate indication of an intermediate research degree with a strong emphasis on research methodology. The traditional Dutch title doctorandus reflects the old ideal of somebody who is invited to strive for the highest honour but actually has become an extended four year bachelor's degree. In any case, the second cycle has a double focus: a final professional degree and an intermediate research degree. It seems to be more international than the first cycle: MBA is a good example (Hugstadt, 1982; Hesseling, 1984). However, in the medical profession there are labour market restrictions and so it seems also in teachers colleges. For increasing international mobility the second cyle offers more opportunities than the first cycle.

The third cycle upon which this book is focused aims at entering the scientific community according to the criteria of discipline, institution or time. The third Chinese imperial degree, chin shih, indicates this entrance in scholarship which has connotations with nobility, wisdom and saintliness in Asian traditions (W. Boot) and may be also in older European traditions. At this level the different appreciation of scholarship between European, American and Asian cultures becomes more pronounced. In its long historical development the European doctorate has become more secular, rational and specialized for individual prominence. It has, however, a broader societal meaning than a purely academic degree and it is not uncommon for mid-career individual distinction or post-retirement reflection. In particular, the Dutch and Scandinavian rituals of ceremonial grandeur are in sharp contrast with the egalitarian customs of their societies. The American assumption of the Ph.D as an exclusively vocational degree for academic teachers does not reflect American reality. Leon Lederman estimates that e.g. about 130 people receive doctoral degrees in high-energy physics in the USA each year. Only some 50 per year remain within the discipline since 1974. The other 80 people are drawn to highly diverse fields, including industrial research, college teaching, other laboratories than high-energy physics, biophysics, computer science, administration, finance and management or ownership of a business. The flow of talent away from fundamental science has been an important resource in large technological projects at least since World War II (in Scientific American, Nov. 1984, p. 40). Also in Time (Jan. 1983) a commission report is quoted to call for a broader conception of graduate education than a pre-academic career degree. Such universities as Chicago, Harvard,

Pennsylvania, Stanford, Virginia and UCLA have set up programmes to retool humanities Ph.D's for jobs in the business world. Humanist Ph.D's possess writng abilities, administrative abilities and the ability to work with values. Theodore Ziolkowski, dean of graduate studies at Princeton, is quoted: 'It is extremely important that some of the graduate schools in the US maintain the *continuity of all the academic disciplines* from Sanskrit and esoteric forms of mathematics to 'hot' subjects like computer science and biochemistry' (p. 38) and I like to add in any case philosophy, the mother of sciences. The Asian appreciation reflects a more collective and recording meaning of a doctorate in contrast to individual originality and rhetoric (see Chapter II). There is a high respect for scholarship and faith in advanced knowledge as a vehicle for civilization, but a reluctance to accept individual excellency. In chapter VIII an Indonesian case study is presented.

Ideal Types

It is of course impossible to generalize about the 6,000,000 students at the 3,600 universities in the extended European Common Market. If we assume some 10% to aspire for a doctorate, we can neither generalize about a European doctorate. Variation is the key asset of European collaboration. There is only a limited number of universities which maintain the continuity of all the academic disciplines and are therefore particularly qualified for a European doctorate. In actual practice there are innumerous networks between European universities for joint study and research. Some 500 joint study programmes for student and staff exchange have so far received support from the European Commission (less than 1%). In 1985 only some 3,000 students are participating in exchange programmes supported by the European Community. Luckily, there are now proposals under way to increase the proportion of exchange students at some stage to around 10% of the total student population from 1992 onwards under the code name ERAS-MUS (the European Community Action Scheme for the Mobility of University Students). Actually doctoral dissertation writers or ABD's in American jargon are the most appropriate subpopulation for internationalisation. Although in the European Community the level of student mobility between member states is at an extremely low ebb (less than 1%), I expect that the mobility at the Ph.D level is much higher. From the 363 doctorates awarded by the Netherlands School of Economics (NEH) e.g. 15% of the doctores between 1918 and 1972 were foreigners. Moreover, 19% of the dissertations were written in an international language and especially after the second World War this percentage has increased. It would be particularly important to create a core of European doctorates within existing networks and regulations. I would strongly plead to reserve a percentage of say 6%, as in German universities, of European doctorates for non-Europeans, mainly from developing countries.

It is equally impossible to generalize about the half-a-million American generated doctorates and the huge population of ABD's. In contrast to the European situation, however, there is a clear ranking of research-doctorate programmes with indications of faculty quality, programme effectiveness, improvement, faculty size, degrees awarded and published articles (The conference Board of Associated Research Councils, 1982). Moreover, individual faculty and research candidates move freely to the most appropriate locus for their particular qualities and aspirations. Ranking, competition, monitoring and differences in facilities and rewards are accepted as academic trade marks. The corporate class exist and every new combination for any price is explored. There is no central authority. A cost-benefit analysis for individual cases is needed because there are large differences in fees. In Hugstad's analysis of 'The Business School in the 1980s' e.g. three levels of performance and adaptation to changing conditions of the labour market are distinguished. In this field of knowledge the 800 doctorates in 1980 constitute only a very small part of the more than 55,000 MBA's and almost 190,000 bachelor's. The attraction of American graduate schools for foreigners is particularly great so that in some fields and institutions one is worried about percentages of 40 or 50, especially Asians on the West Coast. Also employers are clear about their preferences for a particular degree in their line of business and express this preference in differential wages. The Columbia University Seminar on Organization and Management discusses since 1951 in monthly meetings of faculty and key figures in business the Future Challenges of Management Education' (Carter, 1981). In the American situation it is relatively easy to discover the centers of excellence in one's field of study, whereas e.g. in the Dutch situation excellent faculty members are scattered over the thirteen universities because one assumes equality and applies standard conditions.

The Asian situation is for me the most fascinating transformation of European and American practices in a new Asian mold and spirit. The research institute for higher education studies in Hiroshima University has built an excellent platform for observing and analyzing these transformations. During a conference in February 1984 I participated in a conference on Higher Education in Asia with interesting case studies of Indian, Chinese, Thai and Indonesian higher education and Japan's options in Pacific manufactured trade. Since my own exposure to Japanese higher education in 1966 in the International Christian University at Mitaka I have been struck by the particular meaning of individual selection before entrance and the collective pass after acceptance and normal performance. When I was grading examination papers for a Master's degree with the American system of A-E, I discovered that one first has to know what grade a student needs in order to pass, because a 'sensei' has the responsibility for a satisfactory completion after acceptance. The individual originality of a doctoral dissertation does not fit in the Japanese academic tradition. The Japanese occupy a highly strategic vantage point in higher education, one that potentially afford them with a wide angle of vision. Progenitors of neither Eastern or Western traditions, they have little cause to approach the matter with either excessive pride or the sense of superiority that pride often conceals. Since the initial influx of Western knowledge during the Edo period and the subsequent Meiji shift to Western modes of learning were preceded by centuries of training in the achievements of Chinese civilization, the course of their intellectual history has long since placed Japanese to compare the two traditions. Japan's academic tradition has produced little that is original; its influence abroad has been insignificant. But the Japanese have habitually cultivated the faculty of critical choice (Nakayama).

The Japanese higher education system seems an exceptional case within the Asian pattern: the outcome of a hybrid culture (Mitsukuni, 1984). Traditional ties with Holland in Deshima (1641-1858) meant that Dutch institutions were studied first, but as the Education Ordinance of 1872 was being readied, the education ministry undertook a wide-range survey of European and American practice. The early Meiji educational system borrowed the centralized, pyramidal structure of the French system in externals while being largely American in curriculum and texts. After the political change of 1881 however, the 'tilt' towards Germany intensified. New investigations by Mori Arinori and Inone Kowashi in preparation for the Imperial University led to a heightened appreciation of German scholarship. The Japanese university system received its definitive form during a period in which German higher education was being imitated in many parts of the world. However, the graduate school and the introduction of the Ph.D is only a recent addition in the post-war period under American guidance. The Harris School of the Natural Sciences, set up in Doshisha in Kyoto in 1889, was modeled on the American system of the graduate school, but it failed and was discontinued in 1896.

The first imperative was the adoption of the Western type of institution and the introduction of the sciences or *Kagaku* (literally 'classified learning') en bloc. There was no room or interest for individual critical analysis or a comparative examination of paradigms in particular fields. Priority was given in a collective way to certain basic tasks: surveys, standardization, observations, sanitation, printing, railways, military works, all indispensable for the operation of a modern state. One might say that Japan was the first nation to experience the world-wide trend towards state-managed science with which we are familiar today. Science in the sense of *Kagaku* was exclusively utilitarian and pragmatic, planned to enhance the national interest or profitmaking specialized and compartmentalized without debates on science versus philosophy or the two cultures between science and arts. One accepted the paradigms developed in the West as self-evident and was only concerned with mastering them technically. Japanese higher education has thus developed mainly at the undergraduate level of textbook knowledge. The ratio of graduate students is gradually changing from 2.9% in 1974 to 3% in 1982. The proposals on paper for establishing post-graduate and doctoral programmes had, until recently, little effect. The custom of professor-student cliques in graduate studies continues, and so does the graduate student seniority system of waiting in time for a doctorate and for posts obtained through the professorial patronage system, whether one has obtained a doctorate or not (M.J. Bowman, 1981).

However, an older term for science is *kyuri* (literally, investigating the principles of things, a neo-Confucian term) or natural philosophy, being a systematic and fundamental investigation of the nature of things. In recognizing an inquiry into the principles at the bottom of such traditional practical studies as medicine and calendar making, they also grasped the hierarchical structure of modern science, from basic to applied. Above and beyond the culture-bound achievements of Western science, they seem to have sensed that it contained a revolutionary paradigm i.e. the belief in underlying laws of Nature. *Kyuri* represented an understanding of science at the cognitive level. However, less metaphysical than in the West. There is no supreme law or absolutism in Japanese traditional thinking (Daiichi Ito, personal communication). For handling science in institutional terms *kagaku* or 'Fachwissenschaft' is used to indicate the differentiated special disciplines in which modern science manifests itself. In that sense science is something historically quite specific and well-defined. When intellectual activity is understood in terms of the acts of creation, development and transmission of specific information it emerges as a human activity that could and in fact has occurred everywhere. Thus it becomes possible to speak of Chinese or Oriental studies (*yogaku*), Western studies (*seigaku*) and Dutch studies (*rangaku*). Japanese are rather surprised that Western scholars pretend universality whereas they refer mainly to Western sources or to an evaluation of non-Western sources based upon Western paradigms.

This double meaning of knowledge and its application (pragmatic *and* spiritual) seems at the root of discussions about (the lack of) originality in Japanese intellectual efforts and might explain the uneasy position of Ph.D's. There seems to me a remarkable difference between the more than 5 000 books published in 1973 and classified as social science books, each selling several thousands of copies on the one side and the few hundred doctorates as a few percentages of the number of graduates on the other side (Joji Watanuki, 1977). The gap between what is considered a purely academic dissertation and what is considered relevant for the larger public is enormous. The 8,000 Japanese social scientists seem to publish a book every two year. Intellectual curiosity, respect for learning and faith in higher education are widespread in Japan, but the academic tradition of higher degrees is weakly developed and restricted within very narrow boundaries. I am frequently struck by the wide-range creative productivity of Japanese colleagues and the ambivalence or absence of doctorates. I assume that the adoption of Western science and its institutional framework en bloc has alienated the universitas from society. My hypothesis is that the present push to extend doctoral education and research training will lead to a new meaning of originality and frontiers of learning from a Japanese perspective. Presently, the number of four-years universities stand at 45, and requests are pouring in from them to set up graduate schools. However, the addition of new layers does not offer a solution to the conformity in higher education. There is however, not yet an established place for Ph.Ds in Japanese society. The relatively low percentage of doctorates has a large percentage of unemployed: over-doctors as they are called. There are many non-chartered innovations in the second and third cycle of higher education, such as the Matsushita School of Government and Management, which might breakthrough narrow academic traditions. The Japanese have not yet made their own choice what type of doctorate is needed. At a pragmatic level the distinction between the collective responsibility for completion after selection and individual prominence required for offering an independent and original contribution to knowledge has created a yet unresolved dilemma. The present effort to internationalize Japanese higher education will stimulate new transformations.

Finally, one cannot stereotype European, American and Japanese doctorates as if they are fixed and unchangeable. Variety and selectivity are the key characteristics and there is a strong tendency for internationalisation. As ideal types one can characterize the European doctorate as a shiboleth for originality and societal authority, although the actual appreciation varies between disciplines and national systems; the American doctorate is assumed to be a pre-academic career degree or a union card for entering the hierarchy of assistant, associate and full professor but actually there is a trend for broadening the concept of a Ph.D and revitalizing former American traditions as shaped by Gilman and James; the Asian doctorate is still in the process of finding its appropriate function fitting old societal traditions of scholarship, wisdom and holiness on the one side and pragmatic considerations of state-managed science on the other side. The Japanese case seems exceptional, because societal consensus, harmony and conformity have penetrated Japanese standards much more than in other Asian societies. The meaning and extension of family and kinship seem the key as some ongoing Ph.D research of Simon Tam in Hong Kong suggests. Of course, there are many more patterns especially in the Third World. But also the political East offers its own definition of original and independent contribution to knowledge. As the compendium of the history of European universities shows

East-European universities originate from similar assumptions about the scientific community. I know of one comparative study on the intellectual elite in East-Germany (DDR) and WestGermany (BRD) tracing career patterns of doctores. There is only a preliminary publication (Voigt, 1983). The origin of Ph.D's is clearly European. In that sense a revitilization of the European doctorate as is presently launched in the European Community is a vital contribution, if it maintains its international aspirations in the Atlantic and Pacific spheres but also in relation to political blocks and the Third World. The spaceship Earth can only survive by adherence to knowledge at the frontiers of learning as a universal commodity and value.

Life chances

Life chances are, in a somewhat vague sense, the sum total of opportunities offered to the individual by his society, or by a more specific position in a society (Dahrendorf, 1979). The expansion of higher education and especially the entrance of students from less privileged origin than in the traditional elite universities has created more opportunities for those who like to strive for the highest honours in their field of study as Dutch universities put it awarding the first degree of doctorandus. Graduates are not obliged to use this privelege and, if they do, they can select the time and the field of study in coming to the fore. In actual Dutch practice there are few top positions in academia, government, business or profession where one cannot arrive without a doctorate, although it starts to be formally required for academic careers. It is frequently overlooked that especially pre-career Ph.D's reduce the opportunity of work experience in an earlier stage. In many societies apprenticeship and actual performance is more important than formal education. Many of my own respondents in this study did not receive a Ph.D before obtaining top positions, such as Kenneth Boulding, Pete Mitchell and Henk Lambers. There are many substitutes and parallel routes to excellency.

Empirical evidence on social stratification shows that educational credentials are only one of many signals of individual potential under imperfect information (Baron, 1984). They affect position and salary most at the beginning of one's career, but I have seen no convincing evidence that higher degrees in contrast to lower degrees as bachelor or master have a positive pre-career impact. Some evidence in Japan and the UK shows even a negative effect (Meeks, 1985; Mofiat, 1984). Employer rationality is not simply 'bounded', it is sometimes illusory. Casimir told us in the symposium of May 1985 that also in his position of director of the Philips Nat. Lab. a doctorate was only one possible yardstick for selecting candidates. Field mobility (i.e. coping with problems outside one's established field of competence) seems to be more productive than continuing one's specialization from an early start (see also the Ph.D thesis of van Heringen, 1983). Early career attainments are likely to reflect individuals' success in exploiting their ascribed and achieved attributes to pass initial 'tests' (formal and informal) and become effectively socialized. In later stages success is more defined in terms specific to one's organization, profession, community, or other restricted reference group. It may approximate a Markov process i.e. reflecting prior successes and tenure or, as sociologists call it, a self-fullfilling prophecy. A mid-career Ph.D might be instrumental in widening one's scope and reference groups by reflecting on experience, analysing work episodes and opening new perspectives.

However, I don't think that one can force candidates to make the risky shift of a Ph.D journey. It is an individual decision and there are many alternatives for personal development. Of course, one can create formal hierarchies based on a Ph.D completion but this seems to neglect too much human potential and to narrow down criteria of appraisal. Also in academia a stimulating and innovating performance as a teacher and tutor is highly productive although it does not result in printed papers or a dissertation. Contact networks are particularly important for careers in organizations that exhibit task ambiguity, normative control, and intense collaboration (Granovette, Kanter, Collins, Baron, 1984). I have a preference for mid-career candidates. They are a neglected category in most reform proposals which I have seen. Jobs may have an inverted U-shaped performance curve where performance is plotted against tenure. The new employee may lack experience and skill needed to do the job but is frequently enthusiastic and motivated. The more senior employee may have the experience but may now lack the motivation. Thus, performance is likely to be highest at an intermediate level of tenure, in which there is both skill and experience and still a high level of motivation. This inverted U-shaped relationship has been observed in research and development when performance is plotted against average group age. Increasing group longevity tends to produce increased behavioural stability, selective exposure to information, greater group homogeneity, and increasingly differentiated roles within the group. (Pfeffer, 1982, p. 284). It would require a 'knowledge manager' at what particular period in a career of an individual there is fertile ground for developing an independent, original and relevant contribution to knowledge. I assume that decreasing working time, increasing education and life expectancy might create in the future more opportunities for mid-career and early retirement Ph.D's as one option for those who like it. It would need flexible arrangements between learning environment with its own social and cognitive structures in the scientific community and its paradigms, working environment in the industrial community and its learning and induction systems, and the protecting environment in the state and its welfare policies. Such a design would require a special study.

In more practical terms the actual distribution of Ph.D's over careers and occupational classes greatly varies. In the Netherlands e.g. 9% of the chief executives of Dutch major industries hold a doctorate (Dronkers, 1985) and 10% of the members of Parliament. This is much higher than in the UK (Fidler, 1981), but lower than in Germany (Voigt, 1983; Locke, 1985). In Japan doctorates outside academic careers are almost non-existent. In Indonesia the relatively small percentage of Ph.D's is highly concentrated in government, although frequently with part-time or honorary positions as professor. The special case of higher doctorates in the UK on the base of published work without viva or a special dissertation (342 in 1980 against 6,199 Ph.D's; see Simpson) has never been studied. In many societies there are other ways of awarding and recognizing an independent and original contribution to knowledge than the Ph.D. The case of honorary degrees would need a special study. It seems, however, even a more heterogeneous category than the dissertation-based Ph.D. If one analyses the discussions about a honorary degree for the former Dutch prime minister Den Uyl in Amsterdam university, the present English prime minister Thatcher in Cambridge, and to the present Dutch prime minister Lubbers in Seoul university, one discovers a whole range of arguments between political and scientific issues. Another special case is membership of academies. In the English and French situation it is clearly much more important than a Ph.D, whereas in the Dutch situation one seems to need a Ph.D and to belong to an established discipline before one is selected and it has a less important societal value than in the French and English case (see chapter V). Also membership of professional and research associations may substitute for a Ph.D and this is in some disciplines, professions and national systems even more important. Actually, awards and rewards for individual contributions to knowledge are part of the old question of the circulation of elites and counter-elites (Mooy, 1984). It reflects the importance given to knowledge in a society in comparison to political power, wealth and heredity. At the international level Noble prizes (Zuckerman, 1967) and an increasing amount of complementary awards at any level recognize individual or collective contributions to knowledge, usually with a wide spin-off in the scientific community.

Age is a very elusive variable for doctorates. In the Dutch situation one study (Buis, 1983) came to an average age of 36.2 years with an average of 31.5 year in natural sciences and more than 37 years in other sciences. Also the American data base shows an enormous variation in the age of those who complete a doctorate. I discovered only one study, where on tried to distinguish the nature of dissertations written by older candidates in contrast to those written by a younger generation (Lammers, 1964). In this particular case of 66 dissertations it turned out that the older generation has a broader concept of an independent and original contribution to knowledge than the younger generation who sticks to a more theoretical approach according to a particular paradigm (see p. 53). The more general question, whether the age at Ph.D has any predictive value for research productivity as an early career determinant has never been properly tested to the best of my knowledge. In a study of Clemente (1974) a general lack of continuity in research was observed: the findings are not cumulative, but rather ambiguous and often contradictory. Also his study showed a weak influence of age at Ph.D on productivity. My personal experience is that older candidates are rarely interested in a narrowly defined academic exercise but try to include their image of the world and sense of relevance in a thesis proposal, but one cannot be dogmatic about age. There are sufficient examples where original and relevant contributions to knowledge are made at an early age, although not necessarily in the form of a dissertation. There is no stable and symmetrical balance to be found between the age at Ph.D and types of careers, but rather a dynamic ebb and flow of adaptation in disciplines, professions and national systems that substitute for equilibrium. It is partly a self-fulfilling prophecy. Successful Ph.D's in careers trigger off new Ph.D's and a high rate of Ph.D's in certain disciplines, professions or occupations make a Ph.D necessary for careers even without empirical evidence on its effectiveness. It might then become a fetish or union card rather than a relevant contribution to knowledge. The major gap in empirical studies of social stratification is the lack of continuity and of differentiation in the three cycles of higher education. The multiplier effects of Ph.D's in society are unknown, maybe because democratizing and egalitarian forces prevented studies in traditional, academic values. Presently, there seems to be a revival of elite studies, because whatever ideals one pursues in broadening access to knowledge and power one cannot escape selection of the few. Mass higher education makes selection for excellency even more acute at a later stage.

The value of knowledge

In his Richard T. Ely lecture (1966) Kenneth E. Boulding explored the role of knowledge in social systems, both as a product of the past and as a determinant to the future.

'The absence of any unit of knowledge itself .....and, perhaps the intrinsic heterogeneity of its substance, makes it very difficult to think of a piece of knowledge as such and indeed has probably contributed to a certain resistance we feel to thinking of knowledge as a commodity. One longs indeed for a unit of knowledge, which perhaps might be called a "wit" analogous to the "bit" as used in information theory; but up to now at any rate no such practical unit has emerged. It is certainly tempting to think of knowledge as a capital stock of information, knowledge being to information what capital is to income, and to use the bit itself in the form of a stock as the measure of knowledge.....The bit, however, abstracts completely from the content of either information or knowledge, and.....for purposes of the social system theorist we need a measure which takes account of significance and which would weight for instance, gossip and (strategic information).....While knowledge has many of the aspects of property, its capacity for reproduction in many minds and its accessibility in the form of the published word make it a very peculiar form of property.....some knowledge is exclusive, such as trade secrets and patents, and therefore becomes property. What is perhaps even more important, knowledge which has the capacity of generating more knowledge in a single head is also exclusive and becomes property to the individual possessing it.....As far as matter and energy are concerned, we are subject to inexorable laws of conservation.....and even degradation and decay.....It is only information and knowledge processes which in any sense get out under the iron laws of conservation and decay'.

Boulding distinguishes two basic processes in the evolution of knowledge: printing, in which a structure is able to reproduce itself by making a copy of itself out of the incoherent matter around it, and organizing, by which coded information creates a phenotype, such as a blueprint a building, an idea an organization, protocols of research a new theory. The learning process is the real key to development, but we are still too much obsessed by mechanical models, capital-income ratios and input-output tables to grasp its meaning. Even in the 'human resources school' of Schultz and Harbison the problem of learning as a whole outside as well as inside the institutions of formal education has been underdeveloped. For a social system scientist the area of decision making itself in the private sector, in households, business and government is overwhelmingly important. A decision is always a choice among alternative perceived images of the future. The process by which we learn our preferences in decision making is mysterious and fussy. We have what might be called the 'sour grapes' principle - that what we cannot get we decide we do not like or cognitive dissonance. There is also a counterprinciple that might be called the 'Mount Everest' principle, that if something is hard to get, we want it, just because it is hard to get. The epistemological theory of decision making is pretty empty unless we can specify ways in which the inputs of the past determine the present images of the future. Moreover, there is a certain epistemological paradox, that where knowledge is an essential part of the system, knowledge about the system changes the system itself. There is also a great danger in rationality, that is finding and choosing the best position of part of the system which is not the best for the whole. Too many experts devote their lives to finding the best way of doing something that should not be done at all. Despite its epistemological complications the search for truth and limits to science is still more important than a rational approach. Moreover, a judgment about what should be done cannot be isolated from cognition. Soedjatmoko as an intellectual leader in the United Nations University rightly includes knowledge as a source for freedom and self-confidence in human development (Soedjatmoko, 1980).

For the particular piece of knowledge generation that is printed and organized in a doctoral dissertation Boulding's and Soedjatmoko's ideas about global learning systems in evolution are highly relevant. Also the need for interdisciplinary communication as continuously stressed by Mitchell and, in that sense, the need for a full knowledge cycle or a continuity of all academic disciplines, however implicit, cannot be neglected, whatever the operational difficulties. The significance and measure of a doctoral dissertation is based on the judgment of a promotion committee representing the academic senate of a particular university. Of course, this judgment is not failure-proof or true and there are fraudulent cases, but a doctoral dissertation is open for public inspection, though with practical obstacles to access. It is not exclusive. It can therefore hardly be called a commodity. We can put prices on the number of printed pages or on the four or ten thousand hours it took to prepare the manuscript, but in the perfect market that the scientific community is supposed to be the cognitive content of a dissertation is costless or a free good. A successful doctor might be able to publish or edit a commercial edition but it is usually highly restricted in its target audience. Moreover, if a sizable number of copies is required for an academic promotion as in the Dutch case, this restricted market is already satisfied. Also in the case of signing a contract with University Microfilms or similar agencies, one has to pay for one's own copies, be it at a reduced price. Dissertation Abstracts and similar agencies distribute the gist of the information without any remuneration for the author. Publication in recognized international scientific journals of a condensed version is usually also at a price for the author. The measuring rod of money in A.C. Pigou's phrase cannot be applied. The counter principle that Boulding called the 'Mount Everest' principle might be applicable, but then we have to specify why the dissertation is seen as a mountain. In my judgment it is a merit good, although in some cases I don't approve the quality.

Information Markets

A doctoral dissertation is free public scientific information, which is only protected by the convention of Bern or codes of the scientific community. It took from 1450 when printing was invented in the West to 1912 when the Berner convention was approved in the Netherlands before one recognized the property of the producer of information. In some countries the convention is still not accepted. A writer of a doctoral dissertation is in a particularly weak position, when he has been used as a waterboy for the elephant as professor Pettigrew expressed it and the outcomes of his research are simply included in his supervisor's work without proper quotation. The world market of free scientific information is a small, highly fragmented but important market, where English is becoming the lingua franca of our time. The former president of Elsevier (R.E.M. van de Brink, 1985) considers doctoral dissertations for pragmatic reasons to belong to the 'grey' literature in the same category as advertisement. In contrast to the authors of public, educational and professional information he considers the information of a scientific paper or dissertation not to be an economic good for its author. An author publishes the results of his research only if it is considered to be new information. This recognition of providing new or original information has an indirect economic value for its author. It establishes or confirms his position in the scientific community and so helps his career. The publication itself is only for the publisher, editor and bookseller an economic good, that he estimates to consist of 2.5% of the world market of free information. However, some 80-90% of scientific information is supplied to public libraries. For doctoral dissertations university libraries and sometimes the national library have almost a monopoly. There are some specialist bookkeepers and of course microfiches agencies but transaction costs are high.

The actual distribution network of published doctoral dissertations, even if condensed in scientific journals, tends to be highly specific and small. The circulation of a scientific monographe as a dissertation and of scientific journals, even in English, is still some 500-1,500 copies as much as in the sixteenth century, according to van den Brink. Also the number of copies of doctoral dissertations as required or customary in the Dutch situation, some 300-700, has not been increased since the sixteenth century. It seems that scientific networks are highly segmented and restricted, but the number of specialist networks has of course increased in an explosive way. In a doctoral study Michael Wyler (1984) found in a sample of 50 medical dissertations at the Erasmus University an average number of 660 copies. However, most interviewed doctores received only feedback from their own personal network. The actual publication behaviour of dissertation writers depends on the diversity of individual human situation and motives and the complex interaction of the substance of scientific knowledge, broader cultural traditions, and the folkways and structures of particular scientific communities. A large proportion of the scientific community actually publishes very little. Price (1963) estimated that over 50% of the scientific population that publishes at all writes one paper or a fraction thereof per individual life-time, that 10% of the population is responsible for over 30% of all the papers written, and that only 3% of the population consists of highly prolific major contributors. Next, only a small fraction of the scientific journals contains the bulk of the articles read by scientists. Of the vast number of scientific publications, only a few are consulted repeatedly and a large number are virtually ignored (Gustin, 1973).

In the particular case of doctoral dissertations I assume that there is even more skewness in publication rate and rewards in the form of quotations or recognition than in the case of publication of papers in scientific journals. There is an enormous variation between e.g. the Dutch custom of hundreds of copies for an extended network of libraries and colleagues and friends, and e.g. the English custom of some four copies in special 'jackets' and the mere possibility of developing a book from a dissertation. The statistical analysis of scientific publication began as early as the first quarter of this century, but has only recently reached a certain impetus and became of course its own field of study: scientometrics. It analyses the quantitative aspects of the generation, propagation and utilization of scientific information, in order to contribute to a better understanding of the mechanisms of scientific research as a social activity. There is even an international journal Scientometrics published jointly by Elsevier and the Publishing House of the Hungarian Academy of Sciences.

My focus is not on the appreciation of scientometrics or connected fields of study but on the practical importance of information markets for dissertation writers. Despite the impressive technological expansion of the information society (Porat, 1977) each individual member of the scientific community has to cope with a limited capacity to absorb new knowledge and relies on a highly selective communication system. Dissertation writers as neophytes in the scientific community are encapsulated in their own specific network of referees, colleagues, friends and potential clients or users of new information. This network has hardly expanded since the invention of printing, but has become highly specific. Nakayama suggests service research where the potential users of research outcomes become partners in the research process and so prevent the isolation of an individual researcher. I think that this is highly recommendable, although the format of partnership varies in each field of study. Research has become much more of a collective effort than in the past, because of the intrinsic limitations of the individual mind and the explosive growth of the stock of information. In a practical sense therefore the individual dissertation writer needs to broaden his forum and to include potential clients in his writing process. In certain disciplines this might include consecutive publishing stages which at a certain moment become the critical mass for a final dissertation. In the Dutch setting anyhow an academic promotion on conclusions from previous publications has become acceptable practice and this practice gains momentum. A personal computer does not substitute for a personal network, even if it is connected with many others, neither does it substitute for a personal secretary or assistant.

Practical obstacles to a more consumer-friendly dissertation are frequently style manuals and instructions and publication prescriptions. Sometimes one is forbidden to use the personal pronoun 'I' or explanations of a personal nature. There are many more personal elements in each piece of research than we are allowed to express and natural sciences are no exception (e.g. Casimir, 1983). Moreover, if a supervisor refers to a particular style in his institution, it is usually worthwhile to sample a few accepted dissertations in that institution in order to show considerable variation in style. I remember a case where the author presented a concise scientific report of her research but included an explanation for a broader audience. Of course, I do not object to the rigour of proving each statement and of refering to the original sources. Scientific production is usually restricted to what has been published in carefully selected journals and indeed there is good reason for excluding any printed material without selection. However, Japanese scientists are in that sense much less restrictive and publish in widely read quality journals or 'popular' books. In this respect the increase of doctoral dissertations in the narrow academic sence would be counterproductive. Also in Indonesia there seems to be more awareness of science as a societal function, although one frequently tries to copy specific Western academic habits. Of course, I don't expect that academic preferences for a rather esoteric style can be easily changed, but one can commend and support publications which are more open for colleagues in neighbouring fields and for consumers in practice and 'nevertheless' provide tested new insight. Especially professional writers and others in creative work abhor the rigidities of dissertations e.g. a Dutch writer J.J. Peereboom (1984) reflected in 'Hollands Maandblad' a Dutch literary journal.

'As an effort to communicate ideas dissertation writing is the most absurd. The balance between effort of the author and the profit for the public is at the best to compare with mountains and a flea. After five years (of dissertation work) the pale doctorandus presents his evidence of quality which is automatically absorbed by the libraries in their endless system. He slinks off as a doctor and starts a new life. During the promotion ceremonials he is the center of attention during an hour at the price of some tenthousand guilders' (free translation).

Nevertheless his dissertation was well received.

Even if a publisher is interested in a dissertation-as-book, editors will insist that it be changed in numerous ways, the most important involving a 'translation' from dissertionese into a readable language or an acceptable international variation. Moreover, well-research dissertations display frequently a choppy and sometimes contradictory content and style which reflect the candidate's effort to meet the demands of various thesis committee members. Getting a book out of a dissertation is an exception in the American (Sternberg, 1981) and English situation, but reworking some chapters into journal articles of chapters for edited volumes is common enough to be the rule. In some disciplines articles in recognized journals score much higher than a publication as a book or printing a large number of copies as in the Dutch custom or burying the outcomes in University Microfilm archieves. I know of many cases where the authors keep a private stock of copies to be sold or exchanged in the most primitive form of market or as Indonesians would call it 'langanan economy' - a regular network of clients, customers and friends (Kimman, 1981). Indeed in the Dutch system distribution of dissertations can be seen as a subscription system, where the Parliament, libraries, the Royal Academy and faculty members receive a regular supply of dissertations without any market forces. Frequently a waste (R. Arlman). Of course, in university positions it is possible to make it recommended or obligatory reading for students, sometimes to the dismay of university books- hops or sometimes in a direct deal with them.

From a historical perspective printing originated in China and had become common by Southern Sung times (1127-1280), but in the medieval West, where the lack of printing techniques made conversation and scarce manus- cripts indispensable for study, scholars and students travelled from town to town in search of both. It is still an important question, why during the long period between about 250 B.C. and 1450 A.D. the East was superior to the West (Nakayama, 1984). Printing technology does not tell the whole story. The dissemination of technology is decisively shaped by social institutions and neither scholarly journals nor learned societies simply did not emerge from within the Eastern academic traditions. Europeans created academic societies to make the results of their discussions more widely available. Writing a book to announce every new discovery was a burdensome and impractical task. Before the modern scientific journal made its appearance, there were firstly book catalogues and advertising sheets by publishing houses or book markets, such as Frankfurt and Leipzig (with more titles as today), and secondly the recorded proceedings of learned societies. The scientific journal itself is usually assumed to start with the Journal des Sçavans (Paris 1665-1792) and the Philosophical Transactions (London, 1665). These early journals did not emphasize authorship. The articles were not signed, but the work of individual researchers was publicly recognized in hearsay form. There were constant quarrels about who had discovered what first. The role of the university thesis was ambivalent. They were not general- ly available and sometimes little more than repositories of knowledge. There is a whole collection of old dissertations in Holland (S. van der Woude) and German states and also collections of other academic products, which were not for sale to the general public. They can be considered as academic advertisement, but their function in scientific development has not been studied (Nakayama, 1983).

The present scientific article presents the reader with a precisely worded account of original research in the more structured fields of study usually the result of team work, to be appraised and evaluated by the reader withou, explicit reference to the paradigm. Once articles grow out of a single tradition of research, references contain only the most recent previous publications without mentioning the original sources. The mature scientific journal is then the product of the modern merit system and its emphasis on efficiency: presentation of the results of one's work in the shortest possible time with the least expenditure of energy. Scientists report their work in arid style from which all accounts of the research programme and the trials and tribulations encountered in carrying it out have disappeared. Communication is restricted to insiders, whereas the broader public including administrators can only count the pages as bits. Nakayama rightly doubts whether in the process of transmitting an academic tradition, creativity is being successfully communicated through the printed word of scientific journals. The style of the modern scientific article reader gets no feel for what is not known or what failures have been made during many trials. This is even more acute when paradigms produced in one cultural area are transplanted into a remote and vastly different culture (see Chapter VIII). In that respect a more broadly conceived doctoral dissertation especially by mid- or late career candidates, where the origin of the paradigm, its development and future direction is made explicit in explaining the particular focus of one's .research, is highly important. It can never be substituted by articles alone.

New information technology tends to industrialize scientific research itself. When the methodology of normal science is set, the research guidelines specified, the research contracts signed, the funds forthcoming, and the data produced like goods manufactured in a factory, one cannot afford any more to delay the publication or to reflect on doubts or ignorance. On the frontiers of search one looks for the latest information in preprints and news bulletins. Van Bueren (1985) speculates that the new university in the information society will be largely based on a catalogue of prestructured modules where each student selects his own programme and decreases his failure rate. This leads actually to a type of Open University, where normal universities offer received knowledge for the many in a chain of personal computers. In an appendix from the perspective of a scholar in the next century he defines societal utility as what has been left over, when the superfluous has disappeared and refers to a year GD (great depression or 'grand déluge') where a κ-variation of higher education leads through an interactive system with personal computers towards a guaranteed degree and career. His motto from Voltaire 'Le superflu, chose si nécessaire' indicates his concern that development of creativity and strategic insight into the knowledge industry will be at bay in mass universities. The cultural function of the university cannot be expressed in bits or with the measuring rod of money and 'culture parks' as 'science parks' do not exist. Even special institutions as a monastery cannot protect the cultural function as an intrinsic element of academic life. It is therefore regrettable that traditional faculties of philosophy are the first victims of retrenchment policies and that humanities actually stabilize between the rigorous branches of a scientific technological industrial complex.

In the Dutch situation anyhow the number of doctoral dissertations in humanities has stabilized to a hundred since 1937 (see Wyler). Humanities cannot be programmed in graduate schools in a similar fashion as the other sciences. Reflection and maturation are essential, even if it needs longer completion periods and may be higher failure rates. Ignorance and doubts are critical in any research process or as Boulding remarked in the classic 'bon mot' attributed to humorist Will Rogers 'the trouble is not what people don't know; it's what they do know that is not so'. There is even ambiguity in the word 'ignorance'.

Information markets for minorities

It seems useful to consider the dissertation writer as belonging to a minority in the analytical meaning that has been so fruitfully explored by Thomas Sowell (1981). Individual dissertation writers are in an ambivalent position for entering an information market. Individual neophytes in the scientific community who do not belong to a dominant and highly structured department or research unit are in a particularly weak position. Especially if their outcomes do not confirm dominant paradigms (Boissevain, 1974) or provide critical comments on an interest group (Sternberg 1981), there are obstacles in publication or, in minority language, there is discrimination. In Sternberg's case of the professional organization of chiropractors he was indirectly warned that his own health (chiropractic and otherwise) would be best guaranteed by letting the dissertation lie unpublished. One tried to buy his manuscript 'for publication', but in order to get the legal copyright to the materials, so one could prevent it from being published. I do not know whether one can prove discrimination in actual publishing support. It is partly a myth. There are always objective reasons about quality, scope and language and one has to look for autobiographies and fiction as in C.P. Snow's Masters. For humanities and social sciences there is not a lingua franca as in the case of natural sciences and international business. Variety of languages is as much an asset as variety of disciplines. I regret the decline of foreign languages as French and German in the Dutch educational system, whereas one would need a selective expansion in Spanish, Russian, Chinese and Japanese. My plea for a lingua franca in international exchange is only additional and pragmatic for some fields of study. There is always a need for more local studies and service research as Nakayama has put it, where the audience or forum consists of a special language community. In that sense the advantage of scientists in English-speaking countries is also a disadvantage because of an underdevelopment in other languages.

The concentration ratio for publishing scientific information is particularly low. In the Dutch case the concentration ratio 4 (the four highest ranking publishing houses) is 27 for Dutch language and 30 for foreign languages (R.E.M. van den Brink, 1985). For the printing of 170 dissertations between 1964-1967, of which an abstract was published in a chemical journal, Arlman (1968) counted 60 different printing houses. I assume that printing technology will increase the concentration ratio for publishing scientific information, but there does not seem yet a danger for monopolyzing the scientific information market. Moreover, pooling of printing capacity does not need to include uniform publishing outlets. Some universities support special publishing houses.

Of course, not every dissertation needs to be published: the Dutch custom of hundreds of copies is more culture than merit, whereas the expansive habit of a special hard cover for binding the few copies in the English setting is hardly functional for present technology. In the Dutch system the yearly costs of printing the 400 dissertations were estimated at Dfl. 1,000,000, largely subsidized by university libraries, grants and fiscal priveleges in 1968 (Arlman). Wyler's data (1984) indicate the yearly costs of printing the 1,000 dissertations at more than Dfl. 10,000,000. In relation to the integral costs of a dissertation in terms of transaction costs, production time, supervision and opportunity costs this is only a small fraction.

Publishers have played through the centuries a critical role in the reproduction and distribution of scientific information. In the sixteenth century they were even responsible for the documentation (van der Woude, 1963). It would be an important contribution, when publishers would co-ordinate available know-how for the individual dissertation writer as presently seems to happen in the Dutch situation. A European doctorate would need a selective European publishing policy and editiorial support, including translations. We could apply an analogous reasoning for setting the price of a doctoral dissertation as Pen (1985) did for the price of a book. Dutch publishers estimate 40% at the break-even point and only some 1.5% as best-sellers. I assume that doctoral dissertations are much more skewed as publishable material than books. Sometimes one seems to aim at an abstruse language, but we can support valuable doctoral dissertations with editorial service also during the writing stage. It is a myth that readibility and style have a negative correlation with scientific quality.

Doctoral dissertations have also a particular meaning for minorities in the traditional sense of the word. Sowell (1981) stated that the historical and sociological literature is full of accounts of how the one group of immigrant children were the teachers' joy, and the other their despair. Group differences need not to be hereditary in a biological sense to be real in their impact as Thomas already remarked. While it is necessary to be on guard against stereotypes, one cannot dogmatize that cultural differences do not affect economically relevant variables. When education is measured by academic performance level reached, rather than by years of schooling completed, racial differences in the return of investment change substantially. Doctorates for blacks do not show income differences with similar doctorates for whites and the same applies for Chinese Americans (pp. 23-25). Discrimination levels in universities were, in past eras, greater than in competitive industries, but decades later, after national political sentiment turned against discrimination and in favour of ethnic minorities, the swing of the pendulum was greater in the academic world than in competitive industries: blacks received more job offers and higher pay than whites with comparably ranked Ph.D's and the same number of publications. This illustrates how the same institutions that are most discriminatory in one era tend to be the most preferential under changed political conditions. Indeed, discrimination and preferential treatment are simply two ways of looking at the same phenomenon (pp. 47-50).

The case of women and 'women studies' for doctorates is intriguing. Wyler (1984) speculated that the proportional increase of female students has been counterproductive for the percentage of doctorates, but that might be only a question of time lag. Minorities, such as the Chinese in South East Asia, the jews in Europe, the catholics in protestant countries and the reverse, the children of immigrants and so on, seem to have used visible performance in higher education as in the case of doctoral dissertations as a powerful weapon against discrimination. Preferential publishing houses and grants have been instrumental, but this would need special studies, refining degrees of higher education. One has used the term 'higher education' too loosely for specifying its function in careers and information markets (see also Sowell, 1981, p. 23). The general neglect of doctoral dissertations as a 'vehicle of new information' hampers a clear analysis. For a revitilization of a European doctorate we need a selective publishing effort rather than a differentiation of degrees or distinctions.

Research and Development

Doctoral dissertations have an uneasy position in the field of Research and Development, that presently in the Dutch situation covers some 1.9% of the GNP as much as the total higher education system. In the beginning of my study I thought in my naivity it rather simple to discover how many Ph.D's were actually created in R&D organizations as TNO and the major Dutch industries. Figures were not available and the question caused some embarrassment. There is a basic distinction between the nature of advanced knowledge that is required for academic certification as by a Ph.D and that is recognized in R&D organizations as a relevant contribution. In academia the dominant mode of organization is discipline, basically meta-national or trans-national. Theoretical knowledge, i.e. explanation of a particular field of study by specifying relationships between variables according to the dominant disciplinary paradigm is usually preferred. Descriptive knowledge, i.e. data collecting on the historical, actual, formal or virtual shape of reality, is a necessary condition, but one frowns upon an overwhelming amount of detailed description (Clark, 1983). In business the dominant mode of organization is its product or service to be delivered in specific markets and to be produced with differential advantage in relation to competitors. Normative knowledge –based on detailed description of a particular industry and its markets and leading to specific rules of decision and to development, production and distribution programmes– is usually preferred above theoretical knowledge. Trade secrets, patents and other proprietary relationships restrict the dissemination of knowledge. A publication of proprietary information without a price is not acceptable, whereas the scientific community requires desinterestness. Production of new products or new technology is more important for business and business-oriented laboratories than theoretical advancement. In a certain sense a doctoral dissertation of a valuable employee releases him from the company's domain. In actual practice, however, Dutch leading business and R&D organizations have provided a sizable part of academic faculty and doctorates. There is a much more liberal business policy in contributing to human capital in the free scientific market than can be calculated in a rational cost-benefit analysis.

The actual exchange of knowledge and knowledgeable people between business, government and higher education is substantial in the Dutch situation. Part-time, extra-ordinary or particular, professorships are an expression of this amalgation and so is the number of external, part-time aspirants for a doctorate. It makes a clear dichotomy between theoretical and practical knowledge or between pure research and its application illusory. Academia has no monopoly of higher learning. Knowledge is 'positional'. When academics move to positions in government and business, they do not lose their intellectual capacities, but their knowledge gets another position. Administration and management require decision making and programming within its own territory, fussy indeed, but with the best of available knowledge. Policy requires balancing between legitimate support and ideology within budget restrictions, muddling through indeed, but also with the best of available knowledge. Academics have to discover, converse, refine and transmit knowledge within a virtually unlimited range of specialities. There is some conflict of interest between those who apply knowledge for obtaining specific outcomes within boundaries of confidentiality and those who develop and test knowledge for its own sake. But there is a common core.

Historically, there have been objections to grant applied sciences as engineering the ius promovendi. In 1863 the Dutch statesman and prime minister Thorbecke expressed the view that higher education has to educate for those functions which require a 'scientific formation' (the Dutch expression 'geleerde vorming' relates to the German 'Gelehrte Ausbildung') and this is not applicable to the education of engineers who have to prepare themselves for services to society. There is, in his view, a distinction between those who aspire at science as life mission and those who use science as a tool (Lintsen, 1980; de Ru, 1953; Kamp, 1955). Minister de Visser attempted in vain to prevent granting a ius promovendi to the new technical university of Delft (1905). All professors of chemical sciences wrote to the minister opposing against this privilege. The chief editor of the 'Ingenieur' (already in its nineteenth year in 1904) wrote that this a priori judgment that a doctor as such has a broader education than an engineer reflected a period of civilization which we passed already long, long time ago. Our period is one of technological progress (van Sandich, 1904). Also in preparing the new School of Trade in Rotterdam as a private initiative Kreukniet wrote in 1898 a pamphlet arguing that a good merchant needed a broad view and knowledge which should be based on science. In 1903 Dr. Kuyper proposed the Higher Education Law establishing higher education for trade, engineering and agriculture in special institutions. However, the distinction between occupational higher education and scientific higher education remained unclear. Minister Cort van der Linden argued that the university has to care for developing general principles of science independent from direct practical applications, whereas the high school ('Hochschule' in German) starts from the actual state of science and teaches the link with technology and business (Stuijvenberg, 1963, p. 31). But none of the founding fathers of the new higher education institutions accepted this distinction. Merchants, engineers and agriculturalists need not only professional and practical knowledge but also a solid education in theory and methodology. Application is impossible without fundamental research.

The academic promotion was accepted as the final proof of scholarship and science for the few. The first doctor's degree in Rotterdam was awarded to J.A. Nederbragt on the dissertation: 'Pénétration Pacifique in China' for a career in foreign service. Gradually the number of academic promotions increased until some ten in the 1930's. This is still an average score (11 in 1984) despite the multiplication of first cycle graduates. Also the discussions about procedures and quality have not changed. Critiques on the system are as old as the system itself, see the Chinese imperial degree (Dore, 1976). In 1921 it was already suggested to abolish the Dutch title 'doctorandus' indicating that every first cycle graduate had to or could complete his study (Stuijvenberg, 1963, p. 65, 66). Posthumus, for example, argued in the senate for strict regulations, but one concluded that regulations could be never comprehensive. The majority of the 363 dissertations proved to be relevant contributions to the development of economic knowledge in the broad sense, frequently reprinted and quoted. However, at that time there was not yet a scientomatric habit.

Comparatively, each national system had to cope with the two motives of the scientific process: one is to understand nature, man and his world, the other is to control them. Either of these motives may be dominant in any individual learner; fields of knowledge may draw their original impulses from one or the other (Snow, 1964, p.67). Of course, higher education for trade, engineering and agriculture attracted mainly students with practical interests, but for the few the motivation of writing a doctoral dissertation was strong enough even without special courses and support. Locke analysed in detail the differential approach to technology in Germany, France and the UK. Germany was the leader in integrating applied science in engineering and business administration within graduate schools. The Germans were even so eager to follow strict scientific habits in writing a doctor's thesis and a Habilitationsschrift that they almost lost the link with practice. France invented the double structure of higher education with its prestigious Grandes Ecoles and was rather reluctant to develop its universities. The UK only recently included application within the higher education system. Hugstadt (1981) analysed the origin and transformation of the business schools from an American perspective. In this field of knowledge there is a clear preference for second cycle degrees, mainly *MBA*, some 60,000 yearly, whereas doctor's degrees are relatively rare, some 800 yearly, but employers are rather selective where the MBA or doctor's degree has been obtained. However, especially in business administration with its fads and fashions there is a clear need for a broader scientific foundation. Japan has never made the distinction between applied and fundamental science as in the European tradition. However, higher education was mainly seen as a selection device for the top universities without substantial interest for the content. Young graduates had to enter their work organization at an early age for induction and in-house training. Doctorates have not yet a function outside academia, although the corporate class for advanced education and training is growing. Failure at this level is dramatic.

Presently, the pendulum is swinging towards technology and immediate utility away from fundamental science and broad scholarship in most countries (M.W.J. van den Brink, 1985). There are even rumours to replace the traditional doctorate by more manageable stages of methodological and technological exercises without failure rates and within a set period. The problem is that we lack information about the function of the traditional doctorate in Research and Development organisations. Casimir mentions in his Haphazard Reality - Half a Century of Science (1983) how the founder of the Natural Science laboratory in Philips, G. Holst, stimulated publication in order to motivate his research workers. Also Casimir as one of his successors has always emphasized the need for publication. There are examples with other evidence, such as the case of B.C.P. Jansen (1884-1962), who refused an excellent offer from an industrial research organization because he preferred his university position for a free exchange of information. It would need

special studies to discover whether doctoral dissertations written by industrial R&D scientists have made a bridge between the bounded and free
information markets. In most societies there are various linking pin and
gatekeepers organizations and functions which facilitate the exchange. In the
European community new initiatives are flourishing to build networks between industry and university in the field of training, education and research.
In the past we have established the International Institute of the Management
of Technology in Milano but the major challenge seems to be continuity of
effort and institutional anchors within academic traditions.

The function of a Ph.D: a review

For individuals the Ph.D is more a psychic income or human capital than an
economic good in the strict sense. The motivation for writing a dissertation is
complex, sometimes a personal challenge or joy in scientific discovery or
finishing an intricate puzzle, sometimes an ethical promulgation of some new
insight, sometimes artistic creativity or polical and organizational authority
or authorship in the original sense of creativity and originality. One likes to
be recognized and respected and in a society or community where doctoral
dissertations are symbolic expressions of recognition, the doctorate is an
attractive option. It cannot be denied that in some academic careers the
doctorate has a measurable impact on income and, especially in the American culture, this internal labour market explains largely the increase and
decrease of Ph.D's, but the motivation can rarely be reduced to economic
advantages only. As a product in information markets it might be a bridge
between industrial bounded research and free scientific information. Usually
a bridge is open for the public, toll-free.

The Dutch TNO (Dutch organisation for Applied Natural Scientific Research) is a good example. Between universities with Dfl. 2,000 milj. for
research, industrial research with some Dfl. 5,000 milj. for R&D, fundamental
research organizations with some 1,400 milj., and international and foreign
research with some 400 milj. it occupies a linking pin function with some
fifty-fifty support from government and clients, 5,000 employees and some
600 milj. turnover. It finances relevant doctoral studies and offers part-time
professorships. There are many fields of common interest, such as energy,
environment, food, health and building. I am unable to specify the function
of doctorates. Estimates indicate some ten Ph.D's yearly awarded to employees of TNO.

Historically the Ph.D has been connected with teaching. In medieval
universities all resident doctores outside academia were invited to participate
in an academic promotion (W. Frijhoff) and it seems that sharing and
disseminating knowledge for public utilization is still intrinsic in each docto-

rate project. Presently fast and bounded information flows between transnational corporations and public agencies seem to make the doctorate concept obsolete. There is a tendency to rely on information networks in international journals, retrieval systems and commercial data banks rather than on academic products. However, information is not knowledge. Sometimes an informational overload prevents knowledge. One can regret this development, but it seems irreversible in our information society. The function of doctoral dissertations rests on its cultural mission of testing received knowledge in its original setting and exploring frontiers of learning. Some expect a further qualitative reduction of doctoral dissertations as an efficient pre-career device produced in an industrial fashion for a specified number of candidates in prestructured projects and in relation with science policy and industrial markets. In this way one can multiply doctorates as has been done with first cycle graduates. Indeed, there are sufficient indications (OECD, 1986), that the present agenda of policy makers prefers completion rates rather than independency and originality with uncertain outcome. Course-based doctorate programmes will decrease uncertainty and supervisors will be awarded by efficiency measures.

However, I have learned from history (there are no objective lessons) that doctorates or other final degrees have continuously been under pressure of immediate concern and there are periods of decline or ritual exposures of received knowledge rather than originality (e.g. Weisz), but it is only for a limited period. One has sometimes created new more pragmatic degrees for those who need a doctoral degree but not necessarily one based on original research (e.g. Doctor of Arts, Educational Doctor, see Mayhew, pp. 154-164), but sooner or later it becomes a second-class degree or one would eventually need a new superdoctoral degree. The traditional meaning of a Ph.D – i.e. to offer evidence of an independent and original contribution to knowledge and demonstrate one's ability to organize and complete a major research project, verifying old knowledge and searching for new– is already ambitious enough. There is no need for new titles but one has to accept variety and temporal fluctuations.

The market for doctoral dissertations depends on institutional arrangements rather than on supply-demand. In the Dutch case university libraries play a critical role in the number of copies required. If a doctoral dissertation is properly published, it usually belongs to the highly fragmented free scientific information market. A European doctorate which would revitalize good practices in major European universities offers the opportunity of keeping original standards against present devaluation tendencies. Of course, each dissertation is unique and one cannot standardize the number of pages or the period for completion, but one needs to accept pragmatic considerations. There is ample room for improvement of supervision, publication and stages. It needs neither to be a 'magnum opus' nor an obsession over too many years, if we broaden the forum and develop more roles and networks for support and supervision in a European dimension.

Chapter V

Bureaucracy, Clan and Market

This chapter explores a structural approach to the Ph.D. I try to integrate the historical, cultural and functional evidence of previous chapters in describing and explaining structures in the doctorate process. The core is the increasing gap between the complex bureaucracy of science policy, research and development, and the higher education system on the one side and the highly individualized emotional-cognitive structure of a dissertation writer, who needs to complete an independent and original contribution to a particular field of knowledge within a reasonable time on the other side. Weber described a set of conditions that, in his view, clearly make bureaucracy the solution of choice in large organizations or systems of legitimate domination.

'Experience tends universally to show that the purely bureaucratic type of administration is, from a purely technical point of view, capable of attaining the highest degree of efficiency and is in this sense the most rational known means of exercising authority over human beings. It is superior to any other form in precision, in stability in the stringency of its discipline, and its reliability.....The choice is only between bureaucracy and dilettantism in the field of administration' (see Ouchi, 1980).

Weber was deeply concerned with the question of efficiency in public administration and in the relative economic efficiency of different forms of legitimate power. Most organizational theorists base their work either explicitly or implicitly on the Weberian model. Consequently, the terms bureaucracy, complex organization, and formal organization have become interchangeable. However, bureaucracy is but one form of mediation of economic exchange. Market is an alternative mechanism for achieving the same objective under certain conditions. A third mechanism of cooperation is socialization or internalization of values partly substituting for external means of control. The term 'clan' is used here to mean an organic association that resembles a kin network but does not necessarily include blood relations (Durkheim). Markets, bureaucracies and clan may therefore be distinguished as three distinct mechanisms present in any organization: markets based on exchange, bureaucracy based on legitimate power, and clans on congruent, not mutually exclusive, objectives of individuals. There is a rich literature on this distinction, but my objective here is not to engage in theoretical discussions, but to apply these distinctions to the Ph.D phenomenon and its structural context. I focus on the question how bureaucracy can compensate for failures of market and clan, but also for its own failures.

Failures of bureaucracy, clan and market

None of the three mechanisms of organizing minds, hands, materials and time for efficient and contributive work actually provides a perfect solution. The market was seen by Adam Smith originally as the perfect mechanism. The propensity to truck, barter, and exchange one thing for another was for him the necessary, though very slow and gradual consequence of human nature, not of any human wisdom: the invisible hand. A rather esthetic view on the wealth of the nations as J.J. Klant observed. Further developments of these seminal ideas showed many imperfections. The market failure appoach with transaction costs as a rather vague core concept has tried to cope with these imperfections (Williamson, 1975; Pfeffer, 1982). Markets are never perfect. We need counterbalancing mechanisms. Bureaucracy was seen by Max Weber as the most rational known means of exercising authority over human beings. Also here further development developments showed that one cannot design regulations with precision and stability in order to guarantee desired outcomes. There is a paradox in administration, when regulations become too cumbersome. Present discussions on bureaucracy emphasize the imperfections and one could invent a bureaucracy failure approach also with transaction costs as a core concept. Perfect bureaucracies do not exist. The scientific community is the ideal type of an organic solidarity between scholars who share the same ethos and values. It represents the third mechanism of the clan, as coined by Durkheim. The history of universities has made clear that the scientific community has never been completed as a perfect solution. Here again one needs to develop a clan failure approach.

The doctoral dissertation or other final examinations for entering the scientific community pose particular problems for any organizational effort. By definition the doctoral dissertation is seen as a unique, independent and original contribution to knowledge and is consequently never a direct extrapolation of past performance. A science of managing as it has developed over time (Smiddy; 1954) is not concerned with the particular, the unique, but only with the general. That is, with kinds and events, which recur. What we need therefore is an account of the form of the structure. I assume that the particular nature of doctoral dissertations as a concerted effort towards originality has made the Ph.D phenomenon so elusive for systematic scrutiny. It touches the core of any scientific enterprise. It needs an interactive revolving approach.

In a broad historical comparative perspective we can characterize the European tradition of a doctorate as an autonomous expression of the academic clan or scientific community. Judgment of quality is based on some consensus within the guild of scholars which has been given autonomy by the souvereign. Since its origin in the thirteenth century there have been many periods of fragmentation and renewal of the scientific community, such as reformation and counterreformation, the French revolution and the German contrarevolution by von Humboldt. The roaring sixties seem to me a particular example of a breakdown in the scientific community along political lines and consequently the senate as the expression of the scientific community was abolished, suspended or lost its power. The failure of the scientific community as the major mechanism for coordination has led to the present dominance of bureaucracy. One cannot but observe a benign neglect of the academic community in managing doctoral dissertations in any systematic way. Completion rates were held secret and one seemed hardly interested in providing guidance to dissertation writers or offering facilities. It was frequently a purely individual matter. A very loosely coupled system indeed where even insiders did not know the regulations outside their own domain. Moreover, many faculty members were hardly interested in stimulating or supervising candidates. In that sense it is a surprise that the doctorate has continued to be a major yardstick in many higher education systems, but the present concern for completion rates and frequencies in reform proposals through new regulations seems a normal reaction. There are few organizations which could survive with such enormous differences in production costs for a similar product as universities did (see Mertens, 1979). The few empirical studies on the doctoral dissertation did not originate in the university, and their publication did not attract any serious attention. After publication they were discontinued. The European doctorate is characterized by a lack of a clear structure and depends on the various implicit codes of practice in disciplines and institutions.

The American tradition of a doctorate can be characterized as a market-oriented approach. Judgment of quality was based on comparison and competition between different institutions and departments to extend the frontiers of learning. As a European invention it was carefully tested. Before the first doctorate was awarded in Yale in 1861, there was a long tradition of following European patterns. The first bachelor's at Harvard in 1642, followed by master's degrees in 1644 and as an exceptional case in 1696 a doctorate in theology. Ten of thousands Americans were sent mainly to German universities in the last century. One cannot but admire the slow haste of a Gilman to establish the first graduate school in Johns Hopkins. The Americans had a healthy scepticism against diploma's as William James testified: 'a Mandarin disease, a sham, displeasing to American eyes: degrees are secondary incidents in a country of which the recognition of individuality and bare manhood have so long been supposed the very soul' (p. 4). Graduate instruction was at first rather informal. In the beginning of this century there were only a few hundred Ph.D's and before the second world war a few thousand. The sixties showed the most dramatic growth in graduate education with large Ph.D's mills, increasingly impersonal without central purpose or vision: grant-swinging became the name of the game (p. 35).

Especially social science and education became mass producers. Harold Orlans, formerly of the Brookings Institution (1960-1973) observed intellectual crises: 'the simpler certitudes of social scientism, of obligatory relationships that bind ideas to social groups, actions to interests, words to convictions, respondents to words, complex facts to simple theories, and fullible observations to eternal laws like fitted carpets to the floor' (in Crawford, 1976, p. 40). 'Hypotheses pop out every paper, each drawn between two points and confirmed by two others, somewhat off the line. A behaviourist is like a blind man at the corner, cane in hand; he cannot cross the street without an hypothesis, and, for journal publication (and I would like to add for dissertation writers), almost any hypothesis will do'. Pragmatism, empiricism and opportunism became key concepts and these led to coercion and deception e.g. a review of 1,000 studies in psychology found that 17 percent of investigators had given subjects inaccurate or misleading information; 80 percent had given incomplete or no information; and only 3 percent gave enough information for the subjects to know or infer the purpose and main variables of the study (Menges, ibidem, p. 49). Knowledge that is gained by deception is a kind of theft that demeans the taker; knowledge that is used to exploit is a kind of betrayal that invites reprisal. Knowledge, it is said, is power; it is only right, then, for those who seek knowledge to share that power with those from whom it was obtained (Ibidem, pp.55-56). The American market-oriented Ph.D is indeed a remarkable phenomenon with clear structures of competition, comparison and voluntary inspection without central authority. I assume with Kerr that the dramatic expansion of the sixties has been less healthy than the turn-of-the-century reforms, but luckily the American situation allows also internal disagreement with Ph.D mills. Quantity cannot substitute for quality.

The Chinese tradition of a doctorate is not only the oldest, but also a continuity of more than a millenium as a state-oriented selection device. According to Ho (1962) the point of departure in the Confucian social ideology is that all things, including human beings, are by nature inequal. It took a long maturation period, after China reunified under the House of Sui in 589, succeeded by the T'ang dynasty (618-907), to establish certain objective standards by which officials should be selected by competitive civil-service examinations. Through trial and error the chin-shih examination (regarded as doctor of letters) perpetuated itself from the seventh century right down to 1904. The chin-shih curriculum emphasized creative writing rather than mechanical memorization. Since the rise of the chin-shih examination as a major channel of official recruitment, there had been a long series of debates on the relative merits of examinations and other methods of selection, but within China's cultural tradition the chin-shih curriculum remained the best that could be designed: the range of knowledge required for passing was not actually narrow, it was liberal and proved to select candidates with common sense and sound judgment. Accepting hierarchy between the ruling and ruled as a prerequisite, the competitive examination offered the opportunity for all. Of course, in no period of Chinese history the Confucian ideal fully materialized, but the institutionalization of a competitive examination system as the main avenue of socio-bureaucratic mobility and the existence of a large number of state and private schools are probably without parallel in major societies prior to national compulsory education (Ho p. 256). There were no effective legal and social barriers which prevented the movement of individuals from one status to another. Social success depended more on individual merit than on family status and high-status families had little means for perpetuating their success if their descendants were inept. In fact, the examination system's long history of thirteen centuries is a most eloquent testimonial to its usefulness as a main channel of mobility and as a politically and socially stabilizing factor. It is inconceivable for a nation as large and pragmatic as China to have perpetuated an institution if it were truly a sham as some modern scholars, to whom statistical data and complex institutionalized and noninstitutional factors relevant to social mobility are little or unknown, would have us believe (Ho, p. 258). Of course, there were harmful effects, but it is strange that reformers of final degrees of higher education don't seem to need empirical evidence of the past.

Teng (1942) provided impressive evidence that this open competitive examination system in three layers –hsiu-ts'ai at the district level corresponding to BA, chü-jen at the provincial capital corresponding to M.A., and chin-shih at the national capital corresponding to Ph.D– was responsible for the introduction of similar systems into Western Europe, particularly in France and England. However, his description of the European university system seems inadequate.

This broad historical comparative analysis of the clan-oriented European concept of final degrees, the market-oriented American approach, and the hierarchy- or state-oriented Chinese concept of final degrees shows that each of the mechanism has the potential of establishing final terms for selection of the best but it needs to fit national characteristics. The clan or academic oligarchy is a strong mechanism as long as it remains open for deviant opinions and responds to societal and market forces. The market is a vital mechanism but is prone to opportunism and pragmatism. The hierarchy, state or bureaucracy is a stabilizing force as long as one allows the academic community to take its own responsibility and keeps a competitive advantage.

Clark (1983) made a similar analysis of national higher education system, as exemplified in fig. V.1. However, he rightly observes that the higher education system has difficulties in pulling itself together that belie simple descriptions ans answers. 'Tasks proliferate, beliefs multiply, and the many forms of authority pull in different directions.....Even when grouped in national patterns, the many modes of authority leave out much of the story' (p. 136). In any case the explosive growth of higher education in the 1960s and 1970s have seen a general shift from loose arrangements to tighter and more inclusive formal systems, first in the first cycle and in the 1980s in the post-graduate cycles (OECD, 1986).

Disciplines

Most participants in post-graduate higher education are hardly interested in comparative history, evaluation, educational research or management, but look for new structures which can help them in expanding their field of knowledge. Discipline is the dominant mode of organization and determines their view on the higher education system. Psychologists may see it as a place where people undergo personality development; sociologists as an institution for status attainment or mobility; political scientists as a locus of political recruitment; economists as a developer of human capital; medical doctors as the centre for health care and protection and so on. From each disciplinary point of view there are specific frontiers of learning. Attention is the most scarce human resource. The highly skilled and knowledgeable professionals who are attracted by a university career need all their attention for discovering, conserving, refining and applying their own field of knowledge. Interdisciplinary efforts are marginal and so are management and organization in a broader perspective. It is therefore no surprise that there is no natural inclination for institutional management or detailed accounting of costs and benefits. Specialities throughout the academic world multiply with increasing rapidity. They become more internally sequential and require specific and longer tracks of training. In times of retrenchment the disciplinary core becomes sacred.

Whitley (1984) has made an interesting analysis of the intellectual and social organization of disciplines based on degree of dependence (functional or strategic) and task uncertainty. His classification leads to seven types of organization from fragmented adhocracy towards conceptually integrated bureaucracy. I do not expect that one can discover one over-arching typology of scientific fields which is acceptable to all participants. My reading of history of science and some comparative institutional analysis has learnt me that knowledge is fluid and can be divided in various ways. There is always a dual order: one from the inside of the academic community with its own hierarchy and one from the outside by a particular mixture of market and state. In the traditional university the academic community was represented by the senate and at the national level by the Academy, whereas the outside was represented by the board of governors, in the Dutch situation called curators. This dual order is essential and makes universities loosely coupled systems or a garbage can as March called it: an organized anarchy characterized by severe ambiguity, problematic preferences, unclear technologies of teaching and research, and fluid participation. In that sense universities have been always problematic.

Organizational structures cannot compensate for a lack of vision, in this case on the importance of frontiers of learning in a society. Democracy can be applied to institutional management, where all stake holders select regularly their own representatives in decision making councils. In formal organizations this leads to the segmentation of parties and trade unions which try to attract voters with similar interests. In universities with the major part of their activities in the first cycle of four years this leads to a political bureaucracy, where the number of students represent legitimate power along disciplinary lines. One needs fixed ratio's of student-staff-facilities and formal task descriptions for decision making or approval of proposals by governing boards. Democracy, however, cannot be applied to the scientific community in a similar way. Final terms or the frontiers of learning in post-graduate education as exemplified in Ph.D's can only be established by the academic forum and their invisible colleges of references. These terms are based on qualitative arguments, not on numbers or completion rates. In some countries there are trade unions for professors, such as in Sweden, and I wonder whether future developments would not require a new organization of the traditional senate. Of course, the senate has never been an effective decision making body, but the few empirical studies (Lammers, 1974) show at least an important contribution with fluctuating participation.

The tendency today is towards an increasingly professionalized system of doctoral training and research, based more or less on the system obtaining in the USA (OECD, 1986). This might lead to separate graduate schools. There are many advantages, in terms of adequate preparation of the student through training in research methods and such a graduate school creates supportive environments in which collective intellectual activities are possible. An efficient and relevant graduate school tends to be modeled on the natural sciences where it is possible to prepare a doctoral dissertation in 3-4 years. However, in humanities and social sciences and when practical experience is an essential element of research as in management sciences one cannot apply similar standards without relaxing them to a degree which could not but ultimately undermine the value of the qualification. Variety and selectivity are key terms of reference for the Ph.D phenomenon.

How much differentiation in higher education systems is possible without breaking the universitas as a body of scholars and the unity of sciences? In the Dutch situation W.C.M. van Lieshout (1984) expects in the year 2000 a differentiation in four types of higher education institutions: 8 modern universities, 4 traditional universities, 20 'high schools', and 30 specific institutions. He does not specify this development neither its dynamics, but it is a bold effort to extrapolate variation in the Dutch higher education system in institutional terms. The appropriate locus for Ph.D's seems to be the traditional or classical university, even if it is spread over different locations and open for candidates from all higher educational institutions. Present information technology and the seminal idea of an Open University allow the organization of knowledge within a broad range of disciplines. The European doctorate, which has already been proposed by the French former director of education I. Capelle in 1967, might offer a challenging opportunity for revitalizing the old ideals of our university. Of course, this is only a long term solution, but there are sufficient candidates who actually participate in networks between two or more European universities.

The present situation of doctoral research and training is a confused one (OECD, 1986). There is no sound empirical basis due to the benign neglect of the past. Final terms have been rarely specified and available statistics don't give indications of quality. It is the classical dilemma of strategy and structure (Chandler, 1962). One needs first a clarification of strategy, a sense of direction for the whole higher education system. Participation rates might range from the 50% or 40% as in the USA and Japan towards the 25% in Germany or 15% in the Netherlands, but final degrees must be based on quality standards, even if it would mean low completion rates or longer preparation. Of course, there is no point of Archimedes where one can fix the standards of independent and original contributions to knowledge. It is a revolving, interactive process where members of the academic community regularly test the outcomes. There are market forces for hot subjects, such as information technology and biochemical research, but there are many fundamental and esoteric fields of study which need to be protected for the integration of knowledge. There are no perfect solutions for preventing waste and one cannot change too drastically or quickly, but the worst solution seems to lower the standards of final degrees.

New structures

The turbulent environment, massification of higher education, demographic trends and budget constraints have forced modern states to reform universities and recently to design new structures for stimulating and supporting post-graduate research. I do not try to make a comprehensive list of all new structures, but at the generic level I assume that they are all expressions or combinations of national preferences, market forces and scientific priorities. Strategy and structure are two sides of the same coin. If there is a clear overall strategy, structures follow strategy. But if there is no clear strategy, each new structure elicits its own tactics in order to utilize available structures for its own advantage. In the Dutch practice of industrial policy one has even invented a new specialism 'subsidiology' i.e. the knowledge of government subsidies or fiscal facilities which might be attractive for companies. One can also make a living of collecting information about research support schemes for dissertation writers and helping candidates to formulate proposals that fit the regulations. I don't think it a healthy development but it is the other side of the coin.

Presently each modern state seems to be engaged in major reforms of post-graduate higher education. The OECD report (1986) and Altbach's bibliography of higher education in international perspective (1985) provide an impressive amount of background information about new instruments and structures. The rapid succession of partial reforms has made many faculty members embarrassed. At the Ph.D production level the primary teaching-supervising-learning activity by the key actors in the European situation has been until recently very loosely coupled to the administrative-governance structure of universities. This system can suffer through multiple, administrative reorganizations without disturbing the every-day understandings and practices of participants. Even the roaring sixties did not make any impact on the traditional system of doctorates. There were some marginal changes, such as new regulations, suggestions for cheaper publication on recycled paper or for less rituals and the abolishment of distinctions as 'cum laude', but the core remained intact.

However, new structures seem to change the doctoral study in a radical way. It has not so much sense to complain about new structures or to regret certain developments, such as the abolishment or suspense of the traditional senate. There is consensus that quality judgments are to be made by members of the academic community in the most responsible way. It seems much more fruitful to discover strategic good practices in major European universities and develop supportive structures for keeping standards of excellence. There is presently a strong emphasis on normative, instrumental and analytical models which all push the doctorate process in a more programmed direction, such as 'conditional financing' (guaranteeing continuity of finance for approved projects for some five years) and the appointment of temporary research assistants who are expected to complete their doctoral dissertation within some four years and for approved research themes. Each of the new instruments has specific advantages for certain disciplines, departments and institutions. It is expected that the stronger emphasis on concentration of research projects in centres of excellence by hierarchy, on market forces by specifying relevant fields of study and on recruitment of special research assistants will increase the output of doctorates. What is the other side of the coin i.e. the meaning of doctoral dissertations as an independent and original contribution to knowledge?

Within the academic community there is considerable concern that the many new structures of programming doctoral research within specified periods and approved projects might devaluate the traditional doctorate. I see two complementary strategies which might keep standards of quality:

1. The first strategy differentiates the post-graduate degree system. There are various options which have proven to be viable. In the German system of a regular production of doctorates one has added a 'Habilitationsschrift' as a high quality degree after the normal doctordegree. It is mainly used for academic careers. The English practice prefers the presentation of a thesis for a higher degree and after the actual comprehensive examination the thesis can be approved as a M.Phil thesis or a Ph.D thesis, if necessary with modifications. Moreover, there is here an important role for an external examiner. This practice allows completion of research projects while keeping the standards. Also in the American system one needs a special comprehensive examination before one is allowed to start one's Ph.D project. A Belgian practice is to reserve the title of drs. for those graduates (licentiate) who have proven to present a feasible dissertation topic and design for some four years. In all these situations one has actually added intermediate stages. The Dutch system seems too narrowly restricted to the doctoral dissertation as the only option. Moreover, in the new structures the promotor role tends to coincide with the project leader of an approved programme. Given the pressure on completion rates and the difficulty of switching from promotor or university (van Hout, 1986), this system might lead to a second-class doctorate. A European doctorate where one could combine good practices in various national systems seems particularly timely to guarantee quality standards.

    Differentiation does not imply proliferation of degrees. The three cycles in fig. IV-1 seem to provide sufficient scope for variety and selectivity in fields of study and are based on a historical continuity. The higher education system has dramatically expanded but I would strongly plead for the principle of frugality. The bachelor degree can be used for graduates of higher vocational education as has been recently introduced in the Dutch system. The master degree can be used for graduates of four years universities and are either an 'en passant' for the doctorate as in the traditional practice or might be completed for specialist and professional practice. The doctorate can then be reserved for those who are actually entering the scientific community with a concerted effort to contribute an independent and original contribution to knowledge. It needs to be an international passport to scholarship at the level of a 'Habilitationsschrift', but also for general and professional careers.

2. The second strategy aims at improving the structure of doctoral research in a more collective direction. We do not need many more new segmental approaches but linkages and networks between available structures. The major challenge is striking a balance between market forces with the danger of pragmatism and opportunism, the academic oligarchy with the danger of fragmentation and specialization, and the national bureaucracy with the danger of overregulation and fixed targets. In a turbulent environment there is a need for strategical reflection of one's priorities. What unit of analysis is appropriate for such a strategical reflection? For doctoral research the traditional department or chair seems too small. The Dutch reform measures stimulated national disciplinary clusters to design research programmes within work communities and this has led to clarity and cohesion within fields of study. In my own stituation the four core departments of business economics established a strategic unit for selecting priorities and standards of selectivity. There is no uniform solution but one has to look for a critical mass which offers a sound basis for strategic responses. Each new structure and proposal tends to trigger off tactical answers of individual departments for utilizing potential support and this leads to fragmentation and scattered efforts. In the long run only quality survives and this requires a long term strategy where one has the courage to forsake attractive propositions which do not fit the particular nature of one's field of study. A collection of tactical responses does not lead to a clear strategy. The scientific community needs a long time horizon.

Market forces can be made operational by joint research programs with industry and government and by postgraduate courses. It is not difficult to invent a whole range of research activities which start from clients needs. Presently many universities are engaged in market research to assess their image, to evaluate the performance of their graduates and to attract new students. In itself it seems a healthy development, if one has specified one's own strategy. Without a clear sense of mission it seems a dangerous exercise. Academic forces can be made operational by national associations of universities, university presidents, national academies and research organizations. This is not a new phenomenon but the present need for accountability makes it necessary to specify the norms of the scientific community. One would long for a national academy with an over-arching view on the frontiers of learning as in the past, but the world of knowledge has already surpassed national boundaries. National science and unversity policy can be made operational by an increasing number of councils, such as in the Dutch situation the WRR (Scientific Council for Governmental Policy) and RAWB (Advisory Council for Science Policy), but here again one needs to reflect on the critical mission of universities.

Management of frontiers of learning and interdependency

It must be recognized, however, that neither improved procedures and structures nor intermediate degrees nor broadening of the forum alone will be sufficient to solve the problems that beset the credibility of Ph.D degrees, as Soedjatmoko, the rector of the United nations University, wrote me. Rather than worrying about completion rates or the survival of doctoral programmes or the expansion of higher education we need to deepen and intensify the research function of universities. There has been never a time when the research imperative of von Humboldt is more appropriate than today. He proposed that the university should serve not only as a conduit for orthodox knowledge, but also as the crucible for new knowledge (Soedjatmoko, 1985). Of course, in each national system universities must strike a balance between the mass educational needs of society and the highly specialized advanced studies that keep scholars at the cutting edge of new knowledge. My main concern is how to stimulate academic products which are really vehicles of new knowledge based on the whole range of knowledge and offering relevant and original contributions to knowledge. In a certain sense none of the models of the past is really adequate for solving the problems of the present world. Procedures, structures, degrees and academic institutions with all their variation are only means to strengthen and stimulate the learning function. I distinguished three major academic traditions, but of course we have to accept a much more pluralistic system of higher education. No national system of higher education can any longer hope to overcome the real problems of the present world in isolation simply on the basis of national solutions. The role of universities is to build critical capacities to evaluate creatively the various formerly dominant streams of intellectual thought, science and technology for a new international order. A revival of a European doctorate does not imply an increase of Eurocentrism.

One-dimensional analyses, however intellectually elegant, fail to embrace the complex interlinkages of problems as they exist today. We need a more integrative approach. In the past, traditional disciplines have served as the means for organizing knowledge in an orderly fashion. But those same academic pigeon-holes have fragmented perceptions of the larger issues that refuse to conform to limited dimensions. I assume that for undergraduate education these academic departments still offer a solid basis for organizing knowledge but for post-graduate and post-doctoral research we need to develop a more flexible and horizontal approach. Unfortunately, present budgetary concerns have made universities reluctant to continue or start new interdisciplinary centres. They fall back on traditional disciplines and core departments, which have the strongest constituencies. Doctoral dissertations which are restricted to disciplinary centers and are programmed in a way to satisfy completion rates might be counterproductive in fostering integrative thinking and learning.

The most dynamic answer for the creation of new knowledge comes from corporations and other non-chartered institutions. The corporate class as it is called challenges the collegiate class and this seems a healthy challenge. In the United States alone the cost of such corporate programmes has been estimated at more than $40 billion annually – approaching the combined yearly budgets of all American four-year and graduate colleges and universities. Also in Japan there is a huge corporate investment in non-chartered higher education and research. However, there is a big difference in philosophy and purpose. Corporate education aims at the formation of employed human capital and there is a danger of commercialization and secrecy. Soedjatmoko (1985) mentions the example of the Green Revolution which resulted from scientific information developed by a number of international research institutions, primarily founded by philantropic foundations. That information was free and had an enormous impact e.g. on the largest rice importer, Indonesia, which is now facing overproduction, but until recently never expected self-sufficiency, given demographic growth. We are now on the threshhold of a second Green Revolution, a 'Gene Revolution' based on microbiology. But here the decision of the Supreme Court of the United States has allowed the most advanced techniques in biotechnology to be patented. This means that only those who can afford to pay for it will profit from this new revolution. The same applies to information technology and the expensive military research. Freedom of information and new knowledge is indispensable for the university and her products at the frontiers of learning. Corporate research can never substitute for universities and university networks.

I accept the present emphasis on structures, accountability and tight budgets only as a long-overdue reaction on the failure of the academic oligarchy to organize advanced knowledge in an orderly way. Present accounts of universities how they spent public money in handling knowledge show a great improvement with even ten years ago and of course we had to pay for an increase of administration and bureaucracy. However, history teaches me some kind of consolation. It is only a temporal overreaction. I have sufficient confidence in the vitality of academic culture to expect a revitilization of the academic spirit and sense of mission for the tasks ahead. I agree with Soedjatmoko and many other colleagues whom I have consulted during this study that we have been much too timid up to now in dealing with university reforms. The changes have been merely tinkering with marginal modifications of the traditional system. Also the impressive amount of studies on higher education do not touch the strategic issues, but mainly the internal organization of curricula, departments, faculties, universities and ministries of education to cope more efficiently with budget restrictions or decline of enrollments. I am not so much inclined to agree with George Keller's verdict 'If the research in higher education ended, it would scarcely be missed': but I assume that many of us have been trapped in short-term problems of survival and tactical responses to new structures. I regret anyhow that I have accepted some suboptimal solutions or escaped responsibilities of increasing the quality and forsaking quantitative growth. There is no doubt that we need a much more radical self-examination, if universities are to fulfill their critical role of providing new knowledge. The academic nowhere man as described by Staal (1970) might be an ideal, but it is worthwhile to keep this ideal alive.

The critical gap in present universities is the management of frontiers of learning and interdependency. Let me qualify this statement. I don't mean by management a set of models, instruments and techniques which provide ready answers for reaching set objectives in a formal organization. There is no ready answer for stimulating, motivating and supporting graduates to start a long-distance journey for exploring new frontiers in their field of knowledge and experience. Of course, research candidates are confronted with a hierarchy of academic prestige, such as being published in leading journals or utilizing advanced equipment, facilities and models. But the basic motivation seems to me solving relevant problems for people by extending the frontiers of learning. One needs to be fascinated by a problem and possible solutions to start a doctoral research. The universities in the coming decades must confront some serious intellectual, pedagogical, and institutional questions. We need to search for new syntheses allowing to transform avalances of data into new knowledge – and to make that knowledge usable (Boulding). There is a great danger of accepting discipline-oriented, reductionist explanations in models, whose foundations in reality are so insecure that they have no capacity for tolerance of other approaches. This intellectual in tolerance is one of the greatest dangers of our time. It is a source of conflict in itself, between competing religions and ideologies, and it also leads to erosion of commitment to multilateral institutions and undertakings, for it makes collaboration with other parties impossible except on one's own terms (Soedjatmoko, 1985). It is indeed frustrating to observe such strong centripetal movements in universities where one reduces interdisciplinary research projects because they do not fit a particular department or institution. Padgett (1980) came to an interesting set of recommendations for managing university research:

1. Hire rigid analysts for old programmes, but hire uncertain and insecure analysts for new programmes.
2. To the extent possible, reorganize program assignments to divisions in order to segregate high-saliency programmes from low-saliency programmes.
3. Hire only secretaries even more liberal than yourself to run your high-saliency divisions, and only secretaries even more conservative than yourself to run your low-saliency divisions.

I think that the core concept in the management of university research is the gatekeepers function, where one scans new developments in the corporate world, in the many non-chartered institutions and centers of excellence to break through the compartmentalization of knowledge as in traditional universities. In the Dutch practice extra-ordinary part-time professors and external mid-career candidates for doctorates have always played a gatekeepers role. The balance has changed during the last decennia e.g. from 75% external doctorates after the war towards 25% and the present structures might decrease this percentage further. However, the swing of the pendulum has to be pushed again in the other direction, when joint university-industry programmes and new externally supported or part-time chairs are gradually introduced. The European doctorate and some high quality scholarships as e.g. awarded by national academies and international research associations might offer the necessary counterbalance against self-appraisal within narrow disciplinary boundaries. The oldest mechanism for breaking through academic isolation and self-appraisal has been the international exchange of scholars and graduate students. Itinerant students who criss-crossed Europe in search for new knowledge and mentors were rather common in medieval Europe. At the moment inter-European mobility for university students is at a low ebb and when one is asked as external examiner in other countries, one needs to invent other lecturing arrangements or pay for one's own expenses. Only Third World candidates make actually much more academic peregrinations than the members of well-established European universities.

Structures for learning strategies which lead to new independent and original knowledge are indeed a paradox. Graduate learning centers make even control of decisions only partially desirable and one needs periods of temporary relief from control, coordination and communication (March, 1979; Springer, 1985). If we look at the Ph.D as a social experiment in stimulating creativity, we do not need to evaluate this experiment in terms of the degree to which they have fulfilled our a priori expectations, but how they have changed our expectations. We need a matrix of transformations over time, disciplines and national systems. It is more interesting to see how a natural scientist becomes a humanist, an economist a historian, a biologist a political analyst or an engineer a philosopher than how each disciplinary adept tests his hypotheses. It seems a horrifying idea to establish Ph.D mills within disciplinary clusters, where people are trained to strengthen their preferred conception of the world and actually inhibit the serendipitous discovery of new insights and syntheses.

Let me reflect on the nature of evidence which I collected on the Ph.D phenomenon, not so much on the actual product, but on the ideas behind a final degree. The most interesting data on the Chinese experiment with the Chin-shih seem to me the distribution over periods, provinces and types of prominent scholars (classicists, historians, philosophers, men of letters and academics) as provided by Ho (1962). Unfortunately I am unable to read the original sources, but I came to the conclusion that the fluid network of severely tested scholarship open for all has held together this immense empire of the middle. Of course, it was a harsh and almost cruel test, where one was lucky to arrive at fifty year's age. Modern administrators would be horrified to accept the failure and completion rates, but I can't imagine a better mechanism of social mobility on the base of knowledge rather than power or social prestige. The creative period of Europe seems to me, when a network of European universities stimulated scholars and students to search for new knowledge. The degree system was rather unclear but the Doctor Philosophiae et Magister Artium Liberarium provided some core for international scholarship. The European expansion to Asia was not a one-sided experiment, but also challenged their image of the world. In his epilogue, Donald F. Lach (1965) observed, that European characterizations of the natural or regional qualities of various Asian people are a mixture of the factual and fanciful, and, not surprisingly, resemble many of the beliefs still popular in the West (p. 834) and this applies particularly to beliefs about knowledge and the world of learning. Europe had and still has much to learn. China was quickly recognized to be the possessor of unique and effective governmental and educational institutions: examination for public office; state-supported schools; social services; and courier systems; and the law of avoidance or the requirements that provincial governors should never be natives of their own jurisdictions. Japan was an example of physical and mental discipline. 'But perhaps what is most significant of all is the dawning realization in the West that not all truth and virtue were contained within its cultural and religious traditions' (p. 835). From a present-day perspective, this is still the main lesson how to question one's own cultural and disciplinary premises and to initiate fundamental revisions in our own views of the world, man and the future. Also the formative period of the American graduate school seems more instructive than the explosive growth of Ph.D's since the sixties. The first doctoral thesis in John Hopkins was on interdependence of knowledge and the warnings of William James and Gilman are even more appropriate today than at the time of writing.

The core of the problem seems to me that one has failed to accept disciplines and their dominant paradigms only as temporary structures. The traditional center-periphery flow of policy decisions on the direction of post-graduate research has blocked our capacity to learn from localized and fluid fields of knowledge. Disciplines with a strong constituency and a high degree of organization attract the largest number of new research assistants or approved research programmes and thus create an implosion. For power analysis indeed the center-periphery model is useful for understanding and explaining policies, but for knowledge analysis the center-periphery model is counterproductive. The new knowledge required for coping with ambiguity uncertainty, interdependence and field mobility in one's career flows from loosely structured, decentralized networks of problem solvers towards temporary structures of research projects and new paradigms. In that sense interdisciplinary regional centers of Japanese, Chinese or other non-disciplinary studies are seminal for academic development, not peripheral. The traditional structure of a Ph.D is based on an undivided access to the academic forum in its variety and open for resident doctors and there is less reason than ever to reduce this access to faculties or restrict admittance to graduates with particular disciplinary background. If we need to reorganize the university and I think we do, it seems much more healthy to appoint special deans for each cycle of higher education rather than appointing 'discipline bosses' as in the Open University in the UK. In Indonesian higher education e.g. one has appointed special post-graduate deans catering for all graduates from other faculties in some elite universities and, although there are practical obstacles in implementation, I enjoyed at least the discussion in the senate of the Airlangga University in Surabaya with deans of other faculties in awarding the first doctorate on an economic subject.

Chapter VI

Forum, Roles and Locum

In the first explorative chapter I selected three anchor concepts for classifying final products of higher education, such as the Ph.D: forum, role and locus. Historical, cultural and functional explorations of the Ph.D phenomenon and equivalents showed extreme variations from highly segmented or ritualized preparations for a career without any visible meaning for the advancement and utilization of knowledge towards highly individualized long-distance journeys to an unknown destination without guides and sometimes with considerable impact on science, rational thought and public policy. Also at the present moment one observes a broad range of perceptions on what a Ph.D needs to be. The OECD report on post-graduate education in the 1980's (1986) argumented strongly a case for a more differentiated set of qualifications at the doctoral level allowing for disciplinary variation.
Indeed at the pragmatic level I observe many proposals and experiments for increasing the number of doctoral dissertations in an orderly and efficient course-based way tailor made for the needs of waiting corporate professional or public employers and reducing the uncertainty of completion and direction. Public support at different levels seems sufficiently strong to forecast an increase in programmed Ph.D's. The Dutch minister of agriculture and fishery expressed his firm expectation that the recently obtained score of 1000 doctoral dissertations in 66 years would be doubled before the next century and promised a substantial number of 'assistants-in-training' (aio's) for reaching this goal (Braks, in Crombach, 1984). It is no surprise that one offers rewards for highly productive promotors (52 is the top score). Of course I do not imply any causality between the quality of this performance and the quantity. Such studies have not been made.

However, the ideas behind the Ph.D concept seem almost inversily related to this social planning approach. In a doctoral dissertation defended in 1885 at the university of Leyden by Carel van Lookeren Campagne on life insurance contracts one can find a 'thesis' (a customary complement of a docteral dissertation) that a decrease of universities in the Netherlands would improve the quality of higher education and this was before the expansion. Also in Stuijvenberg's history of the Netherlands School of Economics (1913-1963) I have read concerns in the senate about the decreasing quality but never on the small number. Ho (1962) selected twenty-seven case studies of the meaning of chin-shih for social mobility throughout Chinese history. They illustrate the zigzag patterns of social mobility on the basis of scholarship and the permeation of Confucian values also among the poor. 'Ploughing with the writing brush' was the familiar expression meaning living by teaching with meager pay. These case studies might be remote to present needs, but they once shaped the lives and destinies of men and provided a network of scholarship within a huge empire although the number of chin-shih degrees is small (in the Ming period a top of 428 per million for Fukien and in the Ch'ing period a top of 130 per million for Chekiang). If one expressed concerns, it was about possible fraud or quality, not quantity. Concerns about efficiency and production costs of final academic products are only expressed during periods of decline, when universities had lost their credibility in exploring frontiers of learning and became degree mills.

Of course, I accept the drastically changed function of higher education in preparing potential leadership in government, business, service, teaching and preaching for the many, may be for up to 50% of the 18-22 age groups if American and Japanese participation rates are taken as exemplar. This requires social planning, budgeting, new divisions of tasks, educational technology and a more extensive set of beneficary charges and vouchers for direct provision at zero or very low prices in the higher education system (Haveman, 1985). Higher education has become a major public merit good for citizens of the welfare state and the balance between market forces, state policy and academic oligarchy will increasingly move from the cosy shelter of academic clans towards a pluralistic and differentiated set of institutions and programmes in an Open University. There are no other prerogatives for higher education teachers than the attraction of transmitting our cultural heritage to the many than for the teachers of primary and secondary education. As in the health care sector there will be always, I assume, private high-cost higher education institutions for those who can afford to pay for special provisions of close supervision, small groups and excellent scholarship. I don't think there is an optimal balance. Each state has its own history and culture for approximating an appropriate higher education system within economic constraints and political priorities. In the Dutch system one seems to agree presently at some 1.9% of GNP for public higher education, special autonomy for confessional higher education and a rather extensive set of grants or loans for lower-income groups or less-privileged. But 1.9% is not a sacred figure and the participation rate is still rather low and skewed.

However, I don't accept that the ideas behind final degrees as a concerted effort to extend frontiers of learning within the whole range of knowledge for utility, virtue and for its own sake can be reduced to a social planning exercise. Degrees are secondary indeed but the fundamental question is what other mechanism do we need to elicit independent and original contributions to knowledge at the outflow of higher education systems. Or more radically, if universities do not fullfil anymore this critical role, how do we generate freefloating new knowledge at the cutting edge of science by corporate class with its closed shop, internal markets and profit orientation? I felt frequently as a blind man at the cross road, cane in hand, where he tries to sense the direction and intensity of the continuous traffic and the overload of decibels hinders any orientation (to borrow again freely from Harold Orleans' expression). In plain language, I came to the conclusion that the present models for policy making in post-graduate education have created too much noise preventing a clear sense of direction.

Forum

Let me take a second look at the three key concepts. Forum refers to a public place in Rome where causes were judicially tried and orations delivered to the people. It was also a market place. In the 'Mightie Kingdome' of China justice was executed also in public, where judges in all matters of law do nothing but by writing. Every witness is examined before all the concerned parties. In matters of great importance the judges will write with their own hands the declaration of any witness. Public confrontation and cross-examining were continued until the truth is brought to light (and indeed complemented by tormentation, if these examinations fail, no system is perfect). Under no circumstances may a viceroy, governor or councillor be 'a naturall of the country that he is provided for'. This 'law of avoidance' was highly admired by European travellers. In comparison to the prevailing practice in Europe this law facilitated the execution of good justice. The account was so unfavourable to Europe that the censor, or the publisher who brought out his account, excised sections before printing it. Moreover, the description of Chinese government as by Mendoza was too neat to be a faithful reflection of reality, like many constructions of the mind. In some cases the law of avoidance led to injustice. Another observer, Vieira, records, that justices are all from the literati and every member of the literati when he obtains a degree begins in petty posts and then goes on rising to higher ones. A justice born in Kwantung cannot hold an office of Justice in Cantao.....so that those of one province cannot govern another. But in his observation the magistrate of another province administers justice poorly, 'because he does not think of the good of the district, but only of stealing, because he is not a native of it'. According to Lach (1962, pp. 736-759 passim) Vieira, after three years of imprisonment has not inclined either to regard Chinese justice with equanimity or to approve of the law of avoidance which ordained that an official might never serve in his own province.

The special case of the academic forum where causes of what constitutes a relevant, original and independent contribution to knowledge are judicially tried, offers more difficulties in evaluating its performance. The scientific community is too much of an ideal type to be applicable to the grassroot dynamics of science policy and university administration. Let me start with a newspaper item:

'Government decisions about the support of scientific research are supposed to be above politics. Fat chance. In America more and more universities are by-passing the traditional 'peer review' system and relying on political muscle to gain financial support for their pet ideas.....universities with bright research ideas send them to the relevant government department, where they are assessed by impartial experts. The best ones are included in the department's research budget and submitted to congress. Congress sets global spending levels and can influence departments' overall research strategies. But it tries to steer clear of scientific decisions about individual projects. So much for the theory. This year an undignified squabble has broken out between the Association of American Universities, the exclusive club that represents the 50 most prominent research universities in the United States, and Georgetown University, a private Catholic college perched in one of Washington's most fashionable residential areas. The association is furious about a request Georgetown made last month for a whopping $160m. government grant to demonstrate how electricity and heat can be generated by a combination of fuel cells and coal gasifiers. The money is to come out of Pentagon research funds, but the project was not peer-reviewed nor included in the army's own budget request.....For the past two years, universities willing to dip into the congressional pork barrel have done alarmingly well. The National Academy of Sciences is afraid that, if the trend continues, government decisions about financing science could degenerate into the kind of spoils system that already pervades America's public work programmes. But science's high command shows little sign of being able to keep its own troops in line.....the most notorious recent offenders are elite universities which belong to the association: Columbia University in New York and Catholic University in Washington.....for the second year they are to receive millions of dollars from the department of energy to pay for research facilities which the department's internal reviewers had decided not to support. Advised by a lobbying firm the universities got round the department's objections by mounting brilliant campaigns on Capital Hill-.....Thanks to the personal intervention of Mr. 'Tip' O'Neill, the Speaker of the house of representatives, both universities got what they wanted. Inevitably, some of the money was taken away from other universities which had put their faith in the time-honoured peer review system..... According to the lobbying firm tbe number of universities retaining their services on Capitol Hill has climbed to about a dozen' (The Economist, June 30, 1984).

Is this a unique American practice of the scientific community today? It is not difficult to collect a black list of similar cases in each OECD country, I assume, where universities use public relations, lobbying and personal networks rather than the scientific ethos for convincing parliament or directly government officials that their own research projects are more likely to offer a relevant contribution to knowledge, innovation or welfare than those of the competitors. What is science's high command? I think it unfair to blame university presidents, vice-chancellors, deans or other institutional landlords to use various bargaining and marketing mechanisms for attracting support and defending their own domain, if we refuse to analyse the roots of the problem. The scientific community is an inverted hierarchy. The shopfloor decisions on selecting and appraising research projects are the core. I remember one case where as a chairman of a doctoral examination committee (first cycle) I came to the conclusion that the presented doctoral paper did not contain any critical yardstick of scholarship but only an exposition of one particular theory. I informed the examination board that I refused to sign the doctoral examination document, but the chairman of that board informed me that, because the supervisor had approved the paper and all other subjects were properly examined, he would sign the examination document himself without reading the paper. I answered that I would then recuse him for abusing authority but I asked him as a respected colleague and legal expert how and where to appeal. He did not know. Luckily, in this case I could convince the candidate after informing his supervisor to withdraw his request for the examination and rewrite the paper. However, in another situation I was informed the night before an examination that a candidate had hired a consultant for writing his doctoral paper but there was no evidence. The quality was satisfactory. In this case I informed the candidate after the successful defence of his paper (it was an older part-time student who owned a business firm) about the suspicion, but because I could not prove the suspicion or the particular cooperation between him and his consultant I had no other choice than to pass him. I regret this decision. It would have been better to suspend the examination and explore carefully this situation before allowing him to pass. Time constraints are no excuse.

The interests of doctors (scientists, scholars, academics) or doctors-in-the-making do not coincide with scientific interests. Interest is the third personal singular of 'interesse', to be between. The meaning ranges from profit, influence or money towards intentness, concern or curiosity (Webster). The interaction between established scholars, impartial experts, members of examination committees and graduate students, fellows or research assistants in deciding what relevant contribution to knowledge is expected to be made in research proposals and is judged to have been made in a doctoral dissertation, this interaction is very human indeed. Science is a social-psychological activity, even for science students (Zinsberg, 1974). In her observation of undergraduate chemistry students in an English university she concluded that the health of the scientific community depends upon the details of the social transaction of its members. Personal knowledge indeed as Polanyi observed (1958), but also public knowledge (Ziman, 1968). There is a rich literature on the social processes of scientific development in various disciplines, institutions and national systems (e.g. Whitley, 1974), but the question what exactly constitutes justice in the academic community in deciding relevance, originality and independence of academic products, this question is rarely asked.

The debate on the role of knowledge in society and on learning strategies tends in our present universities to be reduced to the question how we can translate the dominant paradigms in the minds of economists, biologists, engineers, physicists or other disciplinary departments in approved research projects which can be efficiently completed by doctoral candidates. My concern about this reduction and denaturalization of knowledge to academic disciplines and research programmes has motivated me to undertake this study. The particular operationalisation into the Ph.D phenomenon and its prototypes as it evolved over time in various cultures and for different purposes is of less importance. If we could abolish the traditional doctorate rooted in philosophy or the whole range of knowledge, we need to invent other means of stimulating and recognizing original and independent contributions to knowledge. There is, in my judgment, nothing wrong in the normative structures of the scientific community and Ph.D's but in the way we apply decision rules. My intention is not to support or propose particular solutions, although I have selected a few available options for recommendation, but to attempt bringing the debate on the role of new knowledge at a higher (or more fundamental) level than that of instrumentalisation of science policy and university administration. I have tried to find and classify the arguments for establishing such a forum. At the moment I do not know where one could debate this type of questions. Traditional senates don't function, academies are split in disciplinary clusters and corporate research centers are engaged in utilization rather than reflection on assumptions. Institutions, such as the Netherlands Institute for Advanced Studies and its exemplars in the USA, could fulfill such a role, if it would encompass the whole range of knowledge and would be equipped with the necessary facilities and guidance. To my regret, the NIAS where I enjoyed such excellent partnership in exploring the mission of higher education operates mainly at an ad-hoc basis of selected fellows who are busy with their own writing within broad programmes and is rather marginal in the world of learning. Even for my Ph.D platform normal universities offer more opportunities for networking than the NIAS can offer.

'A law of contamination' seems to apply in academic institutions rather than 'a law of avoidance'. The same professors who select research projects as potentially relevant and viable contributions to knowledge and reject others as less relevant or viable, become than the projects leaders and supervisors of doctoral candidates. G. Nooteboom, a radiochemist and member of parliament, observed that the same experts who advise the parliament in science policy are actually employed in the particular sector for which their judgment is asked. Because of the highly complex nature of information laymen including members of parliament are not able to judge the quality of information. He suggests an 'advocatus diaboli' as in the Roman Catholic Church where an expert is asked to select all information against approval, in this case of somebody in the past to be recognized as holy (in TNO Magazine, February, 1986, p. 57). The external examiner as is particularly stressed in the anglosaxon system can equally well fullfil this role of countervailing expertise and also the English good practice to suggest another university for postgraduate research than for undergraduate studie is helpful.

In the new Dutch system of a priori clustered research programmes and the appointment of temporal research assistants (aio) the law of contamination might be applicable. It is likely that departmental chairmen will select research assistants from their own own first cycle graduates who have been prepared in the appropriate disciplinary framework and dominant paradigms. Low-risks projects with a high likelihood of completion within the approved period will be preferred above high-risk and salient projects which might not be completed within the approved period. Such a structure facilitates a highly programmed research process but hinders cross-fertilization between disciplines and other competing paradigms. The present emphasis on 'integration' within alpha, beta, gamma and life sciences with their own allotment of research grants will aggravate the 'two-cultures' debate of C.P. Snow. Van Strien has called this preference for integration in specific clusters a bureaucratic idol and he pleads for a more fundamental reflection on the assumptions of research rather than accepting the present external pressure towards 'integration' (TNO Magazine, 1986).

Accepting independent judgment as a conditio-sine-qua-non of the academic community, I cannot but observe an increasing gap between traditional external doctoral candidates with their own definition of a dissertation topic and internal doctoral candidates with special prerogatives in terms of planned supervision for successful completion within departmental research programmes. External candidates become even more peripheral and loosely-coupled than before and they have to compete for attention in a tight time budget of supervisors, who might even refuse external candidates unless they fit into their own programme. It would be a major loss for the academic community.

A second gap will be increased between the so called corporate class stressing problem orientation, field mobility and cross-fertilization and the collegiate class, if it becomes dominated by disciplinary clusters and captive research assitants. Corporate and non-chartered research centers have already occupied much more fertile grounds for advanced learning than the traditional universities which struggle with defense of their image and attraction for their stake holders. This gap can be a healthy challenge if universities keep and deepen their sense of mission that has been always at bay.

Do we need to invent new regulations and new structures for deciding what constitutes an original and independent contribution to knowledge and which selection mechanisms and course programmes reduce the failure risks to such a degree that it can be planned as any other educational credential? The doctorate process is a continual transcending of old and presently existing modes of knowledge production and modes of thinking. We do not have to invent new knowledge 'ex novo', but we stand on the shoulders of giants. I have serious doubts. There is an enormous variety of good practices in many centers of excellence from which we can learn if we are ready to reflect on the assumptions. There is also an enormous variety of new regulations and proposals which have failed to produce quality. It seems the tragic of evaluation officers that one is only allowed to prove what the prince likes.

The external examiner arrangement seems to me a particularly good practice. One has to be pushed outside one's own cosy academic, disciplinary or national organizational climate in order to be considered providing an original and independent contribution to knowledge. There are various ways to guarantee this externality of judgment or the old Chinese principle of avoidance. Let me give examples. In chapter III (p. 45) I mentioned a thesis submitted for the degree of Doctor of philosophy at the university of Oxford by Tasman A. Smith on cross-cultural factors of expatriate managers in Thailand. As external examiner I was rather surprised that the supervisor Desmond Graves was not allowed to participate in the viva. I think that too rigorous but I agree with the assumptions. I had some personal objections against the statistical exercises and I had informed briefly the candidate whom I did not know and who arrived the day before the viva from Bangkok as I did from Rotterdam in an icy Oxford that I might attack the representative quality of the teams in a decision making simulation. I think that is fair warning, although some colleagues are more rigorous. Moreover, I appreciated the Oxford practice where examiners and candidate wear a gown symbolizing the ritual nature of entering a scientific community. There are national and institutional variations but I don't like to see the Ph.D defense reduced to a streetcorner transaction. The forum is a respectable court. The Oxford practice where every fellow with a gown can enter the viva and participate seems to me touching the right ethos of the universitas, but it seems a forgotten practice. In traditional Dutch universities every professor is still allowed to participate in the public defense, but practical problems of space, time and interest restrict the participation to the examination committee. Nevertheless I think it a good practice and I appreciated the full participation of the academic senate in the public defense of Teddy Pawitra's dissertation in Airlangga University Surabaya. Finally, I think it a good practice that the examiners have to write with their own hands why they think the particular thesis to be an original, relevant and independent contribution to knowledge and under what conditions it can be published. Unfortunately, these reports have never been used as far as I know.

A second example is the doctoral dissertation by Ron Naaborg at the Erasmus University Rotterdam on decision making in establishing by-pass surgery in Dutch hospitals. In this case the committee of deans had agreed that the candidate, a doctorandus in economics, defended his thesis in the medical faculty and was to obtain a doctorate in medical sciences because of the nature of the field of study. I think it a good practice that Dutch law is based on the assumption of an undivided doctorate and allows a candidate from a different discipline and faculty to strive for the highest honours in another field of study after approval of the committee of deans. In that case there were two promotors, Dick de Haan, an extraordinary professor and director of the academic hospital, and myself. The co-referent as was regulated at that time as an external examiner on behalf of the committee of deans was a professor in cardiology, P.G. Hugenholtz, with whom we had intensive discussions on the nature of knowledge concerning decision making in distinction to the nature of knowledge in biology and physics. It was not a question of hard and soft but how hard one could make data on human fragility in decision making. I still have a vivid memory of this highly stimulating debate. Cross-disciplinary confrontation is a good practice for the appraisal of research.

> I would commend that research project or programme appraisals would be done in the way that the Marshall Plan started to be implented in post-war Europe. Each participating country's proposals had to be judged by a panel of other countries competing for the fixed overall budget. It would be highly effective if each discipline or disciplinary cluster would be judged by a panel of other disciplines competing for the fixed overall research budget, even if the judges have not read the last paper. Self-appraisal is a rather dubious argument for fair judgment and academics are no exception on the principle of avoidance of interest.

The former minister of public health care had been accepted as member of the examination committee after approval of the committee of deans. I think it a good practice that outsiders with particular experience in a field of study, such as business leaders, members of parliament or government officials are included in academic promotion committees, given proper qualifications. In Dutch practice it is possible, but frequently practical obstacles in getting approval prevent such participation. In one case the former minister, den

Uyl, has been refused as member of a promotion committee for a doctoral dissertation on the closure of the coalmines under his responsibility because he did not possess a doctor's degree. However, there are many members of promotion committees without a doctor's degree in that discipline.

I am tempted to give more examples. Since five years I have held monthly feedback meetings with Ph.D candidates and new doctors. Each situation requires its own definition of the terms of reference and criteria of judgment. Variety and selectivity are the key terms. The increasing collection of egodocuments where new doctors reflect on what they have learned from the Ph.D project leads to an amazing range of learning strategies how individuals cope with the search for originality. Also the recently finished manuscript of Geert Rooijakkers (1986) on the comparative quality of 26 Dutch and 64 matched American and Anglosaxon doctoral dissertations impresses me by the highly personal nature of each Ph.D process and its appraisal by supervisor, referees and candidate. A recent collection of Ph.D reflections in a journal for law students, Ars Aequi (December 1985), where some 25 professors of law were invited to comment on the meaning of their own Ph.D, offers another rich source of autobiographical material. I am mainly amazed to read so many reform proposals on postgraduate education and training without any attempt to establish empirical evidence on history and culture of disciplines, institutions or fields of study in Ph.D production. One seems to assume a common understanding what a Ph.D is supposed to be and freely extrapolates this understanding to one's own preferred graduate school. I don't expect that every reader will share my appraisal of good and bad practices in the Ph.D process, but I hope to convince him that we need to observe, analyze and reflect in much more detail how the academic forum operates in its variations over time, disciplines and national systems.

To prevent misunderstanding, I have no objections against clustering of research proposals in disciplinary and national systems neither against the special allocation of temporary research assistants for elaborating individual post-graduate projects under close and planned supervision. My objection is against standardizing models from natural sciences towards other fields of study and against neglecting interdisciplinary fields of study. My objection is also against piecemeal treatment of stages in postgraduate learning and substituting the product of a second stage for a traditional doctoral dissertation rather than appraising it as a research mastership. My objection is also against the dominance of pre-career Ph.D's without complementary attention to the specific nature of mid-career doctoral dissertations.

I accept the differentiation of the academic forum in special disciplines, fields of study, national systems and their hierarchy of institutions. In the Japanese academic system e.g. one dislikes to sue or to be sued (R. Hatano in a lecture to the Japan week, 3 March 1986, Amsterdam) and, as Dai-ichi Ito told me, this preference for a pragmatic balance in any dispute makes the judgment of individual originality and independence in a doctoral dissertation a particular case, but in the same time Japanese scholars strive for international compatability and equivalence in their new doctorates.

What is the value added by a European doctorate? Actually, a doctorate is awarded by a university with an organizational charter which includes the ius promovendi or traditionally the ius ubique docendi, the right to teach everywhere. The right is given by the sovereign, traditionally king and pope, but now by the legislator, senate and congress or equivalents, and if given, there is autonomy in academic judgment. The university delegates the appraisal of quality to an examination or promotion committee, ranging from two towards six or more members, according to its regulations. There might be stages and degrees of approval. In each national higher education system there are universities which are assumed to guarantee an international passport to scholarship by awarding doctorates. Some still assume an equivalence of universities, such as the Netherlands and Germany, whereas most other countries accept a hierarchy. The international quality is frequently guaranteed by inviting representatives of invisible colleges to participate in the appraisal. A European doctorate implies the participation and responsibility of members of the academic community in two or more European countries in the academic forum. It does not imply Eurocentrism. The value added by a European doctorate is intrinsic, in the sense that it revitalizes the academic peregrination and good European practices. Because there is no European sovereign, there is no need for a special organizational charter. Of course, some universities might recognize a doctorate awarded by another European university, because the candidates prepared part of his research programme in the own university or a faculty member has been supervisor, but I don't expect this development. If one strives for an international passport to scholarship, it depends on the credibility, reputation and care of particular universities to guarantee the appraisal of quality.

Also an American doctorate has no sense, if one does not specify which university and its examination committee have awarded the doctorate. The American situation allows for a clear ranking and a continuous monitoring. There is no equivalence. Similarly the 3,600 universities in the European community cannot be considered equivalent, even if two or three universities in various countries establish joint arrangements irrespective of other qualities. The European doctorate can only be meaningful, if one agrees on some monitoring device in keeping the standards. I expect that many European centers of excellence are reluctant to joint any new bond of organization, but will accept European sponsorship for guaranteeing the quality of individual pieces of scholarship. Also an Asian doctorate has no special meaning, if we do not specify arrangements, such as in Tsukuba university, and guarantee its international quality. There is no need, in my opinion, to invent new Ph.D structures, but there is enormous room for supportive networks and collective arrangements in guaranteeing free exchange of academic products as in doctoral dissertations. In itself the broadening of the forum by including faculty members of other European universities does not increase the quality or relevance of doctoral dissertations, if one would strive for consensus only. The main value of a European doctorate seems to me the revitalization of good practices and a more comparative approach to post-graduate education and research. Self-appraisal within closed disciplinary, national and institutional boundaries prevents critical reflection and cross-fertilization.

It would be possible to select various good practices in Ph.D production, such as external examiners, openness for public inspection and appropriate publication in major languages. It would be equally possible to indicate bad practices, such as disciplinary segmentation, fixed periods of completion, dominance of instruction rather than of research, and scanning within given frames of reference. However, detailed regulations lead to ritualization and standardization. The history of Ph.D's and equivalent final degrees shows too many examples of the counterproductive nature of regulations. In the first standing committee for science (VCW) in our university we tried to agree on essential characteristics for scientific research, such as

1. Search for something 'new', which excludes the mere maintenance of knowledge, application of familiar methods to familiar problems, repetition and popularization as such, but not an emphasis on 'originality' in absolute form;
2. A minimal theoretical basis or content, whereby we exclude routine studies and observation without an effort of explanation, but we include critical and descriptive comparisons;
3. Avoidance of bias or prejudice for a particular explanation or solution, whereby we exclude any data collecting exercise leading to a preferred explanation or solution whatever the arguments;
4. Explicit justification of value judgments, whereby we exclude any set of normative statements without mentioning why the norms were accepted but we include an assessment of the norms themselves;
5. Openness to proof and counterproof, whereby we exclude statements which cannot be falsified, such as tautologies, and
6. Practical criteria, such as utilization of university resources and intended publication.

I do not think that such exercises to establish general criteria for research are particularly helpful for demarcation problems. Of course, such reflection on general issues of the Ph.D phenomenon seems a necessary stage. At the International Christian University in Mitaka I was informed about the endless discussions during many years how to establish standards of Ph.D's before the first was actually awarded in 1984. In specific cases one tends to disagree on the operationalisation of general rules and one needs careful and continuous evaluation of process and procedures.

There is no universal theory of the academic forum as it operates in deciding the entrance criteria of membership of the scientific community. There are respectable proponents of such a theory, such as A.D. de Groot (1985), but one has to accept the continuously changing frontiers of learning. There is a permanent transformation of solipsism towards multi-disciplinary clusters and gradually dominant paradigms, but no perfect solution for deciding what constitutes a sufficient proof for originality and relevance. As in classical Rome and ancient China the academic forum is a mixture of justice, power, propaganda and market. Any concerted action to broaden this forum and strengthen fair judgment as in the case of an European doctorate is helpful but will be never sufficient.

Finally, as a substitute for a universal code of practice I would suggest an Academy of Independent scholars at the European level, such as has been established by Kenneth Boulding c.s. at the American level. Such an academy of eminent senior scholars who do not have any other interest than the advancement of knowledge might serve as a forum of appeal, if individual members of promotion committees have serious objections against awarding a doctorate and normal appeals have failed. Such an academy will have a broader function for the advancement of knowledge and the continuity of the scientific community and its ideals: a countervailing power against dominant politico-administrative regulations.

Role

Role is the presentation of self, in this case, in the world of learning or the academic community. In the first chapter (p. 13) I distinguished various role definitions of a Ph.D candidate: researcher, teacher, professional and generalist. There is no continuum of roles, but there might be a succession of roles in a life cycle. There is no overall and superimposed pattern of doctorates. There is a major distinction between the role set of a fresh graduate continuing his studies as an assistant researcher and that of an experienced mid-career candidate who tries to present his personal research according to university standards. Also the distinction between a local and cosmopolitan orientation determines the nature of a doctoral dissertation.

Role theory belongs to a situationist or external control approach of human behaviour. Its main line of argument maintains that human behaviour can be understood by looking at the conditions of its social context and particularly its situational interactions. Role theory is complementary to the rational or quasi-rational approach which explains human behaviour from an instrumental and utility maximization point of view, but it is also complementary to an existentialist approach, where human behaviour is assumed to be an emergent, almost random process of intrapsychic forces and can be understood only by analyzing the unfolding of these processes over time. This perspective moves away from a stimulus-response logic of interactions and from rationality to a focus on emergent meaning. In general lines, one could categorize the first instrumental and rational explanation of human choice as one preferred by economists, the second role exchange and expectancy theories of human choice as one preferred by sociologists and anthropologists, whereas the third existential and symbolic interactionist approach originates from pragmatic philosophers as William James and John Dewey. I do not believe that we can reduce the particular human choice of writing a doctoral dissertation to one of these approaches. They are not mutually exclusive. I assume that the controversy over the extent to which human behaviour can be explained by rational or instrumental motives, by socialization through role sets, or by emergent action is likely to be persistent and resistant to empirical results. This controversy touches empirical and theoretical nerves and also basic assumptions about the nature of man embedded in religion and philosophy (Pfeffer, 1982; Arts, 1985).

I have selected the role of a Ph.D candidate and the role set with his supervisor and examiners as key concepts for pragmatic reasons. The historical analysis in the second chapter has shown that the three motives for higher learning –utility, curiosity and virtue– have received a shifting attention in the various reforms over time. The present emphasis is strongly utilitarian and knowledge production depends on state science policies. Bureaucratic co-ordination of universities around some central set of research objectives has become increasingly important as the size and the cost of state-supported research mushroomed after the war and science became seen more as a factor of production than just of one component of 'high culture' (Whithley, 1984, p. 295). It is no surprise that also the Ph.D process becomes geared towards specific objectives which require reliable, reproducible and visible results and narrow down research foci around restricted topics. There is no room for life missions. With increased demands for accountability and objective, relevant performance appraisal systems, this encouragement will grow so that granting research assistantships or fellowships may become much more dependent on adopting appropriate administrative arrangements and producing visible, reliable pieces of knowledge at regular, short intervals (ibidem, p. 300). The Dutch 'aio' system is prone to such reduction of Ph.D's as a productive factor without the traditional scope of higher learning.

The cultural analysis of the third chapter has shown the variation between scientific fields, disciplines and professions in producing new knowledge or original and independent contributions to the world of learning. Presently one observes an extension of particular organizational structures predicated upon experiences in natural sciences to human and social sciences and this extrapolation threatens to reduce intellectual pluralism and diversity. Ph.D's belong to the system of free public intellectual production in a society. 'Public scientific knowledge is becoming the product of bureaucratically organized combinations of standardized skills for a variety of intellectual and non-intellectual goals. It is thus beginning to acquire some of the features of industrial, private science. The industrialization of intellectual work which began in the nineteenth-century universities, and was typified by Liebig's knowledge factory, has developed into another phase since the Second World War in which reputational goals and values are established and changed by shifting coalitions of intellectual élites, state functionaries, and administrative leaders in employment organizations' (Whitley, 1984, p. 301). Quotation indices in established international journals and highly structured scientific fields determine the mainstream. Instruction in disciplinary graduate schools about advanced models and methodologies and within approved research programmes will stimulate a regular production of doctoral dissertations. The variety and selectivity of deviant paradigms and multi-disciplinary approaches might be reduced.

The functional analysis of the fourth chapter emphasized Ph.D's as life chances and the particular nature of free scientific information markets. In figure IV-1 I tried to map three cycles of higher education and an Asian, European and American pattern of doctorates in various careers. It has become clear that these patterns are ideal types of the perception of self in producing new knowledge. There is always a sense of disseminating and teaching what one has discovered in a Ph.D journey. From an Asian perspective one's individual contribution is embedded in a societal and collective meaning. Individuality as such is a pejorative and needs to be rooted in social recognition and selection for office and scholarship. Disciplinary boundaries are weak and pragmatic considerations of what constitutes new knowledge are more important than rational arguments. From a European perspective the academic and scientific community seems a paramount symbol of universal validity. The European doctorate has a broader societal meaning than a purely academic degree in many countries. In its long historical development it has become more secular, rational and specialized for individual prominence. The present revitalization of a European doctorate might stimulate a reflection on the original mission of universities, but hopefully prevent Eurocentrism. From an American perspective the doctorate has developed as a pre-career degree with its own cost-benefit balance in a market-oriented society. There are extreme variations, but regular assessment of quality in institutions and fields of study. The American graduate school has become the model for organized creativity. The view of man as an active exerciser of choice and discretion fits the prevailing philosophical and religious tradition in the United States. The Ph.D option is much more pragmatic and individual in the American tradition than in European or Asian traditions.

The historical, cultural and functional explorations of the Ph.D phenomenon lead me to the conclusion that there is a wide variety of roles of Ph.D candidates. The present tendency to select the role of a research assistant as dominant seems counterproductive and might produce role conflicts.

Let us assume that I have selected a research theme with sufficient theoretical and methodological justification in order to get a formal approval from the disciplinary hierarchy. I am allowed to hire research assistants for elaborating individual research projects in the form of doctoral dissertations within a specific period of say three years. The natural inclination is to search for research assitants who accept my theoretical and methodological preferences or are ready to be instructed in a particular programme. As a promotor in the Dutch tradition I am forced to keep the research assistant within the planned sequence of research activities and prevent any deviance in unexpected directions. The double role of project leader who needs to finish as planned and of promotor who needs to assess an original and independent contribution to knowledge creates an intrasender role conflict. Because there is an ambiguity of what constitutes an original and independent contribution to knowledge, I will be inclined to use the completion time as a yardstick, even if unexpected events would suggest another approach. A similar conflict is likely to be raised for the research candidate. If he discovers that his research or the outcomes do not fit the terms of reference of his project leader and thesis supervisor, there are practical obstacles to search for another supervisor and follow his own inclinations. Of course, he might convince an empathic supervisor that another approach is more fruitful, but available evidence (van Hout, 1986) shows that it is highly risky to change his course in another direction or search for another supervisor. In a certain sense, solid craftsmen are better research assistants than original minds with their idiosyncracy.

The most fascinating aspect of the role set between supervisor and doctoral candidate is the changing emphasis over time. In the first stage one has to check whether the candidate has sufficient knowledge and skills in a particular field of studies or discipline for an independent research project. This is a traditional teacher-student relationship, where reading suggestions, seminars and lectures might be the core. In the USA this is a course-based stage with a comprehensive examination as a test. In the UK it is part of the viva and in the Dutch situation there are more informal arrangements. The new structure of a four-years cycle might lead to a more formalised test before one is accepted as a research candidate. This will be an improvement, in my opinion. The second stage deals with the research design, its validity, feasibility and relevance, where tutoring becomes more important than teaching. The third stage tends to concentrate on data analysis and in the fourth stage writing and interpretation become the core of the process. Gradually the candidate gets confidence and develops an independent course of action with feedback sessions as between partners in the exploration. A critical decision is at what particular stage a supervisor needs to leave the candidate alone, supporting, motivating but refraining from detailed comments and new suggestions. In her studies on the Ph.D learning process Estelle Phillips (1984) showed the changing role perceptions over time. She suggests that the supervisor is important in the early stages of the work to act primarily as mediator between the students and their work. Gradually the supervisor can 'wean' the student from his dependence by encouraging self-criticism. Once students have learned the skills and acquired the confidence necessary to assess their own efforts, the students' perception of the supervisors' role changes. Instead of seeing it as one of primarily generating external approval and information, the supervisor becomes somebody with whom they can discuss new ideas and develop earlier thinking: a sounding board and an expert with the ability to proffer the reverse arguments to be encountered.

A European doctorate process where candidates and supervisors from two or more European universities are coupled in feedback sessions will greatly improve and enrich the Ph.D process. There is no standard solution, but there are many complementary styles of supervison and thesis writing. An empirical comparison of the quality of doctoral dissertations and the role of supervisors in various European countries has rarely been done. Rooyakkers' study (1986) in comparing previous university education, the dissertation, personal experiences and the role of supervisors or promotors of 26 Dutch doctores matched with 29 Ph.D's in the United Kingdom and the USA is a singular to the best of my knowledge. The dissertation writing process and the role of supervisors show much more similarities than one would expect given the informal and personal nature of Dutch supervision. Also my own observations in various countries suggest a surprisingly similar process and product despite structural differences in regulations. If we would be ready to accept a variety in roles for candidates and supervisors, each national system allows the production of high quality doctoral dissertations. It is difficult to generalize about the waste and contamination of various systems. Indeed the Dutch system tends to produce doctorates at a later age especially in humanities and social sciences and so does the Scandinavian system e.g. the 822 doctorates awarded in Denmark between 1957-1970 show an average age of forty years. (Ib Haurum in Crawford, 1976). The Dutch system emphasizes public performance and publication, whereas the American and English systems prefer a more private performance within the examination committee and separate publication from the awarding of the doctorate. The American system allows a broader consultation of members of the doctoral committee, whereas the English and Dutch prefer a close, almost monogamous, relationship between supervisor/examiner/promotor and candidate.

Presently there is an amazing variety of roles in research. The study edited by Elisabeth and Norman Perry on the role of research organisations in USA, Britain, France and Denmark (1976) e.g. shows that research has emerged as an important independent valuational base for direct, external allocations to the social sciences and hence is of major influence in shaping the organisational and knowledge structures of most disciplines. Universities have lost their monopoly: the university department is only one of several institutional bases for individuals having research as a full-time or part-time occupation. However, universities have still a monopoly in validating and certifying that people have obtained a specified level of competence, i.c. have provided evidence of originality and independence in a field of study. Of course, there are no failure-proof arrangements for such evaluation, but I am amazed to observe so many efforts for standardizing and 'industrializing' Ph.D arrangements without empirical evidence. There seems a need for broadening and deepening the concept of Ph.D's in various careers outside the academic community. We need the full range of good practices in many centers of excellence and more variety and selectivity rather than a reduction to a so-called American mode of Ph.D production. The European doctorate as a concept, not as a set of detailed regulations, might stimulate this variety and selectivity. The pressures for greater size and an economy of scale and completion in Ph.D production are significant, but the freedom to opt for the more intimate and less economical small-scale arrangements of individual dissertation writers who maintain the momentum of their own research is of paramount importance. Meeks (1985) showed how Cambridge persisted in believing in small scale arrangements: twenty or thirty research students in a faculty of towards a hunderd staff.

Finally, let me select one particular type of research which is likely to elicit role conflicts between academic examiners ane research candidates viz. what Nakayama (1984) calls service science and others action research. In Nakayama's view the role of receivers, assessors or utilizers of knowledge is more important than the role of producers of scientific archievements. Therefore science assessed by people at large is at least as important as academic science assessed by fellow peer group members and industrialized science assessed by public and private sponsors. Service science may be defined as science sustained by a sense of solidarity with and sympathy for local communities, minorities or other powerless groups and responsible to their standards. This type of science is usually field research and involves cooperation with those in minority position in problem solving. It might include various interactive stages of feedback and joint interpretation, where the researcher becomes a partner in coping with specific problems. Forms of publication differ from the scientific report in international journals, because service science addresses directly those who are concerned. It is based on social consciousness and involves members in local communities to select relevant research issues. Nakayama (ibidem, p. 192) rightly remarks, that the traditional Western disciplines of theology, law and medicine, since their origin in the medieval university, have been identified with a group of intellectuals who have given at least normatively intellectual service to the people, independent of political and economic pressure and interest. The new scientific profession lacks a sense of the public as its clientele, and this lack is enhanced by the fact that scientists are usually supported by public or private authorities. Scientific activity remains alienated from ordinary citizens' lives.

My own outlook at the scientific enterprise focuses at the participation of those who have to utilize knowledge for improvement of their own life chances. Bars to freedoms of entry into and exit from the communities of learners and participants and interpreters in the communities of discourse have to be lowered (Nelson, 1974). There are many inherited invidious dualisms between scholars and laymen. Especially in tbe Western concept of a scientific community there is some arrogance in restricting access to those who have the appropriate qualifications in a particular discipline. Indeed, participative and interactive approaches to institutionalized science are not highly respectable in academic prestige and they tend to extend a research project over many years, but I still prefer doctoral dissertations which are based on intensive participation and interaction with the subjects of study above purely theoretical explanations of models and simulations. It is even possible and in my opinion highly respectable to focus on the participation of those who are in less privileged positions, such as the poor or exploited, but one has to strike a careful balance between preference for action and distance from bias.

In the case of Jan Tinbergen for example, he rejected

'The primacy of the narrow economic efficiency objective held to so firmly by important segments of his discipline. He has taught us instead that economics can and must encompass those broader issues which determine whether both the nation and the world are just and compassionate, livable, and at peace – issues such as inequality generated by the market system, inequality between the first and third worlds, and the ultimate danger of a modern technology let loose in a bellicose world.....He has given us a model of the academic's responsibilities. Scholarship is surely necessary, but it is also the scholar's responsibility to teach, to serve, to implement, and if necessary to preach' (Haveman, 1985).

In his selection of Ph.D candidates one cannot but observe the implications of this view. Of course, science and rational thought, models and forecasts, planning and analysis, but all imbedded in his concern to prevent or reduce harsh competition between greedy special interests and warfare of those in power.

Another example is Gé Kruijer (1919-1986) whose inspiration and teaching introduced me to observation, evaluation and problem solving in third world countries. He gradually took the position that science needs to be used for liberating the poor and oppressed from slavery and usurpation and provoked the academic establishment by rejecting a neutral distance and dispassionate analysis. After his retirement in 1982 as professor of applied sociology at the University of Amsterdam he wrote a book with an explicit bias on the third world: 'Liberation Science' or 'Development for Freedom' as will be the English title. It is an excellent personal account how he developed his own outlook from his Ph.D on food expeditions in Amsterdam during the war (1951), country studies on Suriname (1968,1973), and studies on the role of scientific policy consultants (1969) towards lectures in the Caribean and Latin American region after his retirement on his radical reflections. In my personal judgment, it is a respectable perception of the scientific enterprise, which I do not share. In particular the Ph.D concept assumes a concerted effort to present the full range of facts and expert opinion on a selected topic within a specified frame of reference or theory and to argue for a new (re)vision or addition of received knowledge. The search for objectivity and a required variety of opinions and theories is part and parcel of the scientific venture.

There are many legitimate options in the scientific community on the role of a researcher. At one extreme of the continuum one observes a preference for a clean exposition of what one has learned in a Ph.D journey without any reference to personal opinions in style, preface or epilogue or indicating why one is attracted to select a topic or what failures have been made. At the other extreme a promotor or supervisor stimulates a candidate for assessing his own norms and values as explicitly as possible and encourages a personal style, if the evidence seems solid or at least acceptable. What are the academic conditions under which scholarship ferments and becomes creative? Nakayama's answer to this major underlying assumption of the Ph.D system is that it is, pure and simple, tbe proximity of companions with whom one engages in serious academic discussions. Access to a wealth of documents, data, theories or responses is a necessary but seldom sufficient condition (Nakayama, 1984, p. 80). The seminar system of modern universities seems to be the only place for creative dialogue and an exploration of value judgments and the limits of science. But what is the role of a doctoral dissertation as a publishable academic product? Here again there is no agreement, as in the days of Aristotle, because different ideas about the nature of science lead to a variety in expression. The reasons why one takes up certain questions, inside stories about successes and failures, and the bargaining between candidates and the academic forum practically never reach print, but they seem to be extremely important to the maintenance of a creative academic tradition.

My preference is to allow in preface, epilogue and biography much more role reflections than is customary in traditional doctoral dissertations. However, I don't like to generalize. There might be doctoral dissertations in mathematical and physical sciences which are characterized by a high level of dispassionate analysis and abstraction, but even in these fields of study reflections of Nobel prizewinners and other eminent scholars show the importance of role perceptions and their view of the scientific enterprise which are traditionally left out in the doctoral dissertation. In any case a biography as is required in the German practice and becomes customary in other institutional practices e.g. in the Dutch system might add some flesh and blood to academic products. I would regret a development where the choice of a dissertation topic actually reflects bureaucratic-political preferences in a department and available resources without any personal inclination of the candidate. The Ph.D journey becomes then a ritualized and formalized performance showing the application of advanced methodology and theory rather than an attempt to originality and independent judgment. We need a concerted effort to make the Ph.D a more human product related to one's view on knowledge and science or philosophy. I do not pretend to offer a universal solution. In each case I try to strike a balance between the expression of dispassionate analysis and objectivity versus the expression of self with its variations in the world of learners and there is rarely an optimal balance. It is remarkable that most reflections on the Ph.D phenomenon or frontiers of learning tend to be found in general cultural and intellectual journals, such as in the Dutch case 'De Gids', 'Hollands Maandblad', and 'Tirade' rather than in scientific journals which restrict publications to the skeleton of facts and their relationships in theories or models. Besides scientific journals with their rigid regulations and aridity one longs for more fertile combinations between scientific distance and personal involvement. Köbben (in NRC, 20-3-1986) e.g. showed the remarkable parallel between creative writing and anthropological observation and analysis. Indeed, serendipidity as an expression of originality refers to an old tale of the three princes of Serendip, probably in Ceylon.....you must observe that no discovery of a thing you are looking for comes under this description of serendipidity (in Austin, 1978, pp. 195-202). Research refers to many roles.

Locus

The third key concept in classifying and assessing doctoral dissertations is locus, the locality where the Ph.D was prepared and awarded or, in mathematics, any system of points, lines and planes which satisfies one or more conditions or a line or plane every point of which satisfies a given condition and which contains no point that does not satisfy this condition (Webster). The impact of locality –size, quality, flexibility, arrangement, neighbourhood, privacy– on the production of doctoral dissertations has hardly been studied but seems of paramount importance. The assumptions underlying a special graduate school allowing for the necessary networking and interaction for creative work in contrast to mass higber educational institutes are based on the importance of physical arrangements. Technology is a major variable.

Historically the documentary tradition of higher learning in China can be explained by the invention of paper, usually attributed to Ts'ai Lun in about 105 AD which later in 622 AD allowed the civil service examination system with its thousands of answer books. Printing appeared in China in the 10th century. Printing resulted in a wholesale transformation in the scale of values by which scholars were judged. Printing requires a wider readership. Moreover, writing for publication means addressing a large, unspecified audience, but academic products serve a specific highly segmented market (chapter IV). It has been argued that the biggest reason for the stagnation of Chinese science was its geographical isolation from Islam, India and Europe and its consequent isolation from the challenges of a heterogeneous culture (Nakayama, 1984, p. 65). For the Chinese of this period learning was something that was written on paper, something printed. Though they came into contact with many strange artifacts of the West, they encountered nothing that corresponded to their understanding of what scholarly activity was about. Their own system of chin shih provided a network of examinations for aspiring office holders which absorbed the occasional unorthodox ideas of the intellectual elite, but after some thirteen centuries learning itself ossified and favored documents and memorization over disputation and creativity became a dominant pattern.

In contrast to China, oral instruction inevitably predominated in medieval Europe, for printed books were not available and copied manuscripts expensive. Scholars and students travelled from university to university in search for conversation and scarce manuscripts. Had the center of the Western academic tradition remained in Greece, it probably would have come to look more like the Chinese and would have proved incapable of generating modern science. The academic peregrination was an essential feature of the medieval West where the network of universities provided fresh intellectual challenges and accelerated the exchange of information. I would like to add that also the Muslim pilgrimages to Mecca helped to broaden men's knowledge of the world around him and the same applies to the 'Sankin Kotai' system of Tokugawa Japan (Nakayama, 1984, p. 73).

Of course, I do not claim that academic traditions are essentially determined by localities and the communication technology linking centers of learning by travelling or the distribution of printed material and that differences in the West and East can be explained merely by geography and the invention of paper and printing. The Chinese bureaucratic institution was already in existence before the advent of paper and the introduction of paper and printing in the West did not result in any sudden changes in the educational programme of the medieval university. However, one cannot deny that the geographical distribution of centers of learning and communication techno-

logy reinforced, exacerbated and enlarged the cultural and functional differences between the two traditions. The history of the shifting frontiers of
learning is much more complex than the role of shin chih or the university
thesis.

The major question of present reforms in higher education and science
policy is to determine the impact of the explosive growth of mass higher
education institutions with their claims on the ius promovendi and the new
communication and information technology. The Mcluhanist notion that
new communication media are exercising a decisive influence on patterns of
human thought and action does not exclude higher education. Mcluhan's
observations were largely based on a comparison of pre-literate African
people with the demonstrative culture of the West which he found to depend
upon the technology associated with a phonetic alphabet (McLuhan, 1962).
Is there an industrial paradox in higher education, where economies of scale
and standardization of received knowledge for the many will gradually
destroy the search for originality and independence at the edge of scholarship? It cannot be maintained, I assume, that the 3,600 localities for higher
education in the European Common Market are equally fitted to select and
assess the quality of doctoral dissertations. It seems difficult to combine
standardization for the many with the selectivity and variety for the few.
Most innovations in higher education, such as in my own experience the new
seventh faculty in the Municipal University of Amsterdam initated in 1945 by
two historians J. Romein and M.W. Posthumus, become sooner or later
absorbed in traditional structures. Their original intentions to design a new
conglomerate of disciplines integrated in political sciences and open for all
after selection on the base of capacity and knowledge but not of diploma
could not be realized. The minister of education, arts and sciences of that
period, G.J. van der Leeuw, an innovator, suggested even that radical innovations could only be expected from the oldest university i.c. Leyden (F. de
Jong, 1981, p. 45). An interesting suggestion. The more a university is rooted
in history and culture, the more it has the responsibility of extending the
frontiers of learning and of revitalizing the cultural heritage. I would like to
support this nexus between tradition in the full range of knowledge and
radical innovation. Frequently innovations outside the centers of excellence
tend to adopt gradually dominant patterns of organization and paradigms in
traditional centers (see e.g. L.J.G. van der Maesen, 1986).

Data bases, retrieval systems and expert programmes might be linked in
the near future allowing open university networks for received knowledge. In
that sense locality will become less critical. A European university of the
future might consist of such a coupled network for exchange of free academic
information and in an interactive programme individual scholars and Ph.D
candidates might have access to the whole range of academic knowledge.
There is no need for the extensive compilations of past wisdom which

occupied such a large part of traditional doctoral dissertations. In an essay on the future of universities van Bueren, the chairman of the Dutch RAWB, imagined such a future of interactive linked university curricula. However, what are the conditions for satisfying an organizational climate fostering creativity and new interlinkages between disciplines for the traditional Ph.D candidate?

Rather than speculating about a future which Orwell imagined to start in 1984 I prefer to comment on present reform proposals for doctorate programmes. I assume that the Dutch situation is not atypical.

1. There seems agreement to establish only a few locations for selected Ph.D candidates and their supervisors/project leaders/promotors, preferably only one Centre of Excellence, but catering for all participating universities within each discipline. This preference is based on the different organizational climate for tailor made doctorate programmes and for mass higher education.
2. There is a strong tendency to select a few research programmes initiated by project leaders which allow separate but interconnected Ph.D projects for recently graduated candidates who are willing to accept these programmes. They will be instructed in the appropriate theory and methodology. They are selected from those who have followed a suitable four-years first cycle programme.
3. After the first year the candidates will be examined ('prelim') in order to test their knowledge, skills and research design within the approved programmes. If they pass, they will get a three years contract for completing their Ph.D under supervision of their project leader.
4. For financial reasons Ph.D candidates are expected to teach an average of 25% in the undergraduate programme substituting for more expensive senior staff. In the long run the doctorate programme must be fitted within the fixed overall budget. The special allowances for supervisors in the doctorate programme need to be balanced with a higher teaching and administrative load for those in the first cycle programme. It is a zero sum approach.
5. The actual completion of a doctoral dissertation within four years is seen as so important that the traditional scope and quality needs to be reduced to a manageable size. In the final stage one assumes that each supervisor will manage some ten Ph.D candidates and has no substantial commitments in the four cycle programme.

I share the need for differentiation in higher education and if the organizational climate for each cycle is different according to empirical studies, one needs to translate the organizational climate in special physical structures of size, quality flexibility, arrangement and privacy, which might lead to a special location allowing for intensive interactions, cross-fertilization and small group seminars. It is indeed irrealistic to expect each four-year cycle programme to establish its own graduate school or center for higher degrees. Moreover, I agree with the need for special facilities in computing, administrative staff, documentation and travelling arrangements for postgraduate studies. I do not know organizational arrangements and structures which could cover the whole range of tertiary education from induction of fresh 18 years newcomers or sophomores towards electives and research seminars given the present range of specialization and educational technology. If one accepts the three cycles of higher education as depicted in figure IV-1 as a realistic representation, we might need appropriate organizational structures for each. What is the appropriate organizational structure for the third cycle?

The Quest for Control

I started to look at the Ph.D phenomenon as an observer and systematist in the inductive mode of Linnaeus. The metaphore coined by the Harvard professor William James in 1903 gave me the excuse to read about the cephalopods or head-footed animals. I became and am still fascinated by the required variety of the about 150 species of octopuses living in nearly all the seas of the world and since 400 million years surviving in an enormous range of ecological niches. Our present knowledge of how these animals behave is of recent origin and has evolved from patient observation towards advanced experimentation, doubling every ten year. I am still puzzled why William James used the octopus as a symbol to curse the aberrations of doctoral degrees. I assume that in his days popular knowledge was based on Victor Hugo's 'Les Travailleurs de la Mer' (1866) which made the octopus the talk of the day in France or Henry Lee's 'The Devel-fish of Fiction and of Fact' (1875). William James considered the octopus with his eight radiating, supple, tapering tongs, though as steel and cold as night anyhow as a devil fighting against the hero Gilliat in Gustave Dore's famous picture. A time-bound view.

However, the classification of doctoral dissertations or other expressions of 'rites de passage' for entering the community of scholars offers more difficulties than the biosphere. A study visit to Japan in March 1984 put me for the paradox of unemployed over-doctors in a national system of higher education which only in 1953 reluctantly accepted the Ph.D system, of many non-chartered innovations in post-graduate education, and of awarding doctorates to Asian students with another meaning than for internal use. This study warned me against a uniform definition of originality, independency and relevance of doctoral dissertations. I got more blanks than answers. Statistical exercises as such are rather useless, if one does not share assumptions about the meaning of Ph.D's. I still remember how directors of Mombusho were very helpful to explain their impressive computer sheets but became embarrassed by questions about meaning and policy. Recent developments in Japanese higher education show an increasing interest in creativity, originality and independency. The traditional role of Todai selecting on excellency in memorization, comprehension, endurance and an all-round balance for bureaucratic work is declining. The traditional hierarchy of employees drawn from elite universities as Tokyo, Kyoto, Waseda, and Keio is disintegrating (Esaka Akira, in Japan Echo, 1985, no. 3). It is unclear what role doctoral dissertations will play in the formation of the new elite but I expect that selection for creativity and originality or, to quote Esaka, for people with a kind of barbaric brilliance and with the cool courage to hack their way into the unknown, will be critical, probably outside the elite universities.

Fortunately, I found an entrepreneurial student, Michael Wyler, ready to dig out the facts and figures of dissertations for his final paper despite or because of my warning that it would be an unexplored territory. During our many discussions I tried in vain to keep the study within a nice input-output, cost-benefit or demand-supply model. The main conclusion was that a standard dissertation does not exist, but one has to look at the variations over time, disciplines and national systems. Moreover, doctoral dissertations belong to the grey sector of free scientific publications stocked in university libraries and, in the Dutch system, distributed to friends, colleagues and faculty members. Also the literature about doctoral dissertations is scattered over in-house journals, academic newspapers or other grey sources. There is no consistency and continuity in the few studies on the doctorate. It is highly anecdotical. Some studies are initiated to proof a specific issue, such as the disputed quality of Dutch social science dissertations or the cost of printing, but are soon discontinued. I have indeed found many reasons for discontinuing my explorations. There are too many points of view and evidence is scattered. Many university historians do not even pay attention to doctoral dissertations as Renate Simpson warned me allready. It does not seem a respectable, substantive subject of study. It is therefore no surprise that during the defense of this doctoral paper of 193 pages in September 1984 directly after my return from an Indonesian hospital the other members of the examination committee were not particularly impressed because of its descriptive nature without a solid theory. Also another major Dutch study by a student, Geert Rooijakkers, on the comparison of Dutch with American and Anglosaxon dissertations which recently has been completed, was not even accepted for examination purposes because it did not fit a clear disciplinary niche. I discovered also that my own research design of a caucus approach in intermittent stages with experienced supervisors complemented with historical, cultural and functional explanations did not fit any approved research programme. Priority was given to specific evaluation projects of new structures to program Ph.D production in a more efficient way, not to comparative exploration of assumptions and intentions.

Luckily, I had already started some five years ago monthly meetings with Ph.D candidates and recent doctors for establishing a regular feedback network. These rather informal meetings provided a stimulating platform for discussing the elusive but also highly pragmatic issues of the individual long-distance journey, but I realized that there was no neutral observer's role. I had to make explicit my own assumptions and intentions in each individual case, whereas these assumptions can never be made standards for other members of the academic forum. This forum implies equality for all members to express their own criteria in their field of study. A continuous debate with shifting disciplinary boundaries. Candidates are in a very weak position against this forum. External candidates are nowhere represented and can hardly repeal rejections of proposals or drafts. They need self-confidence and access to a supportive, critical, and emphatic network of supervisors and colleagues with more than one option. Despite the variation even within disciplinary clusters there are common elements in exploring unknown territory. There are multiple goals and research is highly interactive. I am persistent in believing the value of Dutch academic tradition with its emphasis on coming to the fore at any stage in one's career, with its freedom to select one's own topic, promotor or faculty, an undivided doctorate, with its public ritual performance for family, friends and colleagues, and with its relatively high publication rate of dissertations. Moreover, I am calibrated in one of the major innovating faculties, the Political Social Faculty in the Municipal University of Amsterdam which I still admire because of its interdisciplinary approach with an explicit societal mission at that time. I experienced in my own career the value of shifting occupational, disciplinary and institutional commitments and became highly concerned with postgraduate education for Third World candidates. Of course, I accept the need for more structure and control in what is loosely called the European tradition of individual, sometimes lifetime missions of doctorates. There is ample room for improvement and learning from other traditions.

Gradually I discovered fundamental differences on what a doctoral dissertation is supposed to be. Let me take the French case which has experienced more radical changes in postgraduate or third cycle education than any other in its long history. In 1954 and 1958 one introduced the doctorate of the third cycle, first in natural sciences, and four years later in social sciences and humanities. In 1964 one established a special preparation for doctorates, the DEA or a diplome for advanced studies in natural sciences, which became generalized in 1974 as DESS or a diplome for higher specialised studies. It was a concerted effort to add to the traditional 'doctorate d'état' with its long duration a more specialised training as professional researcher. Indeed one can observe the substantial increase in third cycle candidates, from 10,000 in 1962 to 25,000 in 1975 for natural sciences, and from 5 000 in 1964 to almost 20,000 in 1975 for social sciences and humanities. Also the actual production of new doctorates increased from 200 in 1959 to some 2,000 in 1974 for natural sciences and from less than 100 in 1960 to some 1,000 in 1974 in social sciences and humanities (Charlot, 1980).

There are two issues at stake, which seem to be confused.

(1) The first issue is the additional training in research methodology and theory. In natural sciences this might lead to the actual post-graduate participation in experimental team research and, for example, applied econometric modelling lends itself well to this natural scientist's approach (Meeks, 1985). In social sciences and humanities this additional training consists usually of taught courses on new developments, paradigms or methodology which cannot be given in mass higher education. I am greatly in favour of this additional research training for those who are selected as assistants-in-training. The output is qualified researchers.

(2) The second issue is the production of knowledge at the frontiers of learning. Here one has to differentiate between experimental modelling and testing as in natural sciences and actual experience in real life situations e.g. as manager, professional or administrator outside laboratories. Of course, one needs to be well-versed in methodology and the state of the art to discover new insights or paradigms, but the application of methodology does not lead automatically to a doctoral dissertation in the traditional sense. It is partly a matter of luck, chance and chase and it is difficult to forecast when there is sufficient evidence of an original contribution.

The two issues in post-graduate research and education are not always compatible. For qualified post-graduate researchers one frequently needs a broad range of search and research strategies and the narrow specialization which a Ph.D requires is often seen as reducing the researcher's versatility. In that sense post-graduate research training is similar to other professional post-graduate qualifications such as M.D., LL.D or registered accountant. It would be even helpful to disconnect research training from the Ph.D and to stimulate a broader cross-disciplinary approach, where the whole range of modelling, experimenting, field studies, documentary studies and theoretical analysis in various disciplines is covered. There is a need for highly versatile and creative researchers who can act as gatekeeper and linking pin between disciplines. In the English perception it might lead to a M.Phil., in the French setting to a DESS, in the American setting to an ABD and in the Dutch setting to a revitalization of the doctorandus, which might be completed with a Phil. The Indonesian solution of establishing a common pasca-sarjana or post-graduate faculty in some top-universities seems to me a better option than separate disciplinary centers of excellence as in the Dutch proposals. The major challenge in each system seems to be selecting for a real concentration of quality, may be spread over various locations, rather than adding to each university its own post-graduate programmes.

A reduction of the traditional doctoral dissertation to a programmed venture has never been a sustaining success. The actual differentiation between a 'doctorate d'état' and 'a doctorate de troisième cycle' has been discontinued. Actually, the reforms since 1954 have also multiplied the number of 'doctorate d'état'. I have seen no empirical evidence how one can differentiate between old and new doctorates, if one keeps the ideal of a concerted effort for originality. Also American reforms in creating special doctorates as doctor of education or arts with less rigour than the Ph.D have failed. I welcome the present Dutch effort to strengthen post-graduate research training by the appointment of special assistants-in-training under guidance of promotors who have actually supported doctoral candidates to complete successfully dissertations. It would be feasible to identify productive promotors with their range of completed doctoral dissertations and offer better facilities for post-graduate research. I am, however, concerned about an actual devaluation of a doctorate, if it needs to be completed within a standardized given period. In some proposals a doctorate is seen as equivalent to one published article in a respectable journal, whereas e.g. in the same field the British concept requires a large-scale undertaking – an original book, typically equivalent in length, if not in sustained quality, to perhaps six substantial journal articles (Meeks, 1985). I assume that the present proposals will lead to a reduced concept of doctorates within carefully selected programmes but I am rather optimistic that the quest for quality will be more vital than the quest for control in the long run.

A European doctorate will stimulate a more comparative approach to post-graduate learning with the required variety. Available evidence shows the variation between disciplines, specializations, careers and remunerations for Ph.D's. Competition with good practices will prevent a degradation but strengthen supportive networks and clustering for quality. In few national higher education systems it has been possible to create and sustain real centers of excellence but one seems to be forced to scatter efforts into too many directions and locations. Equality rather than selectivity. For me the European doctorate is not an abstraction or a separate institute with special regulations, but a revitalization of existing, unfortunately decreasing practices. In my own doctoral dissertation the core was the last project of the European Productivity Agency in Paris to co-ordinate evaluation projects of supervisory and managerial training with participants from many European countries in every stage. If at that time universities had been part of a more formalized European network, the academic forum could have included faculty members of other European universities. Also in many actual doctorate projects colleagues from other European universities participate in supervision and asessment of quality. Formal particpation in examination committees depends on the lack of facilities, not on practices and intentions. I strongly support any effort to obtain European excellency in doctorates, but do not see it as a magic formula. There is at this time a real danger to invent a magic box of the Ph.D as a sufficient and necessary condition for tbe advancement of knowledge confusing research training with original contributions and applying inappropriate standards in quest for control. Any degree is secondary to the learning process. Especially the second cycle as in figure IV-1 offers many opportunities for research qualifications as a M.Phil or non-chartered diploma's or records.

The Ph.D seems to be a rather incidental invention. The Chinese tradition of chin shih with the longest continuing history was based on the selection of state councillors, not on the advancement of knowledge. It was open to all by competitive examinations. Originality was not the key issue, but preventing feudal clans and internal wars. Its influence on Japan, Korea, France and England seems critical in connecting civil service with quality rather than family and power. Mobility of knowledge elites was the main mission. In the European system of higher education one observes many peaks and periods of decline since its origin but no direct correlation with degrees. The distinction between master and doctor was unclear. A detailed concern with degrees indicates a decline of the academic system. Reformation and Counter-Reformation broke the European network and made universities 'instrumentum dominationis' for the souvereign.

If one needs a yardstick for academic vitality, cross-fertilization between disciplines and the percentage of foreigners offer a better insight than examination regulations and statistics. I consider e.g. the period between around 1953 and 1973 in the Netherlands School of Economics as a peak: there were 20% foreigners who obtained the doctorate, a small cohesive faculty, a simple and sober structure where the senate looked for quality and the part-time curators provided facilities. Compared to the present balkanization and the rather unique Dutch structure of a full-time board with a central administration, representative councils with the double function of worker's council and board of external directors (the Dutch commissaris), it is difficult to find an appropriate structure for advanced education and research as a central mission. Officially, the committee of deans has this responsibility but their responsibility as administrator for their own faculty leaves hardly room for stimulating cross-fertilization or internationalization. The case study of Franeker university supports the critical role of mobility in the sense of field mobility between disciplinary niches and international mobility of scholars and students.

Appropriate structure

What is the appropriate structure of a post-graduate learning center which supports the required variety? Presently there is in the Dutch situation a top down project management of doctorate programmes, where public resources are allocated to approved themes under so called conditional financial schemes within national disciplinary clusters. Priority is given to megaprojects of at least 25 assistant-in-training years which have been negotiated between university departments. In September 1986 the ministry of Education and Science will allocate 1,500 assistant-in-training candidates to the Dutch universities, supplemented by 60 more lucrative scholarships awarded by the Royal Academy within four disciplinary clusters. This will gradually grow.

There is a fundamental departure from the traditional Ph.D concept as it has developed over time in various disciplinary cultures and careers. The standard seems to be a laboratory approach as has been seen feasible under assumptions of experimental testing and modelling, not triggering off interesting hypotheses under imperfect conditions of real life situations after field studies and practical experience.

Firstly, the traditional concept of a Ph.D is a concerted effort to cross disciplinary boundaries and transform dominant paradigms. Disciplinary centers of excellence and a priori research clusters pose serious obstacles for new cross-disciplinary ventures. In any case, one would need a complementary interdisciplinary center, such as originally intended in NIAS (Netherlands Institute for Advanced Studies) but open for theoretical natural sciences.

Secondly, traditionally a Ph.D design is initiated by a candidate not by a promotor, although he might suggest the relevance of a particular approach or issue and more so in natural sciences. In my experience, the core of the long-distance journey of a Ph.D is the search for a focus and an operationalization within given constraints. The new concept of a Ph.D is initiated by project leaders who become supervisors and promotors and leaves out the critical stage of exploration. Torben Agersnap observed, that career-oriented university men are so dependent upon the organisation for their job opportunities that they seldom dare to produce a creative or critical report. 'Most Ph.D dissertations contain elaborations of existing theory which follow the ideas of the dominating theoretical school at their university'. (Crawford, 1976, p. 263). The combination of project leader, teacher and promotor will strengthen the inbreeding of research efforts. Of course, there will be always Ph.D candidates and supervisors who conduct excellent research and react against the real and supposed constraints of a planned environment, but the proposed structures strengthen conformity to given standards rather than deviation.

Thirdly, the new structures fit fresh graduates without experience who actually extend their studies within a closed academic climate and expect to be instructed and guided for successful completion. Mid- or second-career candidates who have become fascinated by an unexplored or, in their opinion, wrongly classified problem do not fit in the new graduate centers. After the war 75% of the Ph.D's in Dutch universities were external candidates which gradually decreased to 25% in the seventies. The new structures are likely to direct all effort of senior professors to the attraction of the new research assistants within approved themes. In the full grown situation of 1991 one expects some 8-12 research assistants guided by one senior professor who will be released from other obligations. Those left in the first cycle programme will become full-time teachers and administrators. Because it is a budgettary neutral reorganization, increased facilities for postgraduates and their supervisors need to be compensated with decreased facilities for undergraduates and their teachers. Each teaching hour by research assistants substitutes less than half an hour by senior faculty. So the 25% teaching load of assistants-in-training will compensate for almost 50% of the budget in 1991. External candidates will hardly find an empathetic promotor given the time budgets.

Fourthly, the new structures assume a 50% participation of research assistants in obligatory lectures and seminars during the first years, especially in research methodology. This implies that the new four years cycle is not an adequate preparation for independent and original research as in the old structure. I accept this implication, because one cannot expect the same quality of a four years cycle as the traditional five or six years cycle with more freedom of choice. My experience with the new four years cycle, however, is positive in terms of student motivation, commitment and effort, but not in terms of selectivity through mass lectures and multiple choice examinations. I am optimistic that the second stage will select the better research candidates, but in my field of study, business administration, I prefer graduates to enter the external labour market before starting a doctorate process. There are actually many post-graduate specializations and research training programmes, such as the SIOS (Foundation for interacademical training in management consultancy), summer courses in American Business Schools, INSEAD, IMEDE, etc. which pay off after practical experience. Of course, for graduates in business administration and business economics there are more job opportunities than for graduates in any other discipline in the Netherlands. A younger age of entrance is important and I have great difficulty in advising fresh graduates to continue immediately with a research training. It is more appropriate in a later stage, but then the new scheme does not fit. However, I accept the relevance for some other disciplines. It would have been better to allocate support for post-graduate training and research to major four-years cycle programmes but give them freedom to design their own appropriate structure based on their own momentum and past records. The research component in each university programme differentiates between the various branches and it is highly unlikely to dicover a standard solution with assistants-in-training.

In each previous chapter I actually tried to specify the meaning of doctoral dissertations at the cross road of science policy and higher education administration. Although I tried various consecutive approaches, historical, cultural, functional and structural, but I continued to revolve around a few critical concepts and issues: originality, relevance, serendipidity, creativity, learning strategies, the scientific community, the whole range of knowledge, quality. At a high level of abstraction it seems impossible to agree on an overarching meaning of frontiers of learning, but members of the academic community are regularly involved in a case-to-case judgment of what actually constitutes an independent and original contribution to knowledge. Like justice, health, profit or appropriate management there is no final meaning of what offers a fair amount of knowledge added, but one needs to reach operational consensus how to apply fragile standards of judgment. We do not have a Darwinian theory which sustains that only the best forms of wisdom, knowledge and information survive at the frontiers of learning but we observe periods of decline and peaks. More bits yes, but hardly wits. It is not difficult to select particular cases of doctoral dissertations, but very few productive members of the academic community are inclined to generalize outside their own territory. If one generalizes, it leads to balkanization between academic tribes unless one is ready to specify a particular point of view.

The appropriate structure and process of doctoral research is the resultant of strategy or at what quality of knowledge one aims and the environment or the given boundaries of discipline, institution and national system of higher education. It is my persistent belief that the stragegy of the scientific community implies always the frontiers of learning and includes elements of utility, higher knowledge for its own sake, and virtue. It is a careful balance of teleology which is never reached and therefore requires continuous reflection and monitoring e.g. in national academies of sciences. Particularly esoteric subjects without immediate utility and a strong constituency need protection. The environment of scientific communities is a turbulent one. In chapter V I distinguished three interdependent macro forces in the environment: national bureaucracy, academic oligarchy or clan, and markets.

For national governments higher education and science policy has become since the sixties a major issue. In the Dutch case e.g. there seems now to be a political and financial boundary of some 1.9% of GNP for higher education and 1.9% of GNP for research and development activities. Higher education is almost completely dependent on public finance, whereas research and development is a mixture of public and private expenditures. Doctoral dissertations are squeezed within given resources of rather inflexible university organizations with civil service status for faculty members and a variety of research and development organizations. The quest for control leads to standardization of the doctoral structure and process. The first reformers as Minister van der Leeuw and the special commisioner for higher educational reorganization, professor Posthumus, were careful to avoid a uniform pattern of post-graduate education and research, but the tenacious resistance of universities to change resulted in uniform standards of doctoral dissertations derived from a natural science point of view. Completion rates become the critical yardstick. If e.g. Japanese and Chinese studies of language, culture, history and economy require a longer doctorate process, as I think they do, one is forced to accept lower or intermediate stages for completion.

For the academic oligarchy there were two opposing forces in the recent past. One is mainly demografic, the rapidly increasing number of students leading to economies of scale and mass education in standardized curricula with multiple-choice examinations and an increasing distance between teacher and student. The other one is mainly political, the strong demand for participation and democracy in governing universities leading to the abolishment of the senate and the establishment of representative councils, acting as supreme court within an institutional framework and as workers council for their own constituency. A strong central administration has been established controlled by a Board of Management (CVB) partly appointed by the crown, partly selected by councils, and one member, the rector magnificus, representing the senate or the committee of deans. Because universities had lost their credibility, a host of figures and reports are needed for accountability. The familiar case of information costs in protected markets (Williamson, 1975).

The resulting structure is hybrid and hardly appropriate for a clear strategy. The checks and balances within the system prevent innovative decisions: a stalled bureaucracy (Horringa, 1986). The internal structure of participation leads to many meetings on regulation, allocation and remuneration rather than on the strategic mission of universities. The external pressure of attracting as many students as possible and fixed proportional budgets lead to standards based on numbers, participation and completion rates. I expect an increasing gap between the organizational structure of industrialized knowledge production for the many and the organizational structure of innovation at the frontiers of learning for the few. Some members of the academic community seem to have accepted the quest for control also for doctoral dissertations, which need to be produced in a regular fashion. I have expressed my serious concerns with available evidence, but I do not assume to provide comprehensive evidence of a decisive nature.

There are various markets for the university. The labour market for graduates has always played a decisive role, but only recently universities care for employment rates and career patterns of their graduates. It has been frequently a self-fulfilling prophecy. The growth of universities has created an internal labour market, which seems now to be satisfied. For internal academic careers Ph.D's offer restricted opportunities. An oversupply of doctorates is likely to create blocked careers for newcomers from the first four-year cycle. The corporate class or other para-university competitors at the knowledge market offer a major but healthy challenge for the same product. Especially the American and Japanese situation present prime examples and there is no reason why qualified business universities will not be allowed to award Ph.D's given free competition. The European tradition poses more obstacles, but I expect many joint ventures such as the new information university in the Netherlands. Also in the case of the Netherlands School of Economics private initiative has been critical. It is difficult to identify a product market for the university. Traditional centers of learning offer the whole range of knowledge in distinction to the more limited vocational schools. I assume that each national system has to cover the full range of the human heritage, be it at various locations, but that a comprehensive coverage of advanced knowledge is hardly possible within a national system. Indeed an interdependent world of learning, where in any case the so called Third World will present increasingly its claims to free access. For the third cycle of higher education I expect a growing number of candidates from the Third World. American universities are leading, sometimes in a rather unbalanced growth. The political market is becoming increasingly critical for universities. In the Dutch setting e.g. presidents of the board are increasingly selected because of their political network, such as former ministers or key civil servants in order to guarantee free access to policy makers.

The three macro forces -national bureaucracy, academic oligarchy and markets- have a different strength and speed of change. In a macro perspective the Asian ideal type of the appropriate structure of post-graduate education and research is state-oriented originating from the Chinese chin-shih examinations and adopted e.g. by Tokyo University (Todai). It aims at selecting knowledgeable bureaucrats.

The European type of the appropriate structure originates from the academic community, the guild of scholars and the unity of sciences. After a long maturation period in medieval universities, religious wars and the French revolution, the ideals of von Humboldt have given rise to new strategies. 'Einsamkeit und Freiheit' as Schelsky (1963) coined these reforms: the ideal type of a lonely long-distance journey of doctoral fellows free from direct pressure from state and market. 'Der Universität ist vorbehalten, was nur der Mensch durch und in sich selbst finden kann, die Einsicht in die reine Wissenschaft. Zu diesem Selbstaktus im eigentlichen Verstande ist notwendig Freiheit und hülfreich Einsamkeit, und aus diesen beiden Punkten fliesst zugleich die ganze äussere Organisation der Universitäten' (in Becker, 1985, p. 331). Indeed, beautiful ideals of the academic community: knowledge for its own sake, 'Bildung' or virtue, but outside the direct pressure of industrialization and state. 'der philosophische Kopf, against 'der Brotgelehrte'. This was the beginning of the nineteenth century, but these high ideals actually prepared Germany for a successful industrialization.

The American ideal type of post-graduate education and research can be characterized as market-oriented. No central concept or policy, but free competition in building von-Humboldt-inspired graduate schools upon English colleges with strong religious affiliations in a frontier society. Strong presidents, powerful trustees and freedom in structure, fees, remuneration, contract research, consultancy also for the many European immigrants. The end-of-the-century reforms show an enormous vitality which made the American graduate school the envy of the world. No restriction to pure science but open access to any pragmatic cluster of skills and knowledge. Inventing management science and monitoring quality without worrying about epistemological or methodological problems of measurement. There is no American standard, but many indicators for variety in quality.

I expect that at the next end-of-the-century a new type of university will be shaped originating from the three ideal types but distinct in its emphasis on research and innovation. Although it is a semantic question, I assume that the name 'university' will be kept because of historical continuity and dedication to traditional human ideals of life long learning, character building and societal service. The present strong centripetal forces to build disciplinary post-graduate centers around core departments and the strong centrifugal forces to search for new market-oriented multi-disciplinary and multi-national fields of study will break traditional university structures with their compartmentalization in alpha, beta, gamma and life sciences, with their tenure for established faculty members in a clear hierarchy, with their fixed salary structure, institutional immobility, and elaborate consultation at any level. I assume that the contours of this new type of university become visible in new centers for information technology, artificial intelligence, science dynamics, ecology, space sciences, biotechnology, CAD/CAM, intrapreneurial administration. These centers will result from negotiations between business, government and knowledge centers allowing for a variety of mixed financial support schemes and open to representatives of all stakeholders. A future historian might discover many prototypes since the sixties, such as the Club of Rome, the Milano Institute for the Management of Technology and the many new European initiatives as COMMET, Brite, Esprit, Race and ERASMUS, but the momentum for a real breakthrough is yet to come. Rather than speculating about the outlines and contents of such a new type of university, let me try to indicate its possible impact on the three micro elements of post-graduate research and education which I distinguished in chapter I and VI: forum, role and locus.

The traditional academic forum consists of established members of the scientific community, sometimes completed by qualified members of the wider society, and appointed by university authorities according to specific regulations, in the Dutch case the committee of deans. Access is given to candidates with proper qualifications, such as drs., licentiate, diplom, magister, DESS, master, laurea according to national customs, who have finished a manuscript providing evidence of an original and independent contribution to knowledge in a field of study approved by one or more faculty members, called supervisor or promotor. The forum in operation consists of a private or public defense by the candidate of his dissertation. In a closed session, sometimes before and after the defense or viva, the examiners decide whether and under what condition the doctorate will be awarded. In the Dutch situation one needs to agree before the public performance whether the dissertation is acceptable and can be printed. In other situations the examiners specify in how far or with what changes the manuscript may be published. The Dutch forum is the most open, allowing other languages and in principle outside members of the forum, but all universities are to the best of my knowledge open to foreigners given similar qualifications as national candidates. Evaluation studies on how the forum actually operates have not been made. It is part of oral history, but I assume also of a conspiracy of silence. If one invites a number of experienced supervisors to specify their judgment of quality in science (e.g. in Becker, 1985), there is an amazing range of answers and assumptions, but rarely case studies of misjudgment unless in the safe past. In the new type of university I expect a more regular participation of stake holders outside the university. In the Dutch case part-time appointments as extra-ordinary professor or lecturer offer ample opportunities but also participation at an ad hoc basis might be increased. If one keeps the standard of original and independent contributions to knowledge, I assume that doctoral dissertations become integrated in the new on-line information systems. Since 1984 some 800,000 titles and abstracts are available on line, but European doctoral dissertations are heavily underrepresented. Moreover, the problems of measuring, assessing and monitoring quality are similar in existing scientometric exercises. If one is ready to qualify one's judgment, there are pragmatic solutions to measure output and impact against proposals and to differentiate between new and old concepts of doctorates. However, one needs first a clear policy. Data retrieval systems or scientometric exercises are only means.

The European doctorate can play an important role in preparing the future of broadening the forum for multinational and multidisciplinary quality control. Of course, it is a gradual process with a large cultural variety within the European Community. I assume that initiatives from European multinationals are needed to prepare high quality doctoral dissertations or other joint research projects which revitalize a network of European universities. There are actually a number of trustfunds, such as Leverhulme, which support inter-European mobility between universities, but there is no effective co-ordination and common platform for new ventures. Moreover the role of doctoral dissertations e.g. from an English point of view is marginal as far as I can judge. Publication of joint research projects including doctoral work might be a more appropriate entrance.

The traditional role set of students-candidates-apprentices and teachers-masters-supervisors is based on the assumption of life-long careers, where students like to become masters in the same craft. In old English law it was a barrister considered a learner of law till of sixteen years' standing. A person under legal agreement to work a specified length of time for a master craftsman in a craft or trade in return for instruction and, formerly, support (Webster). In this perception of society one has a clear distinction between those who know and are able to judge and those who do not know and are to be instructed and examined. The Chinese examination system during thirteen centuries is a perfect example of such a harmony in inequality according to Confucian ideals. But ideological and cultural revolutions turned this hierarchy upside down. Judges became to be judged, soldiers became generals, scholars were to be instructed by neophytes. Also the Japanese concept of society was and maybe still is based on life long careers where university education sets the entrance conditions in cohorts. The European concept of guild as applied to the university created distinct degrees for academic careers with tenure as a mile stone and membership of academies for lifelong peers of knowledge. Tbe American concept of frontiers (Turner) prevented the formation of a closed world of scholarship and assumed continuous mobility for those who venture whatever their credentials. It is no surprise that the American graduate school in its variation has become the dominant model of present higher education, but one rarely explores the implications of the underlying assumptions of markets.

The future world of learners will still be based on the research imperative or searching for the unexpected. Institutional academic networks include only a small part of potential knowledge entrepreneurs. The Ph.D itself is not an indicator for this potential. Sometimes orthodoxe Ph.D's block career mobility because of its narrow specialization. However, the original concept of providing evidence of original and independent work or new hypotheses challenging dominant paradigms is still valid, if we are able to open disciplinary boundaries. There is something in academia what I would like to call the 'disciplinary illusion', where one assumes that a separate collection of the best economists, sociologists, biologists of whatever one's discipline-of-origin have the potential of boundary-expanding research. Each discipline extends his framework in a formal analysis of encompassing the whole world. Of course, an economist can treat political power as an economic good, scarce and with alternative utilization without leaving his own discipline, but it seems more fruitful to invite a political scientist and read Machiavelli rather than Adam Smith. I assume that many of the traditional disciplines as economy or sociology have overestimated their claims of explaining the world around us. We need solid training in the origin and growth of scientific fields but at the frontiers of learning one looses confidence in original pretensions.

Role flexibility and role reversal seem to me the critical variables of the new type of university, where tenure is substituted by performance and doctoral fellows on sabbatical leave from business or government become part-time teachers. Paid employment might be possible only for half of the working time and job and role rotation are more horizontal than vertical. Competition will be based on the quality of the learning environment rather than on hierarchy. Situational leadership also in the knowledge business requires lifelong boundary-crossing learning. The distinction between fundamental and applied science becomes blurred, but one needs islands of fundamental reflection and research for long term missions. I do not think that one can escape a critical discussion on what is the role of Ph.D's in various careers or whether one has to invent a completely new type of European doctorate. It is of course impossible to sustain an expensive system of a few thousand man hours frequently during odd hours at night, in weekends and holidays without attempting to assess, measure and monitor the quality and impact within the scientific system. Either one has to accept that the doctorate process is random or one has to make judgment calls explicit. The present lack of trust in the academic system cannot be compensated by normative statements of the disciplinary clans without empirical evidence and reflection on the nature of the problem. I do not belief that Ph.D's can survive only for providing the internal labour markets of universities with qualified candidates neither without searching for viable alternatives.

The role flexibility needed for the new 'post-industrial' society requires new divisions of labour in the world of learners. Traditional distinctions between urban and rural, work and leisure, disciplines, religions, political systems and cultures, center and periphery, developed and underdeveloped, rich and poor become challenged and individuals are to be ready for multiple careers. Doctorates by individual research might constitute a network linking separate knowledge communities and maintaining a historical continuity of the unity of sciences. Of course, no magical solution but a useful complement with some proven value.

The third micro-element of locus is the most dynamic. Universities have spread over the world as necessary complement of civilization, industrialisation and nation building. Each university from whatever humble origin tends to extend from two years towards four years and to add its own post-graduate division. The ten thousands of universities of the present time show a rich variety. Each national system recognizes its own center of excellence and this applies also to disciplinary systems. However, center of excellence is a rather loosely used qualification frequently referring to a particular seif-appraisal ranking of importance. Rip (1985) compared scanning and charting of sciences with ecological mapping and questioned the overemphasis of giants or excellency in scientific fields. In ecological systems one needs a balance between 'dwarfs' and 'giants' and it is understood that the giants stand on the shoulders of dwarfs rather than the other way around. In the world of science we tend to disregard the majority of local, service-oriented studies with a particular biotype which do not reach the international journals but actually provide the infrastructure for giants. There are indeed many local universities engaged in service-oriented regional studies and awarding doctorates based on studies with a restricted impact which sustain the world wide community of scholars. Especially in the Third World one needs to build an extensive network of data collecting, descriptive and explorative doctoral studies which are frequently disregarded as primitive by those in international centers of excellence with their access to impressive data bases and documentation systems. However, originality at the frontiers of learning is not restricted to those in the rich environment of well-established universities.

The major challenge in the new type of university seems to me extending the frontiers towards the weak scientific communities isolated from the dominant centers, not only in the geographical sense but also in the scientific hierarchy, such as community studies exploring the informal sector. Doctorates by laboratory research and instruction rather than by field research tend to focus on the highly sophisticated problems of modelling, experimenting and testing with advanced technology and theory. These doctorates increase the gap between scientific communities and their stakeholders in daily life problems. C.P. Snow tells us in his second look at the epigraphic 'two cultures' that he originally intended to title his lecture 'the rich and the poor'. I think it would have been a better title. I have the uneasy feeling that the present emphasis on post-graduate education and training will result in new centers around formal analysis and advanced methodology isolated from the lower levels of mass education and less structured problem solving. Candidates from the Third World might be welcome but not their ill-defined problems of slums, local farmers or informal economy. Take as an example the doctoral thesis of Cleve (1961) on capital formation in the Sudan. It was primitively produced and multiplied in Sudan and oral history indicates that during the defense of his doctoral dissertation he was attacked about the lack of sophisticated analysis. Luckily his promotor, Jan Tinbergen, had a clear sense of mission to refute this criticism. The nature of data does not allow another level of analysis and other models would not be of use for national policy makers. Also in the case of doctoral dissertations about public administration in a Sudanese town and about a kampung in Jakarta, one has to cope with the criticism of description and lack of sophistication. Scientocracy seems worse than technocracy.

I support the establishment of special post-graduate education and research programmes at the edge of science, where one needs special facilities in documentation, technology and physical structure but I am concerned about the scientific ecosystem with high quality arrangements in splendid isolation for the elite and low quality provisions for the more humble, human, descriptive and explorative field studies. I remember how Ackoff told descending with his postgraduates from Wharton School at the hills of Philadelphia towards local slum leaders in order to help them coping with their own problems. Of course, these problems do not fit the models of the scientific elite and are resistant to a tailor made doctoral dissertation design. Data collecting can hardly be programmed but these community projects touch the core of the scientific mission. In that sense I believe in a double focus approach, where one has to concentrate the best available knowledge for long term missions in discovering artificial intelligence but also in coping with problems of poverty and powerlessness. Dual economy or whatever label one uses to describe the gap between rich and poor, lords and servants, learned and dumbs needs to be reflected in the scientific ecostructure with niches for the dwarfs and the giants. I do not know any other solution than networks as in the Open University and the United Nations University, where one can link these opposing trends. Some call it 'the principle of the pendulum', where each quest for control, based on causality and order needs to be balanced with a quest for variety, based on random process and chaos. Indeed the prototypes of higher education reflect allready this duality: a recording tradition assuming that by careful and precise observation of the past one can become a perfect prince of knowledge and a rhetorical tradition assuming that there is no final wisdom but a continuous debate of pro and contra. Each period, discipline and nation has to cope with this eternal dilemma of closing boundaries for rigid experiments and opening frontiers for new ventures. Some natural scientists at the frontiers of learning become even attracted by eastern religions and the old questions of yin and yang or the good and the evil as in Persian religions.

I am reluctant to accept the scientocratic pressure of prestructured and carefully designed doctoral dissertations but prefer a complementary emphasis on open and almost random exploration of hunches without a planned completion or even without an acceptable solution. Failures are even more critical than successes. It is a pity that the history of scientific discoveries selects the giants and neglects the dwarfs. If I could select candidates for centers of advanced studies, I would prefer to keep the balance between highly sophisticated protagonists of formal analysis and highly motivated explorers of deserts or uncharted territory. The interaction itself seems to me the most fruitful, if one can encompass the extremes of the scientific community. The appropriate locus for a doctorate is a university or network of universities where one encompasses the whole range of knowledge. One can make European maps with the historical and present structure of universities. I do not assume that all the 3,600 localities for higher education in the European Common Market are equally fitted for awarding doctorates as I said before (p. 118), but nevertheless most universities need to be connected with post-graduate education and research programmes and, if they have the ius promovendi, they will use this right. In the USA it has given rise to more growth of doctorates in new universities than in the old centers, but one has solved this problem by a regular monitoring and assessment system actually showing the different quality. In Europe I hope that the new European doctorate would give rise to an increase of external examiners who keep the standards of good European practices rather than to a quantitive growth with unequal standards. I might be too optimistic and that means accepting various levels of doctorates and hopefully monitoring the quality. In any case there will be interactive linked post-graduate training programmes as imagined by van Bueren, but this cannot substitute for the highly individual emotional-cognitive writing process of a doctoral dissertation. There are already many study, research and innovation organizations outside the university, which actually support candidates in developing new knowledge. According to national customs, these studies might lead to Ph.D's and the European doctorate might be an attractive proposition for external candidates.

By way of conclusion, I assume that the present quest for control with its standards and formal regulations will move after some period to a quest for variety, flexibility and informal arrangements. In the third cycle of higher education or the final terms of the higher education system history offers impressive examples of such a law of the pendulum. However, pendulum is a too simple movement to indicate the dynamics at the frontiers of learning. Each period, discipline and culture develops through different experiences particular conceptual worlds. Universities and academies reflect these different worlds in their own language aiming at generalization and the unity of sciences. Our period is one of reorientation and renewal. It has been called an age of discontinuity and information explosion. We need shared learning projects where scholars at the edge of science communicate their insights and conclusions to the practicians. Mid-career doctoral dissertations where practicians reflect on their experiences are only one of the possible means of exchange and new syntheses. Doctoral dissertations are completely insufficient if they do not lead to part-time or second careers in universities. I might have focused too narrowly on doctoral dissertations as an expression of final degrees, but I needed an operational yardstick. There are alternatives. The present impact of the corporate class and joint ventures between governments, business and research centers increase the likelihood of intensified communication between the world of learning and the world of practice and application.

There is also a law of unresolvable ignorance or diminishing returns of more information. I wonder whether a comprehensive European data base on doctorates similarly to the American one would have given new insight. Indeed it would have led to impressive statistics of distribution over time, but these statistics do not indicate what value has to be attached to doctoral dissertations. One measures what one values, I assume. Knowledge of the doctorate system has an impact on its operation. I have come to the conclusion that a clear strategy on what are the final terms of higher education is more important than the existence of comprehensive data bases. Because there is no universal solution of what higher education needs to offer in its final terms, it seems only possible to start a case-by-case and projectwise approach for specific purposes. My own rather broad explorations of the history, culture and function of third cycle higher education are of course highly insufficient for covering the whole field in depth and scope but might stimulate a more fundamental discussion on specific issues than the present quest for control indicates. Hopefully the three macro elements, state bureau-cracy-market-clan, and the three micro elements, forum-role-locus, offer some hinges to search for means to broaden the forum, to differentiate roles and to design more integrated networks. There is an intrinsic quality and vitality in advanced higher education or exploring frontiers of learning which is at the root of human civilization and its heritage. Any concerted effort to extending these frontiers and to share learning experiences between disci-plines and cultures is welcome.

Chapter VIII

The Third World

The fundamental questions about the mission of higher education and its operational expression in doctoral dissertations as raised in the previous chapters become more acute and pointed, when looking at the explosive expansion of universities in the so called Third World. What is the contribution of Ph.D's for development? It would be foolish to generalize about universities or post-graduate education and research in the Third World, because historical evidence, cultural differentiation, functions, life chances and the macro pattern of state bureaucracy, market and academic oligarchy have led to much more variation than in the so called First World. Moreover, universities in the Third World are in transition and there is a much wider choice of all possible permutations of final degrees than in previously developing countries. I prefer therefore to present a selective view on the Ph.D phenomenon with some case studies within a rather exploratory framework of development. My main purpose is to elicit some strategies for shared learning between the various worlds at the level of post-graduate education and research.

Heterogony

There is an institutional paradox in university building in the Third World. The noble objectives of spreading universities over developing countries have led to dramatic disturbances of the ecostructure of traditional knowledge, scholarship and well being. Lambers selected heterogony as derived from the German psychologist Wilhelm Wundt as his key concept in his farewell lecture, when he formally retired as professor at the Erasmus University Rotterdam (1981). In many discussions and joint ventures in coping with industrial conflicts and in supervising doctoral dissertations I have learned from him that there is a fundamental human discrepancy between noble intentions and disturbing outcomes, particularly at the institutional level. In one of the major industrial conflicts around the proposed closure of four factories in a new multinational chemical-textile conglomerate we were both appointed in a commission of external experts. It was actually a case where the nature of decision making on the basis of economic and technical rationality seemed to be incongruous with the social economic condition of plants with their own history of labour relations. During one of the frequent intensive fact finding missions at the headquarters of the company I was phoned by the rector magnificus of my university asking whether I would propose a 'cum laude' for a doctoral dissertation which had been approved and was to be defended in a few weeks time. I consulted him as a senior colleague and regular chairman of doctoral promotion committees. He explained the subtle balance of judgment of quality and the importance of a constraint view. I came to the conclusion that an acceptance of a doctoral dissertation as offering evidence of an original and independent contribution to knowledge is allready more than satisfactory. Although I am sometimes particularly impressed by the high quality, I remain reluctant to add special distinction. The Anglosaxon attitude of specifying one's qualification seems to me more appropriate than trying to differentiate grades in doctorates. The fundamental problem of Ph.D's for development seems to me that one has to start with the research and knowledge community at the local or national level. In the field of higher education this means in action terms: 'a heart-searching critique, an imaginative consolidation, lion-hearted planning for growth, a readiness to face the shockwaves of change, a dramatic breakthrough in strategies of investment and implementation, a rigorous attempt at institution building and organization development, and a massive effort at social engineering and transformation of attitudes' (Bharadwaj, 1974). The creation of local research material and a local network of researchers is essential. Despite the low status at the level of the international research community there is no other way than fact-finding in one's own situation. Abstract or foreign theories are not the measuring rod for quality but the contribution of doctoral dissertations to the existing knowledge community with its isolation and lack of sophisticated equipment and reliable data. I don't see any reason why an independent and original contribution to an existing thinly spread network of scholars, professionals and policy makers is not equally valid as a similar contribution to established centers. Perceptual development and categorizing are essential for decision making. If there is variation in perceptual learning and categorizing because of history, culture and environment, it follows that the creation of learning material in the form of doctoral dissertations cannot be wholly deduced from the dominant paradigms. The role of universities and multinational supervisory networks is then to stimulate, support and nurture this learning process under given conditions of constraint and to offer comparative evidence when it becomes relevant.

Actually my experiences with doctoral candidates in developing countries have made me sensitive to the dominance of scientocracy in deciding what are the criteria for quality outside one's own domain. There is an autonomous tendency in scientific communities to establish a hierarchy based on the level of formal analysis and abstraction, whereas applied and development studies require down-to-earth descriptions and interpretations of what actually happens. Heterogony seems to me a useful concept to describe the discrepancy between intended objectives and unexpected results because of wrongly selected means. In itself 'heterogony' is only a solemn concept from Greek origin to describe an outcome from foreign origin. In the biosphere it might lead to new variations and also in the noosphere. It is not by definition obnoxious. In the particular case of doctoral dissertations or post-graduate education and research one can observe a special type of heterogony. The nature of 'technical assistance' and 'development aid' is from Western origin, especially from the post-war European economic rehabilitation programme, the Marshall plan. Only recently scholars from less-developed countries have contributed to the conceptual framework of development studies. They argue that the alien elements which have been introduced into the subject from the outset have led practitioners into the wrong paths. One has to start all over again from a more eclectic conceptual framework accepting the definition of the situation by the original stakeholders. Moreover, scholarships for the revered institutions in the Western world were mostly offered as a reward to those close to the powers-that-be. This elite group had sometimes a limited commitment to the problems at the grass-root level. It has been observed that their choice of a field of research work was frequently influenced by the ease with which research materials can be gathered and the acceptance by foreign professors rather than by the urge to solving any particular social problem at home (Supachai Panitchpakdi, 1981).

One has to analyse the special characteristics of a scientific community in a particular country to discover what is a relevant and independent contribution to knowledge rather than establish an international, that is a Western set of criteria. In some cases there is a bureaucratic fragmented structure of universities and research institutes, which have grown as counterparts to Western institutes and donor agencies. There is a lack of flexibility and linkages (Beers, 1971, Peres, 1979). Usually researchers are underpaid. The lack of fnancial incentives for research work forces them to moonlight to the extent that can block their pursuing of research lines. There is frequently a distrust in common sense and lack of appreciation of their own history and destiny as a result of colonial dominance in the past. Foreign textbooks have an almost magical meaning. Formulae are quoted blindly and case studies in other societies are accepted as the ultimate truth. The traditional reverence for a national 'guru', 'sensei' or other respected teacher has given rise to rigid programmes of thought without challenging the assumptions. There is a low societal respect for academic knowledge as an independent source of action. In order to be successful, academic researchers have to enter the bureaucratic polity. Quotations of those actually in power are accepted as principles of thought and action. It is sometimes dangerous to refer with too much emphasis to interesting lines of thought of indigenous scholars. Jealousy easily arises and academic success can only be rewarded by positions of bureaucratic power.

Presently there is an awareness of the need for much more radical changes in post-graduate research and education for the new generation. Reliance on foreign aid projects or on research programmes in Western universities is misleading. The North-South dialogue is in a deadlock. The new generation of the intellectual elite shows increasing interest in the cultural and ideological heritage of their own country. Especially in South East Asia a new thrust seems to awake. Of course, this is a personal reflection, not a new theory. I do not like to generalize but prefer to identify in a pragmatic way relevant post-graduate research projects which are embedded in the institutional and societal rationality of each country and region. This search for relevant or, if you like more homogonous, post-graduate programmes requires interpersonal networks between universities within available institutional and governmental arrangements. It is a highly pragmatic exercise where problems and qualified, motivated graduates and supervisors need to be linked rather than launching again another new institutional framework. I have seen only successes if there were supportive interpersonal networks and mainly failures, if there were detailed institutional arrangements at the top level. Universities are an inverted hierarchy especially in post-graduate programmes. Moreover, it is rather healthy for faculty members in established universities who complain or have to cope with drastic changes to be confronted with the much more fundamental problems of universities in transition in developing countries.

History

The proto-types of higher education in non-western countries do not seem connected with modern post-graduate education as shaped in Germany and gradually acculturated in various Western countries. The Japanese hybridization seems the most successful: starting as a disciple of China, carefully selecting a period of distance learning through Dutch intermediaries, plunging in the 1860's into the full translation phase of its meeting with the West, expanding the Tokyo Imperial University concept at an undergraduate level after a brief pilot experiment with a graduate school, and only recently building its own post-graduate university system, balancing between equality and selectivity, harmony and competition, private and public entrepreneurship. Nakayama's interesting analysis of Japanese academic and scientific traditions indicates, however, that the institutional framework has yet to be integrated with new paradigms of scholarship and science. The present proposals to attract some 100.000 students from overseas for the next turn-of-the-century are lofty, but I assume that post-graduate education has first to become a national 'mondai' (recognized problem) before the Japanese model can offer real alternatives. There is no monitoring system to the best of my knowledge how successful are Japanese post-graduate students in American and European universities. I am still greatly amazed how Japanese employers select their post-graduate employees for overseas studies without intrinsic interest in the quality of learning but mainly in the institutional status. There are of course exceptions (Thurley, 1985). The Japanese case of post-graduate research seems to me still rather heterogonous, not only in the Western world but also in other parts of Asia by its extreme emphasis on conformity to standard regulations and discipline rather than on creativity, originality and openness for other cultures.

The origin and expansion of Indian universities since the Calcutta University Commission (1917-1919) do not seem connected with Texila and other 'universities' in the third century before Christ. A recent discussion with professor P.M. Agarwala (Oxford and Harvard educated) informed me that the rise of young Indian Ph.D's (25-30 year) is not seen in itself as a sign of advancement of knowledge. Also in the symposium on 'Culture and the Merchant' (14-11-1984) at the Royal Institute of Tropical Studies in Amsterdam I got the impression that there is still a type of heterogony even between the Indian universities with some centers of excellence isolated from the grass-root problems of Indian society. As in other formerly colonial countries the university system was seen as an extension from the former empire's universities. In the Indian case the link with the original proto-types was already destroyed before the arrival of the English. The Indian elite has followed an Oxbridge tradition since 1860. Presently the whole Indian subcontinent offers a challenging example of advanced knowledge and technology almost disconnected with the grass-root problems of the poor. I am not qualified to judge whether one needs to invent a more integrated concept of higher degrees. In any case comparative studies on English-Indian colonial history and Dutch-Indonesian colonial history seem promising. I assume that one needs more fundamental and detailed studies to discover the archeology of knowledge.

In the Arab world and its expansion through Islam scholars and missionaries the old university of Al-Azhar is still an important center of learning, but it does not easily fit in modern advanced higher education. Discussions with experts as Abdurrahman Wahid (Al-Azhar and Bagdad educated and chairman of Nahdatul Ulama in Indonesia) and with Islam doctoral fellows reveal a fundamental problem of connecting modern advanced learning systems with the traditional wisdom of the Islam. In the Indonesian case there is the special origin of the Islam as a major religion of the region only from the thirteenth century in the context of the Sufi movements. The early Sufi Kingdoms adopted their religious and cognitive orientation probably from regions such as present-day Bangladesh, rather than from Arabia proper. In any case the introduction of the Islam took place after its remarkable impact on Western scholarship and in a mystical shape (in Gunatilleke, 1983). Moreover, in the Javanese case the Islam interacted with Hindu-Buddist traditions. Ray Ghose, working on a Ph.D for the university of London about the history of the Asian region, mentions that I-Ching, a Chinese Buddhist monk of the seventh century A.D., recommends the University of Palembang for anyone interested in Buddhist philosophy (in Kaleidoscope, vol. IX no. 1, 1984). The first Islamic University in Indonesia opened its doors only on July 8, 1945 as the last gesture of generosity of the last Japanese overlords to their Muslim subjects on Java (Benda, 1958). This is a very inadequate view on the history of Arab and Islam higher knowledge but sufficient to emphasize the special nature of heterogony.

The two volumes on Higher Education and Social Change published in cooperation with the International Council for Educational Development (1976, 1977) present an impressive cross-section of higher education's approaches to problems of development. The time has passed when hurried, short term inquiries by Western educators, scholars and researchers suffice. To advance the frontiers of learning is rather a recent function of universities. Historically, most universities in the Third World are transplantations from the West without roots in old national traditions. This origin has created a high degree of heterogony. In pragmatic terms I have come to the conclusion that doctoral dissertations need to include some historical introduction of the nature of the problem and some history of local or national knowledge about the problem or national science history. Of course, this does not prevent heterogony, but it makes the doctoral candidate at least aware of the linkage between the past heritage, the present state of the art, and the gap between national scientific communities and international centers of excellence. The European expansion in the Third World has created a heterogonous level of higher education reflecting the colonial traditions of European countries, such as the UK, France and Holland. It will take considerable effort in the archeology of the noosphere focused on specific regions and periods to trace indigenous traditions of scholarship and to link them with advanced learning, but no national system can survive on 'borrowed' knowledge.

Culture

The cultural differentiation between branches of learning and ecological niches in the Third World seems particularly poignant. At first sight natural sciences and international professional circles as finance and business seem to escape the constraints of national and local culture and the same applies to industrialization, but there is a remarkable paradox in the social implications of scientific concepts and their ramification in international business and industrialization at the grass-root level. The gap between folk knowledge or daily experience at home and different types of advanced knowledge is considerably larger than the similar dichotomy in industrialized countries. The Western beliefs of the Enlightenment that advanced learning, knowing, understanding and thinking 'civilize' are rather naive. Also the assumption that cultivation of human minds and spirits leads to the foundation of a good and economically productive society and that advanced education is a means to a better society cannot be maintained. Frequently universities and their postgraduate extension become mere qualification-earning institutions, diploma mills, ritualistic, tedious, suffused with anxiety and boredom, destructive of imagination and curiosity (Dore, 1976).

Let me briefly review some national cases. The Japanese business world shows an intensive interest in history and culture in the broad sense. The remarkable publications e.g. by the Mazda concern on the Japanese process of modernization and the people's culture from Kyoto to Edo (1985, 1986) are excellent examples of this concern. I remember vividly how a president of a plant for the most advanced textile machinery showed me his personal corner with the production of iron gates according to traditional craftsmanship. Also Matsushita's post-graduate center for government and management links traditional skills of tea ceremony and flower arrangements with modern knowledge. The Japanese concept of science allows an interdisciplinary approach, but the new youth culture seems to create a much more instrumental rationality. The Indian post-graduate excellency in modern science and technology seems almost unrelated to people's culture at the grass-root level. Also modern universities in Arab countries seem islands in splendid isolation without visible connections with people's concerns. The two core themes in post-graduate education are the famous convergence and divergence debate and whether cultural variation enriches or hinders international transfer of knowledge.

The university as the bearer of culture in the Third World faces serious dilemma's. Frequently the university is one of the destructive agents eroding traditional society. Graduates tend to be scorned for their lack of social conscience, their desire to get rich quick, and their lack of responsibility in dealing with their clients (Lewis, in Thompson, 1977, p. 57). The craftsman in countries that have a tradition of fine handicrafts, especially in Asia, are guided by a code: pride in the craft, honest workmanship, honest dealings with the client and perfect quality. However, the new class of graduates do not have a traditional code and it is no surprise that many developing countries impose some form of national service on all university graduates. I am particularly in favour of some type of service research as suggested by Nakayama.

If I had to make a list of criteria by which to judge the quality of post-graduate candidates, ethical criteria as societal concern, commitment, dedication and integrity would be as high on the list than purely intellectual qualities. Even humility, although not a particularly operational yardstick, would get priority above superiority. Soedjatmoko (in Thompson, 1977, p. 535) stresses the need for fundamental structural university reform and suggests a shift from discipline-oriented to a problem-oriented structure. Since his appointment as rector of the United Nations university he has emphasized again and again the fundamental nature of this reorientation. Of course, one needs rapid industrialization for external self-reliance, access to the most recent advances in science and technology, and a viable new international economic and monetary system, but also a sense of moral direction, cultural continuity, self-image, and identity as a nation. It is particularly this duality of objectives – one internal well-being by a careful balance of communal values and the other external independence by access to the real sources of wealth, power and intelligence of industrial countries – which makes the structure of university systems problematic. In any case Third World countries need their own post-graduate system of higher education of compatible quality, but it cannot be a copy of Western models.

Function

The role of universities in developing countries is much broader than in industrialized countries and so is the function of a Ph.D. The first generation of Ph.D's awarded in foreign countries and other graduates had the immediate responsibility of entering public service and key positions in business and industry. Their contribution to university building could be only extensive and at the textbook reproducing level without opportunities for advancement of knowledge. There are still full-time teachers in the university system and other professionals who are longing to complete their own career with a doctorate, particularly in the Dutch tradition. Life chances from a Third World perspective seem to indicate a late development effect at the collective and individual level. Actually the first generation of graduates who studied usually in the universities of former colonial powers have been instrumental in the struggle for independence. They had a clear sense of mission. Presently there is a second generation of post-graduate candidates with a different set of expectations.

It should be realized that as the median age of the population in many developing countries goes down, the social pressures exerted by an increasingly larger youth cohort with undergraduate degrees on jobs and careers will make early retirement policies in a number of areas inevitable. Preparing for a two-career life, for government civil servants especially, will require extending university facilities and offering post-graduate opportunities. Moreover, post-graduate higher education, the very top of the learning ladder, sometimes finds itself at the bottom of the hierarchy when considering priorities in educational spending. Many developing countries have build an extensive educational system, frequently with more universities than available staff and budget could allow. Psacharopoulos (1980) showed that university expenditures in developing countries increasingly move to an emphasis on technical and vocational subjects leaving advancement of knowledge outside their budget which at average tends to be 20% of total educational expenditures.

What is the nature of post-graduate education and research in developing countries? We have to accept, I assume, that the first cycle of higher education increasingly becomes standardized, or if you like industrialized with a clear division of labour and intensive teaching and examination loads. The growing supply of secondary school leavers and the enormous demand for graduates after e.g. a four year curriculum will lead to economies of scale frequently within the same budget. For some qualified professionals such as medical doctors, lawyers, engineers and accountants, one cannot but accept an extension of the study in order to qualify for professional standards. There is no standard solution for the third cycle of higher education but one has to analyse the particular configuration of market, state bureaucracy and isolated academic communities searching for opportunities and projects. I expect that only a projectwise extension will be possible for doctorate projects, after approval and within given budgetary constraints. This will lead to one or another form of special post-graduate programmes frequently with sponsorship of technical aid agencies and scholarships in industrialized countries, but also increasingly as the knowledge or training components in major industrial or ministerial projects.

Multinational Post-graduate Projects

Whether and how post-graduate higher education in industrialized countries has to adopt specific features in curricula, academic requirements, and facilities for graduate students from developing countries depends on the particular mixture of foreign policy, economic opportunities and development aid. In the Dutch case the government established in 1950 a special programme for 'international education' particularly geared to developing countries. The original reasons were rather pragmatic:

(a) Educating fellows of the United Nations (selected foreign officials and experts) in the Netherlands promotes Dutch science and industry;
(b) Sending Dutch experts for missions of the United Nations and for consul-

tation to less-developed countries might create Dutch export opportunities;

(c) Supplying job opportunities for Dutch international civil servants after the loss of Indonesia (van Ravenswaaij, EPIO, 1984).

Presently there are 18 international educational institutes and programmes catering for some 1400 students and fellows from developing countries and supported by 2,4% of the budget of development cooperation (some 100 million Dfl. in 1984). A similar percentage (2,4%) of educational assistance to development is allocated in the UK, Ireland and Sweden (EPIO, p. 23). Some are degree-awarding according to the English system, such as M.A. and M.Sc. and the Ph.D is in preparation in the Institute of Social Studies in the Hague. Recently a federation of all international education institutes and programmes has been established (FION). In comparison to foreign students in Dutch regular higher education (from 4,7% in 1955 it decreased to 1,1% in 1980) this is a substantial contribution. Moreover the Dutch amalgation of international education has a much more pragmatic structure, it includes company-sponsored fellowships and programmes, offers programmes in an appropriate international language mainly English, it differentiates periods of instruction and field studies, it offers housing facilities, language courses and other supportive arrangements, in sum, it is more tailor made for the specific needs of fellows from developing countries than the regular higher education system.

The recent Evaluation Project for International Education, which was commissioned by the Dutch government, in particularly the Ministry of Development Cooperation, delivered in three years time a number of documents weighing no less than seven-and-a-half kilos. The original argument back in 1950 was pragmatic and stressed the language. It does not make sense first to have to struggle for a year to learn Dutch, in order then to be able to follow a course of study that by international standards is extremely long and does not conform with either the Anglosaxon or the French system. Presently, Dutch higher education has become more compatible to international standards in a four-years programme. For post-graduate programmes the foreign language argument is still critical, but not for those who like to get their first degree in Dutch universities. I consider language also of relatively small nations an important asset. Throughout the world there are some 30,000 people who have completed a study programme of International Education. The major contribution of this evaluation project seems to me a concerted effort to develop a central data retrieval system or monitoring system, where field studies in developing countries, follow up of former fellows, quality of teaching and research become linked to strategy and management. Unfortunately, as many evaluation efforts the stakeholders were happy with one of the conclusions that the International Education

System merits being preserved and strengthened, which was accepted by the parliament. Other critical remarks about the lack of research, the lack of coordination between ministries and business, the extreme fragmentation of development efforts, and the need for continuous evaluation were disregarded. The team with its valuable experience was discontinud at the end of 1985.

International trends

It is of course possible to describe in more detail the origin, development and impact of Dutch international education as a particular aftermath of the colonial period and experience but it is better to refer to the original documents of the EPIO project for those who are interested and to concentrate on trends in other industrialized countries. I will be rather selective and emphasize some fundamental issues.

1. *Japan* prepares receiving 100,000 overseas students at the beginning of the 21st century compared to the 12,410 in 1984, establishment open international universities and introducing English post-graduate programmes for foreigners. There is a majority of students from Asia (82,2%). Approximately 10% of the total overseas students will be supported by the ministry of Education Science and Culture. By the year 2000 about 30% of the intake will be at the graduate level while undergraduate level is not expected to change very much. The fundamental problem for Japanese higher educations seems to be clear definition of post-graduate education and research and especially a guarantee of quality for Ph.D's who presently are given more freely to other Asians than to the Japanese because of expectation rathet than because of merit. Moreover, the particular nature of other socio-economic and intellectual cultures poses some unsolved problems. I expect that Japanese continue to go abroad for studies. In the USA some 1,568 Japanese got their Ph.D between 1920–1974. European figures are lacking, although Mombusho specifies the number of candidates admitted in Europe countries, but not how many complete their degree. Moreover, the presumably large flow of Japanese business students is not included. Doctoral degrees itself are rather unimportant from a Japanese perspective, but post-graduate research and education are critical. The main changes are expected to take place in the private, non-chartered sector. Besides the Japan Foundation with its, emphasis on improving the Japanese image abroad and on Japanese language and culture and the Assocation of International Education the main thrust will be in search assocations and joint ventures in the Japanese multinationals (Takayima, 1985; Proceedings Japan-USA business conference, 1983).

   If doctoral degrees become accepted as an international passport to scholarship, I expect a much more fundamental discussion by the Committee on Student Exchange. Japan will never move to a strong market-oriented higher educational system as in the USA, but try to strike a balance between the various macro forces within Japanese society and its international position. Traditionally, selection by entrance was seen as more important than individual completion and performance, but individual selectivity and variety become increasingly more critical. There is a high regard for information, knowledge and scholarship in Japanese society and science. The 100,000 foreign students in the year 2000 and the returning Japanese scholars from foreign universities (only some 250 get a Proceedings, 1983). In the field of management and administration one feels that the leader should realize the natural order of the universe. However, actually there is an increasing emphasis on the development of pragmatic business leaders rather than scholars or researchers (Noritake Kobayashi, in Proceedings, 1983). The major gap seems to me between the world of science, technology and development with its emphasis on the content of learning on the one side and the world of higher education with its emphasis on the process and ritual cultivation of learning. The discrepancy between institutional form and content or paradigms of learning as perceived by Nakayama (1984) seems to me the core. Doctoral degrees belong to the form, not the content. The impressive statistical abstracts of Mombusho present a host of data, but are devoid of the meaning of e.g. a doctoral dissertation or the so called 'old' and 'new' doctorate. There is also no distinction between what is seen as vocational post-graduate higher education and what is seen as scientific post-graduate higher education and this I consider a healthy contribution. One rarely meets Japanese who consider themselves as the excellent lords of a specific scientific domain.

Finally, it is rather surprising to discover the United Nations University in the middle of Tokyo with an amazingly wide network in the Third World but rather isolated from the Japanese world of higher education and science. The 100,000 foreign students in the year 2000 and the returning Japanese scholars from foreign universities (only some 250 get a Japanese government scholarship to study abroad and some 350 are grantees from foreign government scholarships in 1982, whereas private students are not registered) make an uneasy balance for internationalization of higher education. I assume that one needs to define what is the mission of post-graduate higher education for development.

2. The Federal Republic of *Germany* has about 70,000 foreign students as present with a remarkable mixture of development aid and immigrant labour with certain discrepancies at the level of the individual professor and institutional inhospitality, cold and anonymous to the average foreign

student (Roeloffs, in OECD 1985). There is a restrictive tendency in the general immigration policy and a general support for international exchange frequently as part of development projects. The technical university of Stuttgart started in 1984 a two-years Masters program in Infrastructural Planning especially for graduates from the Third World and taught in the English language (OECD, conference, 1985). The International Institute of Management, founded in 1970 as part of the Wissenschaftszentrum Berlin is an excellent feeding centre for interdisciplinary social science research into problems of mutual concern to government, employers and trade unions (Sorge, in Takamiya, 1985).

Germany is the cradle of the doctorate. I have seen impressive sociological studies on the comparison between West- and East-Germany in terms of intellectual elites as measured by doctorates (Voigt, Belitz-Demiriz, 1986) and on the special contribution of the around 1,000 Habilitations in West Germany. There is an enormous range of study centers and data collecting agencies in the field of higher education. The German Academic Exchange Service (DAAD) is one of the most effective academic agencies for foreigners with many branch offices, whereas the Goethe Institutes are world-wide centers for German culture and language. However, I have the uneasy feeling that the present meaning of a doctorate – an independently written scientific or scholarity dissertation for which two to four years are needed as a rule after the first degree, and an oral exam (CEC) – is so different in various institutes and departments (Fachbereich) that it has lost its meaning for an original contribution to knowledge. Higher education institutions are authorized by law to administer examinations leading to higher education degrees, such as Diplom, Magister and Doktor. Some teachers' colleges offer courses of study leading to a degree as Diplompädagoge and provide an opportunity to take a Ph.D in either philosophy (Dr.Phil.) or education (Dr. päd.). There is also a MA, meaning Magister Artium mostly in arts and humanities subjects. Discussions with German colleagues usually lead to complaints about the present quality and the rather independent nature of each Promotionsordnung in faculties or departments. Central issues seems to be 'Bildung' and the amazing variation between and within universities, Hochschulen, Fachhochschulen, Gesamthochschulen each with their own degrees. This observer at least could not come to conclusions about a specific German pattern of post-graduate education and research or the meaning of a doctorate. Statistical exercises about distribution or trends in doctorates seem to me rather dubious. The fundamental problem seems to me that there is no central authority in higher education, a loss of historical continuity and a gap between the excellent Max Planck research institutes and normal higher education.

In the past Germany has been an exporter of Ph.D's, whereas presently many Germans seem to go abroad for post-graduate studies. I don't have figures. In the relation with the USA there has been a change according to available evidence. In the 'Century of Doctorates' it is recorded that some 2,000 Germans got their doctorate in the USA since 1920, whereas 10,000's Americans previously went to German universities for doctoral studies. It would need special studies to discover this changing balance of post-graduate studies.

3. The *French* policy traditionally emphasized the importance of foreign students to export French culture and language (e.g. Weisz, 1983), but in 1981 a policy emerged from the objective of enriching French culture with what the immigration civilizations could contribute. University should not be a mould of settled views but a place where ideas are confronted and cultures of origin do not merge but provide a fresh broadening of outlook for all. There are 106,000 students from the Third World, of which 74,000 from Africa. Numbers enrolled in the third cycle are rising, but falling off in the first cycle and holding steady in the second cycle. Over one-third of students in the third cycle are foreign. The importance of the French language is seen as a major asset. The Ministry of Education urged in 1982 vice-chancellors that a genuine policy of hospitality must include accommodation, tuition support, integration into the life of France and concern how the student will fit back into his country of origin.....The presence of foreigners in your institutions should be a source of enrichment for all our own students. Most academics accept an average of 13 to 14 foreigners per 100 students (OECD, 1985).

There is an impressive number of special arrangements for foreign students and especially from developing countries. University services for foreign students (SUEE) beginning to provide personalised reception, training senimars in information and counselling, language improvement systems, even 'a la carte' training for homogeneous groups expressed by foreign countries in joint missions, and assessment instruments, such as success rates and records of former trainees and students. A liaison bulletin is being prepared to organise meetings abroad between former students who have become professionals.

Also the famous distinction between grandes écoles and universities does not offer obstacles. Presently the doctoral studies reform (stage III) placed different doctoral courses under one system (doctorat de troisième cycle, doctorat d'Etat, diplôme de docteur-ingé), consisting of two distinct levels of scientific recognition:
- A national doctorate recognizing research aptitude and extending over a period of three to five years, of which the first year involves an initiation to research concluded by the DEA (Diplôme d'études approfundies);
- The second level is characterized by the 'habilitation à diriger des

recherche', a certificate recognizing the holder's ability to conduct research, and conferred on the candidate's overall academic work. The habilitation entitles its holders to be directors of research and candidates for professorships. It seems to be more for internal use.

The new French structure of post-graduate education and research seems to be based on a clear vision. There is an emphasis upon attracting more overseas students and one is perhaps more aware than elsewhere of the long-term benefits which may accrue to a nation by attracting post-graduate studens from Third World countries. The overall number of foreign students is expected to rise to some 13% or 14% of the overall university population, mainly from developing countries. However, I have some difficulty in understanding the internal dynamics of the French post-graduate structure and especially the ranking in terms of excellency. La Monde de l'education provides regular comparative statistics, but a data base on doctorate programmes as in the USA is lacking to the best of my knowledge. According to American sources, some 1,000 French students got their doctorate in American universities, but also in this case it would need special studies to make a balance of post-graduate studies. The major attraction of French higher education for foreigners seems to be in the field of literary disciplines (some 60%, according to EEC figures).

4. The *United Kingdom* higher education system has an impressive record in extending its services over the former empire and commonwealth. The origin of the Ph.D in 1917 is directly related to this explicit concern (Renate Simpson), although the English prefer to offer students from overseas high-quality courses of comparatively short duration rather than stimulating long Ph.D journeys. In 1984 e.g. 124,000 students (not including EEC nationals) were granted leave to enter the UK and 65,924 overseases students were given extensions of stay. Since 1980, the subsidy received by British higher education institutions to cover difference between fees and actual cost was gradually withdrawn for overseas students. The present 35 per cent of overseas students among post-graduates is actually a reduction, because of the increased fees. There are centers of excellence as Cambridge which restrict the number of UK candidates to some 25% for higher degrees in order to allow a world-wide mixture of scholarship and forsake quantitative growth despite the high fees (Meeks, 1985). There are many government support schemes for overseas students. In 1984-85 over 16,600 overseas students were assisted under Government and British Council schemes at a cost of £75m.

The English concept of higher degrees does not make a clear distinction between the second and third cycle of higher education. One usually registers for a higher degree, which might become a master's or doctor's depending on the qualifications. There essentially is no labour market for

Ph.D's in the English system and it makes little sense to try to tailor output to expressed needs of employers at any greatly disaggregated level. One looks for intellectual ability, maturity, breadth of experience, initiative and independence and is rather sceptical about highly specialized Ph.D's (OECD, 1986). It is no surprise that Ph.D's as such are not seen as a marketable asset. I feel inclined to agree with this more relaxed attitude to Ph.D's. Post-graduate training and research can be taken up but preferably not as a natural extension of first degree education. If research directly leads to a Ph.D, one prefers an understatement of its importance and if students are too eagre for presenting a final draft for approval, supervisors seem inclined to suggest some rewriting or new points of view. The English academic community accepted the Ph.D in 1917 only by external pressure and until recently a majority of key academics enjoyed an exemption of Ph.D pressures. Higher doctorates are still possible based on academic work rather than on a doctoral dissertation and one is reluctant to accept a publish or perish syndrome.

According to American data some 2,500 English students obtained a doctorate in American universities up to 1974, a much lower number than the more than 9,000 Indian students who obtained an American doctorate in the same period. Presently the Ph.D seems an accepted English custom, there is public concern about completion rates in the press, overseas students expect a more structured approach, the committee of vice-chancellors and principals is trying to strike a balance between market forces and intrinsic quality, the open university has some 1,000 registered Ph.D students, but there is still a healthy scepticism against Ph.D production. For me the fundamental issue in the UK system seems to be whether one develops the Ph.D as a marketable asset in the production of science or keeps it as a personal alternative for offering evidence of an original and independent contribution to knowledge. I am confident that the Engtish system will continue to keep its distinctive flavour, what makes it so highly attractive.

5. *Outside* the three major German, French and English systems there are equally venerable traditions, such as in the Nordic countries, Italian, Spanish and Portuguese clusters, Dutch and Belgian traditions. Country reports for the Centre for Educational Research and Innovation/OECD and for the Office for Cooperation in Education/European Community contain an impressive amount of details, regulations and interesting opportunities for Third World candidates. Of course, there is in each national system a preferential treatment for post-graduate programmes related to one's own history (including colonial heritage), language, culture and particularly national established interests in the knowledge business. Available documentation shows that most countries are developing new post-graduate programmes for students from developing countries. The

American model seems to be a major source of inspiration. Language is a critical variable and there seems an increase in English-language programmes. In general, post-graduate students are ageing and in some countries one observes that a large proportion are part-time mid-career or early career candidates (OECD 1986). Post-graduate programmes become increasingly project-oriented rather than a natural extension of first cycle higher education. In each case one needs specific information about the key faculty involved within the institutional framework.

6. The *European* University Institute in Florence has been established in 1972. It is the task of the Institute to contribute to the development of the cultural and scientific heritage of Europe in its unity and variety. The studies involve the great revolutionary processes and institutions which characterize Europe in its history and development. They take into account connections with non-European cultures. The Institute provides research students an opportunity to attain a Ph.D (three years programme) or a Master's degree (one-year programme) The major question seems to me, whether this doctorate is a model for a European doctorate not only for inter-European mobility but also for students from outside Europe. Presently the small scale (in 1984/85 157 research students, six of them coming from non-EC countries) and the nature of the research programmes do not suggest such a model A European doctorate seems to me more the result of bilateral and multilateral arrangements between individual faculty members in European universities than that it can be contained within new European institutes. The university does not belong to any particular political domain, but its mission includes a concerted effort to extend the frontiers of learning. Frequently development aid and international cooperation have created a special domain for students from developing countries, but I assume that in the coming decades one needs a new integration. Of course, I support efforts for new inter-university cooperation and I accept the necessity of utilizing available inter-regional cooperation, but the major effort seems to me revitalizing the academic community as it has grown in major universities for international cooperation. This leads in each country and university to a business-like analysis of post-graduate projects. Frequently there is a preferential financial support possible within bilateral or multilateral arrangements, but I expect that post-graduate projects become increasingly part of major industrial or governmental agreements as an attractive alternative in transfer of advanced knowledge and technology. A Ph.D is only a means and one has to compare it with other consultancy and training arrangements. The major advantage is the development of independent scholarship and expertise with some additional societal status.

7. The *American* universities are clearly the most important actors in the creation of Ph.D's as human capital for developing countries. From

1920-1959 more than 12,000 students from foreign universities received an American doctorate of which only a few hundred from the Third World, mainly Asian. From 1960-1969 this increased to 22,000 in a ten years period and increasingly more from developing countries. From 1970-1974 this development accelerated again with more than 23,000 in four years and present figures suggest that this continuous growth is creating concern that certain post-graduate courses are coming to be virtually monopolised by foreign students (OECD, 1986). Global trends of the world of learners (Coombs, 1981) suggest that this exodus for post-graduate education and research will continue with the USA as a leading example. It is expected that in the year 2000 80% of the expanding world of learners will be in less-developed countries. Higher education has grown between 1950-1975 dramatically with enrolments of more than ten times and it seems a normal development that future expansion will take place in the second and third cycle of higher education in search for quality.

These statistics illustrate the magnitude of the invisible transfer of knowledge, but do not touch the fundamental problem of the nature of foreign higher degrees and foreign research experience. One would like to have more insight into the learning process and the emotional-cognitive structure of dissertation writing in a foreign culture. The American situation is highly competitive, market-oriented and pragmatic and one can only speculate about the impact of a particular research style as exemplified in some American universities. Of course, the American practice does not lead to easy generalizations despite some stereotypes. In any case for developing countries there is a need for striking an acceptable balance between import of foreign research traditions from various sources and the gradual development of one's own post-graduate traditions which can never be a copy from abroad. I assume that especially tbe highly individualistic and pragmatic nature of American post-graduate performance might offer an obstacle to one's culture of origin.

Strategies

In a previous publication 'Effective Organization Research for Development (1982) I selected a particular strategy for connecting indigenous learning strategies with post-graduate programmes abroad. The core is a shuttle-service programme of research. The *first* stage consists of intensive local programmes on the identification of relevant problems e.g. by ministries, local administration, business or universities. Post-graduate candidates are selected and senimars are organized with visiting professors to identify, conceptualize and operationalize relevant problems. This leads to preliminary descriptions of projects. The *second* stage consists of offering selected candidates research fellowships in the home university of the visiting professor. In two to four months these preliminary projects become full-fledged designs with definition of units of analysis, sampling, methodology and candidates participate in seminars, tutorials and work on special reading and visiting assignments. The *third* stage consists of a field study in the home country of participants according to the approved design. This requires institutional backing of national institutes and, if necessary, supervision, operational support and back-stopping service. It might be functional to integrate the project in a bilateral or multilateral Technical Aid Project. The duration might be some ten months depending on the design. It will need intermediary stages for reporting and adaptation. The *fourth* stage consists in offering the candidates again fellowships in the university of the second stage for the dissertation writing, data analysis and interpretation. The core are individual tutorial sessions and seminars with other Ph.D candidates. Editing and translation services may be required. The duration of this stage will vary from 5-8 months. The output must consist of solid research reports which satisfy scientific criteria. If satisfactory, the research report leads to a Ph.D either at the foreign university or preferably at a national university.

The basic design of such a bottom up strategy where research candidates in developing countries select their own project and move in intermediate stages with support of a foreign university towards a doctoral dissertation seems solid. The few manuals on doctorate research, which I consulted (David Sternberg, 1981; Howard and Sharp, 1983; Gordon B. Davis, 1977), distinguish similar stages and it is possible to make more detailed arrangements for each stage. However, this bottom up strategy of shared learning between candidates in developing countries and supervisors in industrialized countries does not easily fit the present top down strategy of post-graduate education. The criteria for selecting relevant projects in developing countries are based on the needs and the particular state of scientific communities in developing countries and not on the themes selected by scientific communities or disciplinary clusters in industrialized countries. This raises the fundamental question what is the nature of original and independent research. My own explorations of history, cultures and functions of Ph.D's have made me conclude that higher degrees are only means for stimulating and developing a particular scientific community in its societal connection. One needs to assess first the needs and the state of the art in particular disciplines and problem areas in developing countries rather than starting from some international scientometric comparisons. We need science dynamics in order to select the appropriate balance from the vantage point of a particular developing country.

As an example of such an approach I present the case of Indonesian economic studies. It is no more than a first approximation that needs to be refined. The Indonesian situation shows a remarkable mixture of various scientific schools. I tried to make some profiles from the Indonesian collection of dissertations in LIPI (1981). For humanities, such as literature and philosophy, there seems a clear Dutch dominance, whereas for languages and history the American and Dutch impact are equal. For social sciences, such as law, there is a Dutch orientation, whereas in economics and sociology the American impact has become stronger than the Dutch one. For psychology one discovers an Indonesian development. For natural sciences and applied sciences there is a strong American impact. For medical sciences there is a strong indigeneous development from Dutch origins. It would be interesting to make a balance of post-graduate training and research and to show how the Dutch impact centered around medical, legal and administrative applications with a strong American re-orientation since the fifties gradually moved towards a broader range of post-graduate studies (Australia, Philippines, Japan, W-Germany, France). Presently, a particular style of Indonesian post-graduate education and research is gaining momentum.

The Case of Indonesian Economic Sciences

Proto-types

In Western civilization the origin of economics as a coherent structure of explanations, assumptions and methods in the allocation of scarce resources, is usually attributed to Adam Smith. Around 1750 he wrote moral essays for ladies and gentleman in Scotland. In his 'Theory of Moral Sentiments' (1759) he perceived society as a great, immense machine with harmonious movements. 'Sympathy' functions as the law of gravity in a newtonian cosmology. There is a propensity to truck, barter and exchange which keeps the balance. In his 'An Inquiry into the Nature and Causes of the Wealth of Nations' (1776) this mechanism, the invisible hand, becomes the basis of economics. Another source of economics is the French medical doctor François Quesnay who modeled his economic lifecycle (1758) upon bloodcirculation as described by William Harvey. Quesnay assumed an ideal order of agriculture, trade and industry (J.J. Klant). The literature on the origin of economic ideas is extensive and there are many histories (e.g. Guy Routh).

In Eastern civilization a similar origin of economics as a coherent structure cannot yet be traced. Before colonialization 'Indonesia' belonged to a Southeast Asian archipel in continuous exchange with other civilizations. It would need studies as those by Needham on Chinese civilization to trace the roots of economic ideas in the past. The concept of *pamong praja* offers a reasonable start for an exploration. 'praja' means land, people, and the economy, and 'pamong' is from 'among' which means to guide, to care for, to protect, to guard, to educate, to develop. Pamong praja means therefore 'Custodian of tbe Country'. It already existed in the empire of Majapahit and was well organized under the leadership of Prime Minister Gajah Mada. This empire stretched its power to what are now Indonesia, Philippines, Thailand and Indo-China. The style of leadership can be formulated from the following principles:

1. Tan hana mangua: there is no place for double loyalty. In practice it means that one should not make a distinction between personal loyalty to the superior and organizational loyalty as existing in modern organizations.
2. Hing karsa asung tulada: in front, to give the example. In practice it means that the leader should be the example in everything that concerns the performance of job, duty, mission or work. Regularly there is an 'upacara' (ceremony), where the leader gives his 'amanat' (message): explaining policies, issuing warnings and expressing his expectations.
3. Hing madya manguan karsa: to be amongst the people and from there to stimulate their ambitions/desires. In practice it means that any job, work or duties should be distributed and the authority delegated as far as possible, in such a way that every member of the group can get the opportunity to participate as actively as possible. It means also, that the one who are not involved by the leader have a serious problem. If this problem is not solved in a personal discussion, it may be interpreted as lack of interest.
4. Tut wuri handayani: to influence society, yet at the same time following or observing the path of its development. In practice it means that the leader should trust his subordinates and let them do the job without interference. It is expected that subordinates report to their superior when problems arise and ask for advice 'penunjuk' or his blessing 'doa restu'.

The roots of these leadership principles are so strong that the influence of Hinduism, Buddhism, Islam, Christianity, and modern science are only phenomenal. 'Rukun' is the basic organizational unit meaning familially or communally being together with feelings of affection. Since the Japanese occupation one has divided people into Rukun Tetangga, the neighbourhood unit. It consists of 10-25 families. The role of the elected chairman is very important He (or she) is not a public servant and not paid for services. There are many organizational principles embedded in the proto-Indonesian culture, such as 'gotong-royong' (mutual help), 'musyawarah' (collective decision-making, arriving at a consensus rather than agreement through voting), and 'arisan' (mutual credit arrangements). This is only a brief sketch from Indonesian sources (Atmosudirdjo, Tjondronegoro, Mulyono).

It would need special studies in the field of economic anthropology (E.E. Le clair) to identify how economic relationships are still influenced by these patterns. Especially to understand the large informal sector in Indonesia such studies to link economics with traditional behavioural patterns seem relevant.

Colonial knowledge

With the disbandment of the VOC (the Dutch East India Company) on 31 December 1799, Indonesia became 'a state' in the broad sense of the word. The VOC system before that time was based on political and trade contracts. The company's servants had only to check every time whether the bupatis and other chiefs complied with the provisions of the contracts. Armed troops and Chinese businessmen were the instruments of the VOC. Daendels, doctor of law, served in the French army under Napoleon. In 1808 he was sent by King Louis Napoleon of Holland to organize the defence system of Indonesia against a possible invasion by the English. He improved the postal services and the overall communication system, the administration of finance and the General Secretariat. In 1811 Raffles, Lieutenant-General, ruling on instructions from Lord Minto in Calcutta, wanted to by-pass the bupatis, and instructed the European administrators to deal directly with the village people. He abolished the compulsory delivery-system of export crops by the village people, and replaced it with a new land taxation system, the land-rent system, which in a modified way still exists today in Indonesia. Daendels and Raffles were the founders of the modern Administration in Indonesia. Their ideas were very advanced at that time and therefore hardly viable. There was no well-qualified administrative staff to put the regulations and instructions into operation. Van den Capellen made the first steps in Education and Training of the Indonesian Administration (1819), mainly public administration and regional languages. An Institute for Javanese linguistics was established at Surakarta in 1832, after a study at the Military School at Semarang in 1818 was felt to be inadequate.

In 1843 the Royal Academy at Delft was founded. This was the start of Indology. This field of knowledge was characterized by a minimum of differentiation (LIPI I, 167, LIPI II, 368). It had a strong legal orientation. Only three branches of specialization emerged, i.e. the studies with a dominantly literary-historical orientation, those with a dominantly socio-political orientation, and studies with a dominantly socio-economic orientation. It was in fact a European mode of pamong praja. I will not describe here the various changes in this type of education in Delft, Leyden and Utrecht. In 1942 there were 850 European civil servants who had passed this type of education.

Economic education was in this development part of the Law School in

Batavia (Jakarta). From 1924-1928 J.H. Boeke was the first teacher in economics before he was appointed professor in 'Colonial Economics' at the university of Leyden. He coined the term 'economic dualism'. After Boeke, J. van Gelderen and subsequently G.H. van der Kolff held the chair in economics at the law school in Batavia. After the war the chair was briefly held by D.H. Burger, a former student of Boeke. The discussions between Boeke, van Gelderen, van der Kolff and Burger on the possibilities for Indonesian economic development have exerted a great influence on Indonesian intellectuals, particularly lawyers, who received their university education during the 1930s. However, economics was only a supplement to the main courses in law. Training at the law school was geared to produce qualified lawyers, and in so far as courses were offered in economics, they were only intended to provide the law students with some basic understanding of economics required for their future jobs. According to the LIPI survey, "only an handful could enjoy a full-fledged university education in the Netherlands, such as the Netherlands School of Economics in Rotterdam. People like former Vice President Moh. Hatta, Aboetari, Hidajat, Saroso, and Sumitro Djojohadikusumo were among the few Indonesians who were able to pursue their university training in economics in the Netherlands before the War", (LIPI, II, 1979, 227. See also Sukadji Ranuwihardjo, 1982). However, available evidence shows that 13 Indonesians obtained their doctorate at the Netherlands School of Economics between 1923 and 1945, or almost 10% of the doctorates. I have no figures how many Indonesians studied at the Netherlands School of Economics or other Dutch economic faculties, but if one assumes that only 4% graduates (drs) continue with a doctorate as for the total population of economists, it seems a substantial number. Of course, other assumptions are possible, but it would require a special study.

The Independence Period

The revolutionary period between 1945-1950 is particularly interesting. The guide for the academic year 1949-1950 of the University of Indonesia (Dutch) gives some insight in the new venture of establishing a comprehensive university. The introduction places the 'Universiteit van Nederlandsch-Indië' established in 1940 as a comprehensive structure for all existing institutes of higher education in a wide historical perspective. The design was based on the particular needs of 'Indonesia'. In stead of a rector magnificus as in Dutch universities there would be a president as in European medieval universities (chancellor) or as in modern American universities (p. 6). The Japanese occupation from 1942-1945 destroyed almost everything in the field of existing higher education. Already in January 1946 a temporary university (Nood-universiteit) was officially opened with five faculties and some 200 students. In March 1947 this temporary university was transformed to the

University of Indonesia with gradually nine faculties, 75 professors, 1300 students and located at five different towns: Jakarta, Bandung, Bogor, Makassar (Ujung Pandang), and Surabaya. This new university with its unique structure is explicitly placed in a West-European historical perspective modeled after Paris (1215) with its nations and tribes from all over Europe (p. 2). Indeed, if one reads a recent detailed study as 'The Origins of the University: the schools of Paris and their critics, 1100-1215'(S.C. Ferruolo, 1985), a comparison between the turbulations in medieval Paris and the environment of the new university seems revealing. Also a comparison between the five original Dutch universities and the new Indonesian university is made with the example of promotion rituals (see p. 26).' Internally very progressive but externally strongly conservative institutes'. After a description of these rituals the author remarks that many of these traditional customs have remained in Indonesia. In this period seven academic promotions were held and 18 inaugural lectures, presumably with all the rituals, but only six by Indonesians.

For economics the official opening of the first faculty of economics in Indonesia at 8 October 1948 on Sulawesi (Celebes) offers an insight in the motivations of that time. The first speaker during the official ceremony in the parlement, the president of the University of Indonesia prof. Cense, mentioned the start with an occupational training for teachers in economics in 1947. Makassar (Ujung Pandang) had been selected as a centre of trade and shipping. The second speaker, J.J. Mendelaar the representative of the crown, stressed the objective value of science "Without objectivity there is no future for country and people of Indonesia. Economics more than other disciplines focuses on the reality which is so pregnant visible in the environment..... Economics is a link between theory and practice". The design of this faculty is based on the co-operation between East and West, faculty and students, white, brown and yellow; study material that is the product of universal minds. He warned against a scattering of the rare scientific resources and pleaded for an overall Indonesian policy in higher education and scientific research. (At that time the Dutch government proposed a federal structure for an independent Indonesia). The faculty of economics is not the start of an East-Indonesian university, but an exponent of a general Indonesian idea connecting the various states.

Various other speakers, dr. E.A. Kreiken, Tjokorde Rake Soekawati, E. Katoppo and the first dean prof. J.J. Hanrath, stressed the need for a practical economic education with high standards but without scientific perfectionism. A content analysis of the three inaugural lectures by Hanrath, A.H. Stikker and C. de Heer would indicate the nature of economic studies as programmed at that time.

The actual developments prevented the operationalization of this programme. On the 19th December 1949 the Gadja Mada State University was officially recognized as the first Indonesian university, seated as it was in the capital city which was the center of the struggle of the Indonesian nation during the revolution. It consisted of six faculties with economics under the Faculty of Law. On 30 January 1950 the Emergency Act no 7 created the Universitas Indonesia with Ir. Soerachman as first president. This university was a fusion of the 'Balai Perguruan Tinggi Republic Indonesia' (Higher Education Institute of the Republic of Indonesia) and the Dutch 'Universiteit van Indonesië' with all its branches. It consisted of ten faculties, one being the Faculty of Economics in Makassar. However, the Dutch staff left en masse so that the Faculty of Economics had to close in 1950. (Koesnadi Hardjasoemantri, Leyden, 1981. p. 11).

Period of expansion

The institutional growth of economic faculties shows a remarkable pattern. According to Sukadji Ranuwihardjo (1982) agricultural economics in IPB-Bandung started in 1946 and economics in Hasanuddin-Ujung Pandang started in 1948. Here the transfer of power from the Dutch to the Indonesian government created some discontinuity. In September 1950 a separate faculty of economics was establbed in Jakarta as part of the Universitas Indonesia. The first dean was a professor in law, Sunorjo Kolopaking. In 1951 he was succeeded by professor Sumitro Djojohadikusumo, who obtained his doctorate in 1943 at the Netherlands School of Economics. He was able to recruit qualified Dutch professors and lecturers through his past association. In 1957 Djojosutono succeeded Sumitro. The fourth institutional setting for economics was Sriwijaya in Palembang in 1953. The fifth separate faculty of economics was established in Gadjah Mada, Yogyakarta in 1955.

The period of expansion, as described by Koesnadi for state universities, shows a wide regional scope: Andalas at Padang and Padjadjaran at Bandung in 1957; Lambung Mangkurat at Banjarmasin in 1958; Tanjungpura in Pontianak and Syiah Kuala in Aceh in 1959; Diponogoro in Semarang in 1960; three more in 1961 in Manado, Surabaya and Medan; one in Riau in 1962; six more in 1963; one in 1964 and one more in 1965. These twenty three faculties of economics up to 1965 are part of the explosive uncontrolled increase of institutions of higher education. According to Koentjaraningrat and Harsja W. Bachtiar this quantitative expansion was a reaction against the extremely limited opportunities to achieve social mobility through education during the Dutch colonial period. The staff was usually recruited from available local professionals whose main occupation was outside the university. Moreover, simultaneous to this tremendous increase in the number of economic faculties at state universities, the proliferation of an unknown number of economic studies in private universities occurred. Some of these private universities, for example based on christianity, were better equipped and staffed than many state universities. Some other private universities turned into commercial institutions with profit as the main motive while academic quality was of minor importance. The history of private universities has not been written.

It is therefore understandable, that only six doctorates in economic science were awarded by the Universitas Indonesia, starting in 1954, all of a high quality but without academic distinction (Kumpulan Nama Doktor, UI). Eleven doctorates were awarded to Indonesian economists by American universities, starting in 1960, two in Germany, two as an after-math still in the Netherlands School of Economics, and one in Switzerland. The data don't allow statistical analysis. Compared to the situation before 1945 with 13 doctorates in the Netherlands School of Economics and one in the USA, Azhari in Indiana University (1945), the period between 1945 and 1965 showed a transition towards the American Ph.D. The promotors in the Universitas Indonesia were largely foreigners. Compared to the prewar situation the quantitative expansion of higher education is indeed impressive.

'In 1940 there were only three colleges and no single university; 28 years later Indonesia had 563 institutions of higher education, divided into 40 state universities, 87 colleges for Islamic theology, 236 recognized and registered private universities, and over 200 vocational colleges. Among the 255 state institutions of higher education there are 81 faculties of education, 45 faculties of agriculture, 40 faculties of science and technology, 24 faculties of economics, 21 faculties of law, 17 faculties of medicine, 14 faculties of social-political science, 9 faculties of letters, 3 faculties of psychology and a faculty of philosophy..... Universities became attributes of provinces, like having a provincial budget. Universities came to be regarded as status symbols, regardless of the intrinsic value i.e. the academic status of the institutions. Quite often they were universities in name only'. (Kusnadi, 1981, p. 20).

Economic studies were part of this system. As a discipline it covers in Indonesia a broad field: general economics, business economics, business administration, agricultural economics, and lately also public economics as a variant of public administration. Those studies are housed within the faculty of economics as departments, but also in the faculties of agriculture, industrial engineering and political and social sciences. Moreover, the first generation of economists were heavily drawn into government service so that their involvement at the university became severely limited (Sukadji, 1982, p. 2-3).

Period of reorganization

Since the Basic Memorandum on Higher Education of 1967 the emphasis has been changed from expansion towards consolidation and manpower needs. The policy of donor agencies such as the Ford Foundation, US-AID, the Rockefeller Foundation, the Colombo Plan Programs and World Bank Programs became very strong in the actual development of economic studies. During 1966-1985 I have identified 69 doctorates under the term 'Economics' awarded to Indonesians. The majority (45) by American universities, the next cluster (15) by Indonesian universities, and around nine by various other national systems, such as Philippines (2), France (2) and the others scattered over the UK, Belgium, Japan and the Netherlands (KIDI, LIPI, 1981 and additions). However, I do not know how comprehensive is this collection in LIPI. There is no regulation, as far as I know, for a national collection of dissertations or for a national documentation. It would be possible to extract Indonesian dissertations from the American data bank. In 'A Century of Doctorates' the baccalaureate origins of 1920-1974 Ph.D's are recorded and indicate 243 of Indonesian origin over all disciplines, but other countries lack a similar comprehensive documentation system.

In June 1979 the Minister of Education and Culture issued a fundamental reform bill on higher education. Similar to the French system the minister established three levels of tertiary education:

1. The first stratum (S) is a four-year programme leading to the title Sarjana.
2. The second stratum (S2) is a one and a half to two year programme leading to the title Sarjana Utama, and is supposed to be equivalent with Master or Magister. It is designed as a first stage research degree.
3. The third stratum (S3) is a full-fledged doctoral programme of one and a half to two years leading to the doctorate.

There are also non-degree programmes, popularized as So at the undergraduate level, and Diploma programmes.

At the doctorate level there are two co-existing systems.

1. One requiring an independent and original contribution to knowledge presented to the senate in a public session and prepared with casual consultation of an appointed promotor and sometimes co-promotor. This is usually called the continental system and is of Dutch origin.
2. The other requiring a full course-work Ph.D programme of three or four semesters, a qualifying examination and writing a dissertation under full supervision. This is called the American system.

It is difficult to assess the emergence of an appropriate Indonesian style with available evidence.

Evaluation and perspective.

In terms of forum, role and locus the present Indonesian doctorate is compatible with international practice. The present forum is in two stages, the first private in the form of a comprehensive examination according to American practice and the second in the form of a public defense according to Dutch tradition. One might consider a more sober and less expensive public defense but this is more a social than a scientific problem. The same applies to the levels of distinction. Nowhere I have found an operational definition of originality, quality or relevance. It is somebody's judgment and one needs the proper balance of the forum in terms of external examiner or the principle of avoidance. The regulation that both the rector magnificus and the dean of graduate studies are involved implies a broad range of knowledge. There are no obstacles to the participation of foreign co-promotors or the use of an international language. There seems a broad interest for doctorates in Indonesian society also outside academic careers, but one needs more supportive structures for part-time external doctorate candidates. The tendency to make participation in post-graduate courses obligatory might be counterproductive. The selection of a few (nine presently) postgraduate centers has prevented explosive growth, but one needs more multinational and multidisciplinary links between foreign and national doctorates.

As an empathic observer of Indonesian post-graduate research and training I consider the gradual change from a supply oriented approach, based on available scholarships by donor agencies, towards a demand oriented approach, based on explicit needs and priorities in the Indonesian scientific community, healthy. Particularly in the public service sector I discover many proposals to design post-graduate research and training programmes for their own graduate staff and based on an analysis of operational needs and assessment of capacities. The present concern for unemployment and decreasing budgets because of the low oil prices might stimulate early retirement and second-career opportunities for civil servants rather than multiple jobs. I assume that quality of graduates will become more critical than the increasing quantity.

The balance between vocational and scientific higher education or horizontal and vertical integration has been historically rather skewed to intellectual qualifications mainly because of the Dutch influence. The Teachers Colleges (IKIP) are a particular example, where one might consider more professional qualifications in teaching performance rather than Ph.D's. I assume that operational skills become increasingly more critical than theoretical sophistication. There is in business economics an old debate between the so-called Amsterdam school, associated with Limperg and his normative approach to the 'true' concept of profit; and the so-called Rotterdam School, associated with Nico Polak and his empirical or inductive approach to effective practice. Although this debate is not anymore localized in Amsterdam or Rotterdam, it seems still to touch a real problem of science dynamics. As a protagonist of the Rotterdam School I am strongly in favour of empirical studies and experience in real-life situation as an entrance point for conceptual frameworks, theories or images rather than starting from theories and models and looking for confirmation. The core of business administration consists of practical assignments and problem solving after some classical introduction, which gradually lead to new insights and hypotheses. Brezet's doctoral dissertation in 1986 at Leyden university after decennia as teacher and professional is for me a solid example of a late career Ph.D and at least equally valid as a pre-career Ph.D. His effort in identifying and classifying the operationalization of profit from a micro-economic and business economic point of view is for me a useful guide. A more empirical approach to business practice in Indonesia would be useful for curricula development in Indonesian universities.

The balance between public and private universities is becoming an issue of considerable concern. Presently the top state universities set the standard for other universities, but one needs to allow more alternative and pragmatic efforts in developing tested knowledge in an Indonesian setting. The present interest seems to be in professional degrees in the second cycle, such as the prestigious MBA. However, in the long run one cannot escape a more inductive, case research approach to discover culture's consequences in work-related values and decision making (Hofstede, 1980, 1982). Knowledge cannot be transferred as capital or technology. It requires a long process of creation, adaptation, maturation and utilization at the local level. Individuals can be trained and educated even abroad, but local institutional networks of shared learning between the public and private sector and between universities and their stakeholders need their own timing. Societal recognition of academic knowledge takes even longer. There is no time left for massive new research programmes, but we have to start from available human capacity and build up, case-by-case, issue-by-issue, problem-by-problem, a modest and coherent set of operational rules. There is a rich structure of post-graduate research coordination with minimal and discontinuous output, but one needs project-wise utilization of available opportunities. The Ph.D might be instrumental.

The most critical factor seems to me the management of post-graduate research and training. In a previous assignment for the World Bank I produced a manual on the management of R&D but a major need seems to me an assessment of present practices and gaps rather than a collection of foreign tools. It seems a fair judgment that many graduate candidates have been educated in a highly standardized way due to the lack of faculty and books. The relatively small amount of professors has to tutor an increasing amount of doctorate candidates without proper facilities. The present period of the new post-graduate system is experimental, where the 'American' and 'continental' style of Ph.D programming are tested in order to find an Indonesian style. Recently a doctoral dissertation on the critical factors in the research climate of Indonesian universities has been completed by Bob Waworuntu in the USA. Although I have not yet seen the final copy, I assume that it contains a large amount of empirical data and their interpretation. A major contribution would be a guide for available post-graduate programmes in various European and American universities and in Indonesian universities. Such a guide should contain a selection of relevant manuals for dissertation writing but emphasize the pragmatics of post-graduate research at the interpersonal level. One could start with briefing, monitoring and feedback sessions with Ph.D candidates in various stages and some disciplines in order to establish a solid base for such a manual. My own experience suggests that a clear vision of what a doctoral dissertation is supposed to be focused on an issue and on the expected audience is of major importance before one elaborates the pragmatics and formalities of each doctorate process. In contrast to first cycle higher education one needs to stimulate candidates for an independent journey rather than for copying some examples. A major difficulty seems preventing impressive scholastic compilations of received wisdom and footnotes and stimulating an empirical search in an unexplored area.

Publication, distribution and utilization of doctoral dissertations need special attention. The central library of the Indonesian Institute of Sciences has already an impressive collection, but there are no regular new editions of the catalogue (Katalog Induk Disertasi Indonesia). Moreover, one needs to develop dissertation abstracts and reviews. There are excellent publication services in Indonesia, and it would be an important improvement, if publishers could agree on some joint venture in publishing academic products rather than establishing separate publishing services within universities. It is a question of policy rather than of scientific quality to stimulate a readable style of doctoral dissertations for a wider audience. Also textbook editions of parts of doctoral dissertations seem useful to substitute or complete foreign textbooks with Indonesian learning material.

Finally, I assume that the French 'habilitation' or an explicit training for managing and supervising research will find an Indonesian equivalent in the future, although I am hesitant about adding new degrees. The major task will be to create a stimulating research climate with full-time supervision and to monitor completion rates.

Towards Multinational Doctorates: Some proposals

Translation of available evidence on history, cultures, functions and structures of research-based doctorates into practical policy requires a sober, imaginative and patient mind. Of course, this study could be completed by special studies along disciplinary lines and limited to periods, institutions and national systems, but there are sufficient indications for commending some actions and practices focused on the revival of multinational doctorates in particular the design of a European doctorate.

During my explorations I have become less inclined to generalize about the contribution of a doctoral dissertation. It is possible to select cases and periods where doctoral dissertations have become merely ritual compilations of received wisdom. It is also possible to indicate the value of pre-career doctoral dissertations in highly structured fields of knowledge. My own calibration in a Dutch promotion culture and preference for experience and practice as a platform for theoretical reflection lead to a particular type of doctoral dissertations. The major danger of the present quest for control is that one tries to apply one's own standards to other domains or cultures. Without empirical studies of science dynamics and the transformation of paradigms one cannot arrive at feasible designs of post-graduate studies. Strengthening of multinational networks of partners for shared learning experiments might prevent a scientometric imperialism.

Historical continuity or at least reflection on past experience in the search for excellency seems of paramount importance. One has never been able to agree on the parameters of excellency, quality, originality or creativity. It is somebody's time bound judgment. It is equally elusive as one's culture of origin. Reflection on the sense of mission and clear targets rather than operational definitions are needed. Each of the major reforms in higher education has been based on a sense of direction. The future of higher education depends on the nature of post-graduate research and none of the national systems has found a satisfactory solution. Practices have widely varied and I cannot discover a Darwinian theory showing a growth in excellency. We cannot teach or instruct excellency. The university is an old idea and history teaches me that vitality of scientific communities has been continuously threatened, but has survival value for the frontiers of learning. I did not find any real alternative for higher degrees. It seems like democracy, the best choice from fragile solutions.

The cultural variations between institutions, disciplines, nations and periods is impressive. It is remarkable that frequently natural scientists by training become interested in the discrepancy between the two or thousand cultures at a certain age. Field mobility or tresspassing one's original field of knowledge is still a major difficulty. Presently there is a belief that the so called alpha, beta, gamma and life sciences constitute their own domain, but I assume that transformation is the key term and that each field of study needs the whole range of methodology and technology. There is a strong tendency to separate advanced research from university teaching. The noble profession of teaching and sharing learning experiences is in disregard and individual research performance has become the yardstick for prominence. I consider this growing gap disastrous. At the present time it is possible to program inventions and in that sense doctoral dissertations, but the impact of new technology on human behaviour escapes the quest for control. One cannot apply an industrial engineering approach to the human-machine interface or separate natural sciences from learning strategies. The interest in aquarian and other conspiracies might be healthy, if we could escape the simple dichotomies which are gaining momentum. I sometimes wonder whether the absence of philosophy and history of science in many curricula has created these false dichotomies and the sense of crisis and stress for fundamental human issues. Causality has never been a simple concept.

The academic community is squeezed between market forces and state bureaucracy and one needs self-reliance in one's particular field of study to keep the original standards of free exchange or shared learning. Post-graduate research is not a natural extension of first cycle higher education, but needs a projectwise selection of candidates and research themes. I don't think that there is a particular labour market for Ph.D's as such like for professional degrees in accountancy, law, engineering, research, and medical practice, but I assume that each society needs particular arrangements for stimulating originality, creativity and independent thought in the whole range of knowledge. There seems a tendency to confuse the second cycle of professional specialization with the third cycle of entering the scientific community. Independency is vital but has been always at bay. The growth of the corporate class requires new interlinkages but not a loss of free exchange of knowledge with graduate students. Of course, I do not claim a particular solution but try to trigger off a discussion about what contribution the scientific community ought to make to the society of the future.

The Third World is for me not peripheral and a frequent participation in Indonesian higher education has made me aware that the nature of doctoral dissertations and post-graduate education and research is the most sensitive indicator for the role and function of universities and knowledge. Also there one can observe an industrial engineering approach to pre-structured research themes and a more humanistic approach to extend the frontiers of learning in unexplored territory. Each individual Ph.D candidate puts me for the fundamental question what could be his contribution to the scientific community. One needs a business-like approach to specify in each case potential contributions to the local knowledge infrastructure by a particular candidate and to offer all the support and guidance needed.

I consider the core of post-graduate education and research individual candidates with their specific qualifications and interests. It is possible to teach methodology and theory, but not interest, motivation and a focus. For the first cycle we have to accept programming within given constraints of curricula and budgets, but for the third cycle I see the university as a public service institute, where one tries to offer a supportive climate for shared learning, for testing interesting hypotheses or hunches or for exploring new problems. Present reform proposals intend to structure post-graduate education and research according to criteria and dominant paradigms of the scientific establishment rather than according to the needs and issues of individual candidates. There is a strong normative approach and a belief in new structures without careful observation of actual practices.

Let me specify some issues and possible actions:

1. The situation of post-graduate education and research is a confused one. There are so many extremes in the actual meaning, process and product that one needs a clarification of goals and purpose. Higher education has to be differentiated in three cycles and the balance between general and specialist or occupational and scientific orientation is different in each national system. In some disciplines and proposals one might actually select the doctorate as an immediate extension of first cycle higher education, but then one needs in a later stage special degrees for a broader capacity to direct research, such as the French 'habilitation'. In other disciplines one might prefer doctorates as an individual qualification after experience. A good instrument for such clarification is a code of practice regarding doctoral training and research by committees of Vice-Chancellors, Principals or Presidents, such as published in the UK in 1985. This code does not propose a uniform system but commend good practices which are widely followed in many institutions. One does not need a final consensus on what exactly constitutes a good dissertation, but one cannot escape careful observation of existing practices and variety. The present interest in a European doctorate provides an excellent opportunity to build such codes of practice in each national system. The European regulation to change every half a year the presidency leads to a revolving process, where after some six years one has a comprehensive view on existing and desirable practices. Actually the number of external, part-time candidates for higher degrees is growing and they are becoming older.

2. Available information about doctorates is scattered, although there are many documentation services. In the European Community one might launch complementary information services which might underpin joint doctorate training and research. Gradually one might establish a European Doctorate File compatible to the American one. There are many European and international information networks in various disciplines and fields of study, but they need to be connected. I am amazed by the many reform proposals without any systematic scrutiny of available practice. Sometimes one declares the Ph.D concept obsolete without trying to clarify the nature of the problem. Bildung or other concepts of cultivation are seen as irrelevant. The new information technology allows floppy discs for dissertation writers and new publication outlets, but does not change the nature of the problem. At the level of concepts, intentions and strategy one does not easily reach consensus, but one can observe and classify practice, outputs and structure.

3. Graduate support networks for individual dissertation writers exist in various degrees and usually within disciplines or around individual supervisors. These networks are very loosely coupled with higher education systems and hierarchy, especially for the increasing number of external candidates. Actually I have seen no reform proposals where Ph.D candidates have been consulted or represented. These networks are to be based on human concern and empathy for individual capacities, interests and life chances. Most Ph.D work is, and I assume, will remain a lonely long-distance journey but one can offer a platform for sparring partners in discussing progress, obstacles and pragmatics. Institutes, such as the small scale Netherlands Institute for Advanced Studies, could offer facilities for such a platform and periods of writing and reflections. A multinational and multidisciplinary constituency seems to be healthy and prevents solipsism. A European extension of similar networks within available structures and including the corporate class would be welcome. We do not need new institutions but we need to mobilize clearing house functions and interlinkages from the bottom. The English Graduate Network in management studies with yearly rotating conferences in one of the participating universities is also a useful format and can be easily connected in a multinational way e.g. with support of European multinational business.

4. We have to accept variation in supervisory styles and the mixture between taught courses and research, but there is ample room for improvement of supervisory practice, accepting variety and diversity as an asset. Completion rates are a sincere concern, but one needs patience, a long term vision and a more inductive than normative approach. The English Open University with its 1,000 Ph.D candidates and its supervisory seminars pre-

sents a useful format for small scale pilot experiments with a multinational dimension. A serious practical obstacle is that many faculty members do not have any facility or budget for intensifying or extending supervisory or tutoring activities. I consider supervision of Ph.D candidates as one of the most rewarding duties or privileges. The present ERASMUS project launched by the European Commission might offer complementary facilities for joint supervision. There is also an enormous variation in time budgets allowed for supervision.

5. Actually more Ph.D candidates from the the Third World make a European academic perigrination than Ph.D candidates within established European universities. In the Dutch system there is even a tendency to keep one's best students within an institutional or disciplinary network. This seems highly counterproductive for creativity, field mobility and independent thought. Ph.D's become then an extension of professorial claims. The decline of Franeker university is characterized by an introverted attention to professorial privileges and a loss of international interest. There is a danger for implosion in present reforms. At the doctorate level one could establish multinational supervisory systems for candidates from the Third World with an emphasis on institution building in developing countries for a knowledge infrastructure but not isolated from the mainstream. Language is a major obstacle and one needs special facilities and courses in international languages as English, French and Spanish. Compared to American practice Europe lacks a comprehensive guide for post-graduate facilities and practices at the interpersonal level. Available manuals for dissertation writers do not seem very helpful. Heterogony is a major concern if one tries to copy the Marshall plan. An explicit concern for the nature of isolated research and knowledge communities, late-development life chances, and for societal service is required. This is not a soft concern for sympathy but a pragmatic concern for the changing world balance of power, knowledge and information markets.

6. I do not expect consensus or an immediate implementation of proposals, but hope to offer arguments for a more fundamental revision of the present scientocratic trends towards a more humanistic concept of the university and its role in stimulating multi disciplinary and multinational transformations. We need a restraint, bottom up approach issue-for-issue which can be continued over time rather than triggering off too many comprehensive initiatives which will be discontinued. The concept of university and its prototypes and its expression in higher degrees and knowledge products are rooted in human civilization. It relates to life long learning patterns, apprenticeship and maturation and cannot be easily reduced to scientocratic exercises or industrial technology.

Finally, I started with the metaphore of an octopus as coined by William James of Harvard in 1903 to curse the evil of specialization and to stress the humanistic value of Ph.D's. I observed and tried to classify the amazing range of variation in the practice of final degrees over time, nations, disciplines and institutions. Selectivity indeed, but without any true value of excellency or standards. During my explorations of the Ph.D phenomenon and its proto-types I encountered many other metaphores, such as fetish, union card, driving licence or credit card. From European mythology Cordasco sugges-ted the god of the sea, Protheus, indicating the ever changing shape of the actual product and process: the Protean Ph.D. The most appropriate symbol seems to me the Promethean Ph.D, referring to the Greek god who took pity on the misery of mankind, stole fire from heaven for their benefit and became chained to a rock. The aim of a doctoral dissertation is to ignite received knowledge and experience with sparks of new insight. It might be minuscule, maybe a new concept, a single relationship or refinement of observation and experimentation. Fire might be destructive or be extinguished. Human civili-zation is characterized by the invention and utilization of fire as Goudsblom develops as an attractive hypothesis. For the noosphere, the world of lear-ning, we need also some fire or intended new contributions to knowledge and scientific communities. A Promethean Ph.D suggests a much more readable report of an individual long-distance journey in unexplored territory than the standard article in scientific journals. My preference is indeed for a more humanistic concept of a Ph.D where candidates are allowed to integrate personal observations and experiences in their particular field of study, even in the natural sciences. Practices of final degrees have varied and will vary, and so do judgments about these practices, but a concerted effort to extend the frontiers of learning and share the results freely through universities is a precious human heritage. Maybe it is our only hope for development.

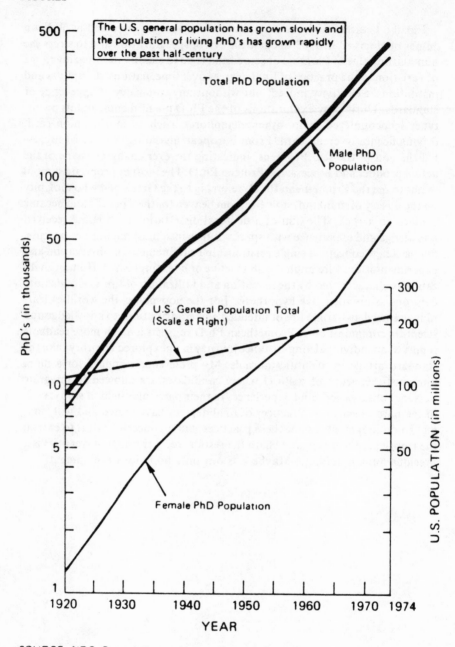

The U.S. general population has grown slowly and the population of living PhD's has grown rapidly over the past half-century

Total PhD Population

Male PhD Population

100

50

PhD's (in thousands)

U.S. General Population Total (Scale at Right)

10

5

Female PhD Population

1

1920   1930   1940   1950   1960   1970 1974

YEAR

U.S. POPULATION (in millions)

300

200

100

50

SOURCE: NRC, Commission on Human Resources

Fig. I-1 Ph.D population against general population in the USA

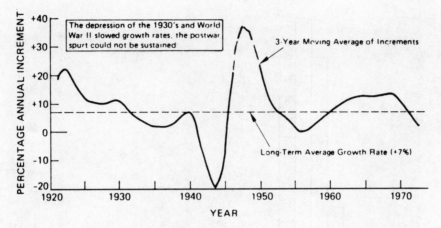

SOURCE NRC, Commission on Human Resources

Fig. I-2 Fluctuations of growth

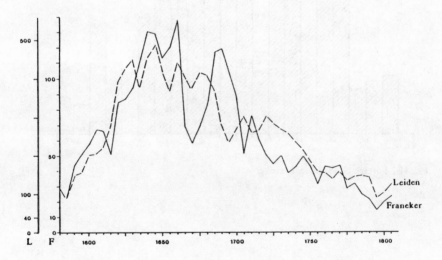

Fig. II-1 Entrance of new students in Leyden and Franeker

190

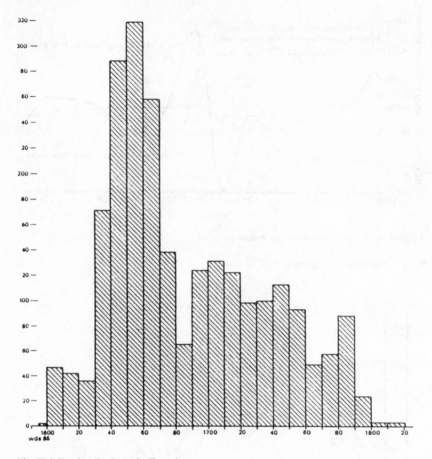

Fig. II-2 Foreign Students in Franeker

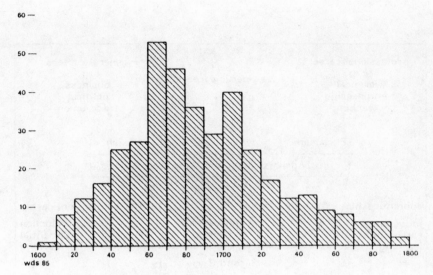

Fig. II-3 Doctorates of foreigners in Franeker

192

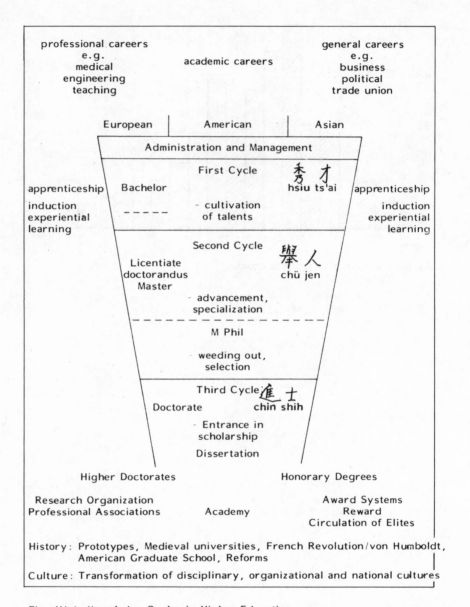

Fig. IV-1 Knowledge Cycles in Higher Education

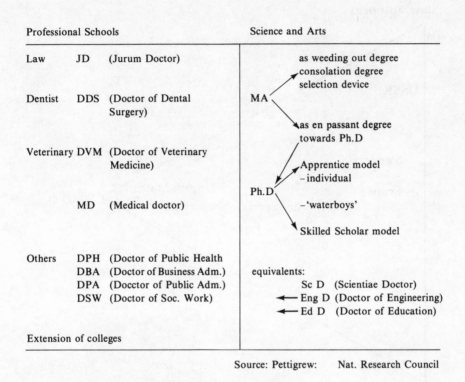

Fig. IV-2 A preliminary taxonomy of higher degrees (USA)

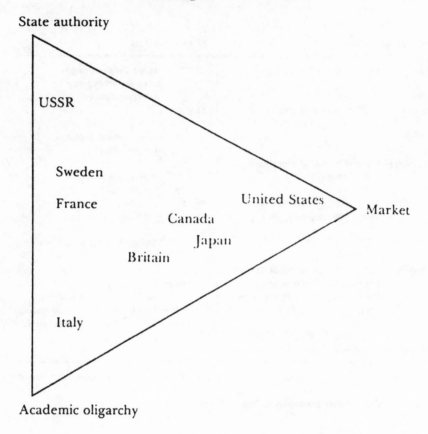

194

The Triangle of Coordination

State authority

USSR

Sweden

France

Canada

United States

Market

Japan

Britain

Italy

Academic oligarchy

Fig. V-1 The Triangle of Coordination (B.R. Clark)

SELECTED BIBLIOGRAPHY

Altbach, Philip G. and others,
  Academic Supermarkets: a critical cast study of a multiversity, San Francisco, 1971.
Altbach, Philip G. and David H. Kelly,
  Higher Education in International Perspective, London, 1985.
Amaya, Naohori and Nishio Kanji,
  "Educational Reform: How far, how fast?", *Japan Echo*, vol. 12, no. 2, pp. 50-56, 1985.
Arlman, R.,
  "Het drukken van proefschriften: geldverspilling", *Chemisch Weekblad*, vol. 64, 9
  augustus, pp. 11-19, 1968.
Aristotle,
  On Man in the Universe, ed. by Louise Ropes Loomis, New York, 1943.
Ars Aequi,
  Op Gezag van . . . , Nijmegen, 1985.
Austin, James H.,
  Chase, Chance and Creativity, New York, 1978.
Balderston, Frederick E.,
  "Challenge for the Universities", *Int. Journal of Institutional Management in Higher
  Education*, vol. 3, no. 1, pp. 21-32, 1979.
Bauman, Z.,
  Culture as Praxis, London, 1973.
Bauerfeind,
  "Aretè", *Wörterbuch zum neuen Testament*, vol. 1.
Becker, H.A. and A.F.J. van Raan (ed.),
  Kwaliteit in de Wetenschap: een Meetbaar Begrip?, Leiden, 1985.
Benda, Harry J.,
  The Crescent and the Rising Sun, The Hague, 1958.
Ben David, Joseph,
  Centers of Learning: Britain, France, Germany, United Stated, New York, 1977.
Benezra, Geneviève,
  "Influencing the direction of university research, some problems", *Impact of Science on
  Society*, vol. 29, nr. 2, pp. 231-239, 1979.
Berghe, Pierre van den,
  Academic Gamesmanship: How to make a Ph.D. pay, New York, 1970.
Bevers, J.A.A.M.,
  Een Staalkaart van Veranderingen in het Hoger Onderwijs, Den Haag, 1981.
Boer, J. de,
  De wetenschappelijke gemeenschap, Amsterdam, 1981.
Boot, W.,
  De Philoloog als Politicus, Leiden, 1985.

Boulding, Kenneth E,
"The economics of knowledge and the knowledge of economics", *Proceedings of the American Economic Association,* pp. 1-13, 1966.
Boulding, Kenneth E. and Lawrence Senesh,
The Optimum Utilization of Knowledge: Making knowledge serve human betterment. Boulder, Colorado, 1981.
Boulding, Kenneth E.,
Evolutionary Economics, Beverley Hills, 1981.
Boussevain, J.,
Friends of Friends, Oxford, 1974.
Bowman, M.J.,
Educational Choice and Labor Markets in Japan, Chicago, 1981.
Braun, T. and others,
Scientometric Indicators, Singapore, 1985.
Brink, R.E.M. van de,
"Antwoorden over Informatie", *ESB,* vol. 70, pp. 1227-1233, 1985.
Bueren, H.G. van,
"De Universiteit in het Gedrang", *De Gids,* vol. 148, no. 9/10, Amsterdam, 1985.
Buis, P.,
"Het Schrijven van een Proefschrift", *Academische Raad,* 1983.
Calcoen, R.,
"Ontwikkeling van de Wetenschappen", *AGN,* vol. 4, Middeleeuwen, pp. 363-365, Haarlem.
Carter, Richard, D.,
Future Challenges of Management Education, New York, 1981.
Casimir, H.B.G.,
Het Toeval van de Werkelijkheid, Amsterdam, 1983.
Charlot, Alain et Roland Mimouni,
La Formation par la Recherche et l'Emploi: les Docteurs de troisième Cycle, Paris, 1980.
Clark, Burton, R.,
The higher Education System, Berkeley, 1983.
Clemente, Frank,
"Early Career Determinants of Research Productivity", *American Journal of Sociology,* vol. 79, no. 2, pp. 409-419, 1973.
Cobban, A.B.,
The Medieval Universities: Their Development and Organization, London, 1975.
Commission of the European Community,
Higher Education in the European Community, Brussels, 1985.
Compendium,
Historical Compendium of European Universities, CRE, Genève, 1984.
Coombs, Philip, G.,
Future Critical World Issues in Education, International Council for Educational Development, 1981.
Cordasco, Francesco,
Daniel Coit Gilman and the Protean Ph.D., Leiden, 1960.
Crane, Diana,
Invisible Colleges: Diffusion of Knowledge in Scientific Communities, Chicago, 1972.
Crawford, Elisabeth and Norman Perry (ed.),
Demands for Social Knowledge: The Role of Research Organisations, London, 1976.
Crombach, Charles (ed.),
In het Laboratorium van de Nederlandse Landbouw, Wageningen, 1984.

Dahrendorf, Ralf,
    Life Chances: Approaches to Social and Political Theory, London, 1976.
Davis, Denis J.,
    "Some Effects of Ph.D. Training on the Academic Labour Markets", *Higher Education*,
    vol. 5, pp. 67-78, 1976.
Davis, Gordon, B.,
    A Systematic Approach for Managing a Doctoral Thesis, European Institute for Advan-
    ced Studies in Management, Brussels, 1977.
Derksen, W.,
    Tussen Loopbaan en Carrière: Het Burgemeesterambt in Nederland, 's-Gravenhage, 1980.
Dogan, Muttei (ed.),
    The Mandarins of Western Europe, New York, 1975.
Dore, Ronald,
    The Diploma Disease: Education, Qualification and Development, London, 1976.
Dronkers, J. (ed.),
    "Nederlandse Elites in Beeld", *Mens en Maatschappij*, vol. 59, 1984.
Eco, Umberto,
    Hoe Schrijf ik een Scriptie, Amsterdam, 1985.
Ferruolo, Stephen C.,
    The Origins of the University, Stanford, 1985.
Fidler, John,
    The British Business Elite: its Attitudes to Class, Status and Power, London, 1981.
Frijhoff, W.,
    La société Néerlandaise et ses gradués, 1575-1814, Amsterdam, 1981.
Frissen, P., e.a., (ed.),
    De Universiteit: Een Adequate Onderwijsorganisatie?, Utrecht, 1986.
Geertz, Clifford,
    The Interpretation of Cultures, New York, 1973.
Gudykunst, William B. (ed.),
    Intercultural Communication Theory: Current Perspectives, Beverley Hills, 1983.
Gustin, B.H.,
    "Charisma, Recognition and the Motivation of Scientists", *American Journal of Sociolo-
    gy*, vol. 78, pp. 1119-1134, 1973.
Hannan, Michael T. and John H. Freeman,
    The Population Ecology of Organisations", *American Journal of Sociology*, vol. 82, pp.
    929-964, 1977.
Harmon, Lindsey, R.,
    Century of Doctorates: "Data Analyses of Growth and Change. U.S. Ph.D.'s – their
    number, origins, characteristics, and the Institutions from which they come.". *National
    Academy of Sciences*, Washington, 1978.
Haveman, Robert H.,
    Does the Welfare State increase Welfare?, Leiden, 1985.
Heeringen, Arie van,
    *Relaties tussen Leeftijd, Mobiliteit en Productiviteit van Wetenschappelijke Onderzoe-
    kers*, 's-Gravenhage, 1983.
Hiroshima University,
    Comparative Approaches to Higher Education, Hiroshima 1983.
Ho, Ping Ti,
    The Ladder of Success in Imperial China, New York, 1962.
Hodges, Lucy,
    "Universities on Blacklist", *Times*, 1-11-1985.

198

Hofstede Geert,
Culture's Consequences, Beverley Hills, 1980.
Horringa, D.,
"Verlamde Universiteiten", *Bestuursjournaal,* april, 1986.
Hout, J.F.M.J. van,
"De Diversiteit in de Cognitieve en Sociale Organisatie van Wetenschapsgebieden en Universitair Onderwijs", *Frissen.*
Howard, K. and J.A. Sharp,
The Management of a Student Research Project, Aldershot, 1983.
Howorth, J. and Philip G. Cerny,
Elites in France: Origins, Reproduction and Power, London, 1981.
Hugstad, Paul S.,
The Business School in the 1980's: Liberalism versus Vocationalism, New York, 1981.
James, William,
Memories and Studies, London, 1912.
Jantsch, E.,
"Inter- and Transdisciplinary university", *Higher Education,* vol. 1, pp. 7-32, 1972.
Jencks, C. and D. Riesman,
The Academic Revolution, Garden City, New York, 1968.
Jensma, G.Th. and others (ed.)
Universiteit te Franeker 1585-1811, Leeuwarden, 1985.
Johnson Abercrombie, M.L.,
The Anatomy of Judgement, London, 1960.
Joynt, Pat and Malcolm Warner (ed.),
Managing in Different Cultures, Oslo, 1985.
Jong, Frits de,
Macht en Inspraak: de strijd om de democratisering van de universiteit van Amsterdam, Baarn, 1981.
Kamp, A.F. (ed.),
De Technische Hogeschool te Delft, 1905-1955, 's-Gravenhage, 1955.
Katz, Joseph and Rodney T. Hartnett (ed.),
Scholars in the Making: The Development of Graduate and Professional students, Cambridge, 1976.
Keller, G.
"Trees without Fruit: The Problem with Research about higher Education", *Change,* Jan./Feb., 1985.
Ken'ichi, Koyama,
"An End to Uniformity in Education", *Japan Echo,* vol. 12, no. 2, pp. 43-49, 1985.
Kidu, Hiroshi,
"Can Education Survive Liberalization", *Japan Echo,* vol. 12, no. 2, pp. 57-61, 1985.
Kimberley, John R. and others,
The Organizational Life Cycle, San Francisco, 1980.
Klant, J.J.,
Spelregels voor Economen, Leiden, 1979.
Klein, P.,
De Nederlandse Hogeschool, 1963-1973, Rotterdam, 1974.
Lach, P.F.,
Asia in the The making of Europe, vol. I and II, Chicago, 1965.
Lambers, H.W.,
Uitgesproken Institutioneel?, Rotterdam, 1981.
Lammers, C.J. and H. Philipsen,
"Ars Promovendi", *Sociologische Gids,* vol. 11, no. 1/2, pp. 52-83, 1964.

Lammers, C.J. and others,
  Menswetenschappen Vandaag, Twee Zijden van de Medaille, Meppel, 1972.
Lane, Frank W.,
  Kingdom of the Octopus, London, 1957.
Lawrence, Peter
  The Ph.D.: A Study in "National and Professional Location, Ph.D. Platform, December 1985.
Lederman, Leon M.,
  "The Value of Fundamental Science", *Scientific American,* vol. 251, no. 5, pp. 34-41, 1984.
LIPI,
  Social Sciences in Indonesia, vol. I and II, Jakarta, 1975, 1979.
Locke, Robert R.,
  The End of the Practical Man: Entrepreneurship and Higher Education in Germany, France and Britain, 1880-1940, Greenwich, 1984.
Luria, S.E.,
  De Weg van de Wetenschap, Amsterdam, 1984.
Macintyre, Alasdair,
  "A Mistake about Causality in Social Science", *Philisophy, Politics and Society,* P. Laslett and W.G. Runciman (eds.), Oxford, 1964.
March, G.J. (ed.)
  Handbook of Organization, Chicago, 1965.
Masurel, Jean Louis,
  Entrepreneurism and Large Corporations, lecture, Inauguration of the new Euro-Asia Centre Building, Fontainebleau, 15 nov. 1985.
Maury, C.
  Reflections on the Duality of the French Educational System, Rotterdam, 1985.
Mayeur, Jean-Marie,
  "Analytical Afterword", *Howorth, J.,* 1981.
Mayhew, Lewis B. and Patrick J. Food,
  Reform in Graduate and Professional Education, San Francisco, 1974.
Meeks, G.,
  Graduate Economics Training in Britain, Rotterdam, 1985.
Mertens, Peter,
  "Comparative Indicators for German Universities", *Int. Journal of Institutional Management in Higher Education,* vol. 3, no. 1, 1979.
Mitsukumi, Yoshida and others (ed.),
  The Hybrid Culture, Hiroshima, 1984.
Mooy, J.J.A.,
  "Elites en Tegen-elites", *Hollands Maandblad,* pp. 14-19, Mei 1984.
Nakayama, Shigeru,
  Academic and Scientific Traditions in China, Japan and the West, Tokyo, 1984.
Nauwerlaats, M.A.,
  "Scholen en Onderwijs", *AGN,* vol. 4, Middeleeuwen, pp. 366-371, Haarlem.
OECD,
  The Role and Functions of Universities: Post-graduate Education in the 1980s, Paris, 1986.
OECD, *Higher Education and the Flow of Foreign Students,* Zoetermeer, Nov. 11-13, 1985.
Ouchi, William G.,
  "Markets, Bureaucracies and Clans", *Administrative Science Quarterly,* vol. 25, pp. 129-141, 1980.
Panitchpakdi, S.,
  Underdevelopment of Development Economics in Thailand, University of Malaya, 1981.

200

Pen, J.,
   Een Voertuig voor de Beschaving, *NRC*, CS-Supplement, 31-5-1985.
Pfeffer, Jeffrey,
   Organizations and Organization Theory, Boston, 1984.
Phillips, Estelle,
   "Learning to Do Research", *Graduate Management Research*, 1984.
Phillips, Estelle,
   Higher Degrees by Research, Open University, 1984.
Polak, J.M.,
   Rechtsvergelijkende Opmerkingen rond de Wet Universitaire Bestuurshervorming, Deventer, 1974.
Porat, M.U.,
   The Information Economy, Stanford, 1977.
Price, Derek de Solla,
   Little Science, Big Science, New York, 1963.
Psacharopoulos, George,
   Higher Education in Developing Countries, World Bank, 1980.
Rashdall, Hastings,
   The Universities of Europe in the Middle Ages, Oxford, 1895, 1936.
Ravenswaay, Boem van,
   Evaluation Project International Education, The Hague, 1984.
Rip, Arie en Peter Groenewegen,
   Macht over Kennis: Mogelijkheden van Wetenschapsbeleid, Alphen a/d Rijn, 1980.
Rooyakkers, Geert W.J.M.,
   Proefschriften onderzocht: Een Onderzoek naar Kosten en Baten van Proefschriften op Sociaal-wetenschappelijke gebieden in Nederland en in de V.S. en G.B., Leiden, 1986.
Salam, Ardus,
   "The Isolation of the Scientist in Developing Countries", *Minerva*, pp. 461-465, 1966.
Second Japan-United States Conference,
   Proceedings, April 4-6, Tokyo, 1983.
Smiddy, H.F. and L. Naum,
   "Evolution of a Science of Managing in America", *Management Science*, vol. 1, 1954.
Smith, Tasman A.,
   Cross-cultural Factors affecting the Management Performance of Expatriates: Thailand Case, Oxford, 1978.
Snow, C.P.,
   The Two Cultures: and a Second Look, An Expanded Version of the two Cultures and the Scientific Revolution, Cambridge, (1959) 1964.
Soedjatmoko,
   Development and Freedom, Tokyo, 1980.
Sowell, Thomas,
   Markets and Minorities, New York, 1981.
Staal, J.F.,
   "De Academicus als Nowhere Man", *De Gids*, pp. 96-159, Amsterdam, 1970.
Steenkamp, T.B.M. and others,
   "Taakverdeling en Concentratie", *E.S.B.*, vol. 70, pp. 1198-1201, 1985.
Sternberg, David,
   How to Complete and Survive a Doctoral Dissertation, New York, 1981.
Stone, L.,
   "Prosopography", *Daedalus*, pp. 96-159, 1971.
Stuyvenberg, J.H.,
   De Nederlandse Economische Hoogeschool 1913-1963, Den Haag, 1963.

Sukadji Ranuwihardjo,
"Teaching and Research in Economics", *Indonesia, a Country Report*, 1982.
Sulleiman, Ezra N.,
Politics, Power and Bureaucracy in France, Princeton, 1974.
Takamiya Susumu and Keith Thurley (ed.),
Japan's Emerging Multinationals, Tokyo, 1985.
Teng Ssu Yu,
"Chinese Influence on the Western Examination System",
Harvard Journal of Asiatic Studies, vol. 7, pp. 267-312, 1942.
Thompson, Kenneth W. and others (ed.),
Higher Education and Social Change, vol. I and II, New York, 1976, 1977.
Touw-Otten, F.,
Wetenschapsbeoefening en Huisartsgeneeskunde. Een Analyse van Dissertaties en enkele Wegen tot Structurering van Huisartsgeneeskunde als Discipline, Utrecht, 1981.
Trompenaars, Fons,
Culture and Organization, Milano, 1985.
Veld-in 't Langeveld, H.,
De Financiele Aspecten van de Academische Promotie, Amsterdam: Prins Bernhard Fonds, 1953.
Versey, L.R.,
The Emergence of the American University, Chicago, 1965.
Volbeda, Sjoukje,
Pionierssteden in het Oerwoud, Nijmegen, 1984.
Voigt, D.,
"Zum Bildungsniveau der Eltern von Promovierten im Deutsch-Deutschen Vergleich, 1950 bis 1982", *Progress-report*, Jan. 1986.
Wahid, Abdurrahman,
"Islam, the State and Development in Indonesia", *Ethical Dilemmas of Development in Asia*, G. Gunatilleke (ed.), Lexington, 1983.
Weiler, A.G.,
"De Ontwikkelingen in Filosofie en Theologie in de Late Middeleeuwen", *AGN*, vol. 4, Middeleeuwen, pp. 426-436, Haarlem.
Weisz, George,
The Emergence of Modern Universities in France, 1863-1914, Princeton, 1983.
Wheatcroft, M.,
The Revolution in British Management Education, London, 1970.
Whitley, R. (ed.),
Social Processes of Scientific Development, London, 1974.
Whitley, R.,
The Intellectual and Social Organzation of the Sciences, Oxford, 1984.
Wilkins, L.T.,
Social Policy, Action and Research, London, 1964.
Williams, Raymond,
Keywords, London, 1976.
Williamson, Oliver E.,
"The Economics of Organizations, the Transaction Cost Approach", *American Journal of Sociology*, vol. 87, no. 3, pp. 548-577, 1981.
Woude, S. van der,
"De Oude Nederlandse Dissertaties", *Bibliotheekleven*, vol. 48, pp. 1-14, 1963.
Wyler, M.L.,
Aspecten van Academische Promoties, Rotterdam, 1984, (unpublished).
Zi, Etienne,
Pratique des Examens Litteraires en Chine, Chang Hai, 1894.

AUTHORS INDEX

(Selection of main resources)